IT'S AWESOME, *Baby!*

75 Years of Memories and a Lifetime of Opinions on the Game I Love

Dick Vitale

With Dick Weiss and Joan Williamson

ASCEND BOOKS

WWW.ASCENDBOOKS.COM

"Dick Vitale is one of the great ambassadors we have in college basketball. In *It's Awesome, Baby!*, Dick brings us along on the ride that has taken him to the top of his profession. Dickie V's enthusiasm and passion continue to inspire me, coaches, and college basketball fans from coast to coast."

— Villanova coach Jay Wright

"Most people know Dick Vitale for his unmatched passion for basketball. And while that is certainly remarkable, what truly impresses me is his passion for life and for helping other people. It's a lesson that should serve as an inspiration to us all."

— Michigan State coach Tom Izzo

"For more than 35 years, Hall of Famer Dick Vitale has been a primary voice in college basketball and a true friend to the sport. His latest book is a must-read for all basketball fans."

— Duke Hall of Fame coach Mike Krzyzewski

"There is no better ambassador for the game of basketball than Dick Vitale. His enthusiasm for the sport and the people in it is unmatched, but it doesn't stop there with Dick. He has championed a fight and used his platform like none other in helping to raise millions in the fight against cancer. He is a true PTPer for the game and in life."

— Kentucky coach John Calipari

"There has not been a better ambassador for college basketball over the last 35 years than Dick Vitale. He's unique because he's been able to take his vast basketball knowledge, being a coach, to the public in a way nobody ever has before. Dick has also used his platform and popularity to do what is most dear to him—to raise money to fight cancer through the V Foundation. It's remarkable what he has accomplished professionally and personally in his lifetime."

— Kansas coach Bill Self

"From a coaching perspective, I have always appreciated what Dick Vitale has given back to the game. I have always respected what he has given to the community through his work for cancer research. This book tells his whole story."

— Florida coach Billy Donovan

"In the over 40 years I've known Dick as a high school, college, and professional coach and announcer, I've never seen anyone sustain the passion, enthusiasm, and drive for the game of basketball that he has. He is truly a modern day inspiration."

— Louisville Hall of Fame coach Rick Pitino

"No single individual has done more to spread the good word about college basketball than Dick Vitale. Any fan would love to read about the sport's many exciting personalities and events over the years as seen through his eyes."

— Syracuse Hall of Fame coach Jim Boeheim

"An event is bigger, better, and most importantly, much more fun when Dickie V is involved. He's a joy to be around and his love for the game of basketball is infectious. He's forgotten more basketball than most people will ever know and is as genuine, passionate, exuberant, and thoughtful a human being as you will ever meet. Very few people have done more for college basketball than Dickie V."

— UCLA coach Steve Alford

10 9 8 7 6 5 4 3 2 1

ISBN: print book 978-0-9904375-3-6
ISBN: e-book 978-0-9904375-4-3
Library of Congress Control Number: 2014951600

Publisher: Bob Snodgrass
Editors: Mark Stallard and Claire Reagan
Publication Coordinator: Christine Drummond
Sales and Marketing: Lenny Cohen and Dylan Tucker
Publicity: Bob Ibach
Dust Jacket and Book Design: Rob Peters

All photos courtesy of Dick Vitale unless otherwise indicated
Front Cover and Larger Back Cover Photo courtesy of Kristine Foley Photography
Back Cover Photos courtesy ESPN and Dick Vitale
Every reasonable attempt has been made to determine the ownership of copyright.
Please notify the publisher of any erroneous credits or omissions, and corrections will be made to subsequent editions/future printings.

The goal of Ascend Books is to publish quality works. With that goal in mind, we are proud to offer this book to our readers. Please note, however, that the story, experiences, and the words are those of the authors alone.

Printed in the United States of America

Visit www.ascendbooks.com for
more great titles on your favorite teams,
coaches, athletes, and celebrities.

TABLE OF CONTENTS

So many people have helped me fulfill my dreams along the path of my life, and I know how lucky I am. From the institutions who hired me as their basketball coach to all of my fantastic colleagues at ESPN, to my friends, great fans, and especially my beautiful wife, daughters, and grandkids—this book is for you. Thanks for putting the "Awesome" into my life.

—Dick Vitale

For Howie Schwab, a good friend and an encyclopedia of sports knowledge who is an MVP in his profession.

— Dick Weiss

For Marge.

— Joan Williamson

FOREWORD
BY MAGIC JOHNSON

I remember first meeting Dick Vitale when I was in high school. He was recruiting me to the University of Detroit. He told me I could own the Motor City if I played for the Titans. Sorry, Dickie V, I became a Spartan…and the rest is history!

Dick has always had so much enthusiasm and energy. Now, he is showing his passion in his new book, *It's Awesome, Baby! 75 Years of Memories and a Lifetime of Opinions on the Game I Love*. This book chronicles his rise from schoolteacher to coaching in the NBA. He tackles a number of controversial topics on the sport he loves, college basketball.

Dick also gets into why he is so passionate about the battle against cancer. I've seen firsthand during one of his galas how he carries that energy into his efforts to raise money for cancer research. It was a touching event for a very special cause. He is one of the most enthusiastic people I know.

Dick Vitale is a great friend and someone who I respect and admire. This book is a special look at his full and remarkable life.

—Magic Johnson

Magic Johnson, all smiles as usual.

INTRODUCTION

So I hit this milestone, this "magic" number of life. And I've thought about it, maybe too much. My life.

The ups and downs, the highs and lows, the gifts I've received, the things I've lost, friends I love, the people I admire. My gorgeous, wonderful wife, Lorraine, my two fabulous daughters and their families. My incredible grandkids.

I work every day to give back more than I've gotten—that's the easy part.

Still, this number is with me. I think I finally made sense of my 75 years—at least what this long passage of time actually means to me—and I realize it all comes back to one thing.

The only way to sum it all up is very simple.

The Rock (the basketball).

I have an awesome life that happened because I love basketball.

I consider myself a lucky man, but I also know hard work and the ability to make connections with people have made a big difference in my career. My coaching experience— even more so, my people experience—gave me the confidence to be myself while broadcasting. My success has given me the opportunity to share my love and enthusiasm for the game of basketball all across the United States and even around the world.

So, here they are, memories from 75 years, stacked together in one place. I've included a lot of stuff.

My many opinions? They're in the book. Celebrities? Yes. My all-time favorite basketball games? Affirmative. I've covered everything, including where I think the game is headed.

And, baby, my biggest thrill concerning the Rock has to be my induction into the Basketball Hall of Fame. Greatest disappointment? The Detroit Pistons job.

One of most important lessons I've learned is how much basketball can transcend into "real" life. The best part is when you have the chance to make something better, and for me, that meant using my "basketball skills" to raise money to help children with cancer. I've aspired to be even more successful in giving back, to win the game of "making a difference."

And that's the best part of what I've been able to accomplish as a basketball analyst for ESPN.

As for the 75 years, they're mine, but I'm glad to share them.

For the rest of the highlights from my life—and a lot of other things—turn the pages. And, remember, this isn't just a good book…

It's an awesome book, baby—enjoy!

—Dick Vitale
August 2014

Photo courtesy of ESPN/Rich Arden

Me and the Rock—it's an awesome thing, baby.

LIFE CHANGING EVENTS

I wouldn't have the kind of a life I've lived without several life-changing moments. Sure, I have things happen that change my life almost every day, but there are a few experiences that have left more than just a lasting impression—the major events of my life that I share in the next few chapters have changed me, they've shaped me. And the Rock made almost every one of them possible!

It's been an awesome ride, baby!

CHAPTER 1

THE CALL FROM THE HALL

The Naismith Memorial Basketball Hall of Fame. To me, it is the Holy Grail of basketball.

Founded in 1959, the Hall is located in Springfield, Massachusetts, where James Naismith invented the game in 1891 by putting up a peach basket in the local YMCA. The Hall honors the best of the best in basketball. An exclusive "club," it has inducted over 300 players, coaches, major contributors, referees, executives, and teams worldwide.

I was first honored by the Hall in 1998 when I received the Curt Gowdy Media Award. I was singled out as a member of the electronic media for my contributions to basketball.

Then, the Hall came back in 2008 and inducted me as a contributor to the game.

Wow! I really was living a dream, and it was "Awesome, baby," with a capital A!

To get into the Hall, you need 75% of the 24 honors committee votes. Because I thought there was an element in the committee that strongly favored the NBA and I have mainly dealt with college hoops, I didn't think it would ever happen for me.

I had been nominated three times before 2008, and each year, the phone would ring with the same message: "Dick, you realize what it's like, what an honor it is to even be nominated for the Basketball Hall of Fame?" John Doleva of the Hall of Fame, who is a friend of mine, would say to me. "Don't feel bad it didn't happen this time."

I was starting to feel like Susan Lucci, the soap opera star from *All My Children* who was nominated 18 times for Best Actress starting in 1978 and finally won the prize in 1999.

Let's move forward to 2008. Once again, I'd been nominated but had really given up hope. I was getting ready to go to the Final Four with my wife, Lorraine; I was running to the car when I heard the phone ringing in the background.

I said to myself, "Should I answer it? Ignore it? Let it go to voicemail?"

For whatever reason, I ran in and grabbed the phone.

"Dick? John Doleva."

I was getting ready to hear the same speech.

"Dick, sit down," John said. "You've been voted into the Naismith Hall of Fame." I was to be honored for my contributions for promoting college basketball.

"What?!"

The thoughts started flashing through my mind: all the greats who are in the Hall, being in there with all the giants, being part of the Holy Grail.

I was at a momentary loss for words—Hard to believe, right?

Five minutes later, Jerry Colangelo, the chairman of the nominating committee, called me up to congratulate me, telling me how happy the committee was that I had been selected.

It was one of the greatest moments of my life. I ran outside, jumping for joy and screaming like a little kid.

I received a lot of calls when I got into the Hall, but one still stands out. It came from former NBA superstar Bob Lanier who told me, "Dickie V, we weren't together long with the Pistons, but, my friend, we are now on another team, one of the greatest teams you can ever belong to—the Naismith Hall of Fame."

The way he put his congratulations really touched me.

I was in awe. I cried like a baby.

The Final Four was in San Antonio that year, one of my all-time favorite cities for hosting a Final Four. They were to make the formal announcement on Monday, April 7, the day of the championship game. Jim Nantz of CBS would host the event. I was part of seven people inducted in the class of 2008. My fellow members were Patrick Ewing from the Knicks; Hakeem Olajuwon of the Rockets; Adrian Dantley, the scoring machine from DeMatha who was a star for Notre Dame and my buddy Digger Phelps before he went on to excel in the NBA; Pat Riley, who invented Showtime with the Lakers and won three straight NBA titles; Cathy Rush of Immaculata fame; and Bill Davidson, my former boss at the Pistons.

The induction took place on September 5, 2008, at the Hall of Fame building in Springfield. All my family and good friends were there. ESPN was there to do the telecast, too.

I asked Bob Knight, who I have always admired, to introduce me. He walked me to the podium, and we embraced. One of the first people I saw when I got up to speak was Earvin "Magic" Johnson, who was sitting in the front row next to "The Logo," NBA legend and Hall of Famer Jerry West, and smiling a smile as only he could do. When I saw Magic, I told the audience how I'd tried to recruit him back when I was coaching the University of Detroit Titans and he was a star at Lansing Everett High School. I would have given anything in the world to coach him because, as good as he was, even I couldn't screw him up—that got a good laugh!

As I was talking, I felt like a guest on *This Is Your Life,* the old TV show with Ralph Edwards.

I had been told I had five to eight minutes to speak.

Were they crazy? I'd just be taking my first breath at that point!

All of the people in my class were told the same thing, but everyone seemed to speak for at least 25 minutes or so…I took nearly 27 minutes.

Who else but The General? Robert Montgomery Knight was my presenter at the Basketball Hall of Fame.

What they told me to do was be myself, to talk from the heart with no notes, and that's exactly what I did. First, I thanked Coach Knight for his loyalty and applauded his character as he played a big part in supporting me for this honor. I also got to thank him for allowing us to honor him at my gala several weeks before (we'd honored both Knight and Pat Summitt, who were the two winningest coaches at that time) where we raised $1.2 million for kids battling cancer.

I went on to tell the crowd how, when I was coaching, I was just a gym rat, constantly trying to learn from guys like The General (Robert Montgomery Knight), John Wooden, John Thompson, Jack Ramsay, Hubie Brown, and Chuck Daly, attending clinics just to hear those guys speak and watching their games just to see them coach. I shared how I'll never forget sitting in the third tier at the Garden the night Knight's Army team upset South Carolina.

My biggest fear at the induction ceremony was forgetting someone who had played a vital role in my life. It's tough to mention everyone, but I certainly had to mention Howard Garfinkel, who convinced Rutgers coach Dick Lloyd to interview me. Both guys were responsible for opening doors for me when I was a high school coach, trying to become a college assistant. The day he hired me, I was so excited I didn't even bother to ask how much I'd make. I was getting about $12K back then, coaching high school and working summer camps. I called back to talk salary, and he asked me how much I was making. When I told him, he said, "That's fantastic, you're only gonna take a thousand dollar cut, baby!"

Talking at the Hall, and man, this was the moment. To be honored with all of the greats of the game, well, it's awesome, baby!

I also explained how the same thing happened at the University of Detroit because I was such a financial dummy. They asked me what it would take for me to become their coach, and I told them I was making eleven thousand, but if they gave me $15, I'd come. They said, "That's great, man. We're a Catholic school, and we've got $21 thousand budgeted for the job." So, I landed my first college head-coaching job not because of my ability, but because I came cheap.

I also told the crowd about my run at the University in Detroit. In 1977, we made it to the Round of 16. We'd won 21-in-a-row that year. Even after losing a heartbreaker in the last minute against Michigan, I was on top of the world in 1978 when I was hired by the Detroit Pistons—Think about it! Sixth grade teacher in 1970, and in 1978, I was coaching in the NBA. I remembered looking at Jerry West on the other sideline and thinking "Shouldn't we get a picture? Should I get an autograph?" But it wasn't meant to last.

I told the audience how I hit rock bottom when I was fired my second year just twelve games into the season. I was always about getting it done immediately, but as an NBA coach, I was impatient. They had no choice but to fire me. Interestingly, Bill Davidson, the guy who hired me and then fired me when I was with the Pistons, gave his speech before I gave mine that evening. Mr. D. certainly was a fantastic contributor to the game. His being there at the induction brought back a lot of memories. Before I got up to speak, I went over to him, and we spoke for the first time in 30 years since the day he came to my house and told me about Detroit's "coaching change." I shared part of our exchange with the audience in my speech; I told him I was so sorry because if there was one emptiness still on my resume, it's the fact that I let him down, I let the people of Detroit down. I told him I never did what I wanted to do in my heart and what I really planned to do when I was named coach of the Detroit Pistons. Then, I thanked him because he put on my resume three important lines—that I have been a high school coach, a college coach, and a pro coach, and I will never forget the role he played in my journey in getting to that Hall of Fame induction ceremony.

But it was not a night for regrets. It was a night for celebration.

I went on to explain how two weeks after I got the ziggy I got a phone call from ESPN, what was then a new sports broadcasting network, asking me to announce their first broadcast game. After a little hesitation and taking the advice of my always wise wife, I announced my first game, DePaul and Wisconsin in Chicago. And I was hooked—my time as a broadcaster for ESPN has been 35 of the most incredible years that anybody could ever have.

I got to thank George Bodenheimer, not only for being a great leader but also for his friendship in tough times and in good times. I also got to tell his inspiring story. How about this: I had a driver in my early days at ESPN in 1981 by the name of George Bodenheimer. There was something about him. I knew he'd be a success. He told me how he wanted to go somewhere in life and that all he was doing was working in the mailroom and driving guys around. I encouraged him. Then, one day in 1998, I couldn't believe it. I was looking at a paper during a flight delay in Atlanta, and there it was in headlines: "The new president of ESPN—George Bodenheimer."

Along with thanking and acknowledging all the people I've worked with at ESPN who have been invaluable in helping me in so many ways—producers, directors, play-by-play announcers, audio people, those involved in the telecast—as well as everyone who has helped raise a phenomenal amount of money to battle a disease that affects us all, believe me, I made sure to mention my No. 1 priority, my family—my wife, my kids, my grandkids, and certainly my brother, John, and sister, Terry, they're Hall of Famers as parents and people, just like my wife, Lorraine, and my daughters, Terri and Sherri. I shared with the crowd how Lorraine and I met: In sports, we've all heard about the miracle in 1969, the miracle of the Mets; well, there's also the miracle of Richard J. Vitale, I told them. I still can't forget the first night I laid eyes on her. I even shouted out to Magic Johnson that I may have lost a battle for him in recruiting, but I didn't lose the battle for that beautiful red head—I won that one, baby!

I talked about my parents, who taught me to be good to people and never to believe in "Can't." About my love for my family, my personal dream team. My parents may not have been educated, but they had doctorates in love. I shared how I can remember the words of my mom to this day: "Don't ever, Richie, don't ever ever believe in can't. Richie, chase those dreams." You don't get to the top of the mountain in your profession without a super team surrounding you.

I got so emotional about it that night.

It had been a very emotional year. I was dealing with the lesions on my vocal cords. I thought my career was over, but all I could think about was my family. That night though, going over all the people and stories—like meeting Olajuwon in an elevator in New Orleans when he was a freshman at the University of Houston. He was so down after being overwhelmed early in his career; I shook his hand and remember saying to him, "Son, someday, you're gonna be special because you're agile, you're mobile, you're hostile, and you're not fragile." The crowd had a good laugh since I know that was one of the first times in my life I was ever right with an analysis.

That night, through all those memories, I thought, "To get to this moment, to stand here in this exclusive club for talking about a game I love…I'm one lucky guy."

Being there among the game's all-time greats, to have my bust up there with people I idolize—people I'm in awe of—people like John Wooden, Dean Smith, Bob Knight, Mike Krzyzewski, Oscar Robertson, Jerry West, Bob Cousy—is unbelievable. I think about the fact that a guy like me, a sixth-grade teacher from New Jersey, is living the dream. Never a great talented player. Didn't have a big name as a coach. But because of ESPN and George Bodenheimer and all the basketball people I work with, I have gotten an opportunity to do something I love. Until about 10 years ago, I didn't think I could be considered for induction as a contributor to the game. Really, all I've been is a guy with one common denominator: a love of the game. I can't run. I can't jump. I can't shoot. But I've always had a terrific passion and enthusiasm for whatever I've tried to do in life.

I would have given anything, anything in the world if my mom and dad had been there, and so I ended my speech by thanking them. Even though they weren't there to share in the celebration, I knew they were there in spirit. I said, "I love you so much, love you so much for giving me that drive, that determination, that desire, to chase my dreams, to believe that a simple formula in life: passion + work ethic + good decision-making in your personal life = W, Win in the game of life."

At the end of the evening, I joined all the other inductees on the stage. I couldn't believe I was going to be inducted with the people I used to go to see play in Madison Square Garden, sitting up in the third deck, cheering. It seemed like yesterday I did that. And, here I was, getting to be among those people. It was just incredible. I felt like a little kid on Christmas, whose every wish had been granted by Santa Claus.

My Hall of Fame jersey—it's awesome, baby!

CHAPTER 2
AN AUDIENCE WITH THE POPE

I've never had a bucket list, but if I did, then meeting the Pope would surely be at the top of it.

Well, in 2011, I did just that.

I was having dinner with Bishop Frank Dewane of the Diocese of Venice, Florida, and during the meal, I mentioned I was going to be in Italy in the summer.

"Would you like to meet the Pope?" he asked me.

"Come on, really?"

Bishop Dewane told me he couldn't guarantee anything, but he would write a letter to the Vatican on my behalf, and we'd see what would happen.

The bishop paved the way for Lorraine and me to have a Papal audience during our 10-day trip to Rome, Florence, and Venice with my daughter Terri, my son-in-law, Chris Sforzo, and their children, Ryan and Sydney.

We got a letter back, saying to bring it to the Vatican. We did and were told the Pope would not be in residence there that summer. He was in his summer home at the Papal Palace at Castel Gondolfo, a 17th-century palace 15 miles southeast of Rome. They gave us a date to bring the letter there and said there was a chance he would meet with us.

We did, and he did.

I tell you, it was one of the biggest thrills of my life. I was in such awe that I was speechless; my hands were shaking. I'm an Italian-American Catholic, and this was a huge moment for me, the fulfillment of a lifelong dream. I remembered my mother, who, after her stroke, still walked almost two miles with her friends to St. Leo's of Elmwood Park to hear daily Mass. My only regret was that my parents weren't here to know I had an audience with the Holy Father; I wish they'd been able to join us. I know they would have cherished the immense honor just as much as I did.

It wasn't a general audience either, not a large crowd. Lorraine and I were sitting there with four clergy from South America. We looked up, and I couldn't believe what I was seeing: There was the Pope, walking down the stairs. He was about 20 feet from us. I swear to you I got goose bumps. Lorraine and I were just amazed. There were a ton of Swiss Guards there, too. I said, "Oh, man, no one is going to believe I'm one-on-one with the Pope," since we weren't allowed to take photos.

We lined up. The clergy went first, then us. We all talked to the Pope in our turn. Remember those goose bumps I mentioned? Well, they were so prominent that Pope Benedict started the conversation. Lorraine and I both kissed his ring. He gave us rosary beads that were blessed and asked us who we'd like him to pray for. I replied, my family and for peace in the world.

When we finished talking to him, I said to Lorraine, "I'm just going to stand up there with the Pope. Snap a picture."

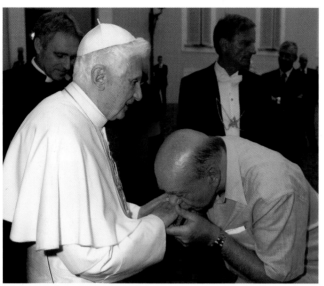

This was the memory of a lifetime, meeting His Holiness, Pope Benedict.

She started to take a picture and the Swiss Guard was signaling "No, no." Then, a Vatican official came over and handed us a card. He told us to take the card and go to the Vatican photo shop tomorrow; we would be able to get all the pictures we wanted because somebody had been shooting while we were there.

We went there expecting it would cost us hundreds of dollars—or lots of euros—for the photos, but it was very inexpensive. We bought CDs. We got all kinds of photos with the Pope.

Afterward, I felt bad I hadn't had the nerve to joke around and ask who was more popular in Germany—His Holiness or Dirk Nowitzki?

The only thing that crushed me was not being able to take my daughter Terri and her family in with us for the audience. But then, the Pope came out on the balcony of the palace. He spoke to the people outside in five languages. My daughter and her family were able to get up front so they could take pictures and see him.

Judging from the tweets I sent that day, I was still in a state of shock and giddy after the experience. A couple of samples: "Goose bumps as it was a moment I will treasure. Usually a non-stop talker, I was in such awe that he started the chatter," and "Dickie V from New Jersey had just had an audience with Pope Benedict XVI. I still have to pinch myself that I'm awake and that it really happened."

The rest of the trip was fun, too. I love Italy. I was blown away by the ruins of Rome and the Coliseum, the statues by Michelangelo in Florence (I know now why I call Dean Smith the Michelangelo of coaching), and those gondoliers in Venice are Surf and Turfers on the canals. I loaded up on pasta, pizza, and gelato—three of my favorites, baby!

I know I've met many celebrities in my life, but the highlight of all highlights was meeting the Pope.

Another example of strong personal faith who had a positive influence on me is Father Mychal Judge, a Franciscan I'd met when I was a young coach at East Rutherford High School. He was a priest at St. Joseph's Church in East Rutherford, New Jersey. He was gregarious with a special voice and a natural way of communicating with people.

Whenever I wanted inspiration, I talked to Father Mike. He was very, very special.

Unfortunately, we lost touch.

About a year ago, one of my former players at East Rutherford High School, Kim Becker, who played on my state championship teams, came to Florida, and we went to dinner while he was in town.

"Geez," Kim said, "isn't it a shame what happened to Father Mike?"

"What happened to Father Mike?" I thought with a confused look on my face.

"Didn't you know? On 9/11, he was the priest everybody talked about—the priest who went in and tried to save all those firemen."

Father Mike had become a story in *The Daily News*.

A lot had happened to him since we'd had our talks in Jersey.

In 1992, he became the department chaplain to a fire station on West 31st Street in New York. He had moved to the priory across the street from the station—where he ministered to the men. He loved his life. He loved his firemen. He was even known to climb a ladder in his sandals—his brown habit billowing. He ministered to the homeless, the addicts, people with AIDs. Everyone loved him.

In the summer of 2001, close friends noticed a change in the once ever-cheerful priest. In retrospect, they sensed he knew his time would be up soon. But that was fine with him. He didn't want to grow old and infirm. He wanted to go out the way he'd lived: strong, capable, happy, helping people.

On September 10, 2001, in what would prove to be his final homily, he reminded the firefighters that, even in the midst of danger, God was near.

When the first plane hit the World Trade Center, Father Mike was relaxing with several off-duty firemen. Just an ordinary day—a Tuesday—following the usual routine.

They rushed to the site, the North Tower.

Father Mike was in front of a large window. He saw victims falling to their deaths. A French documentary company just happened to film Father Mike's last moments. He was praying for the victims, absolving them of their sins.

When the South Tower exploded, the force shattered the window and threw Father Mike across the lobby. A fireman, who'd stumbled over the body, recognized him. He was put in a chair and carried outside. But it was too late.

Father Mychal Judge was the first recorded victim of 9/11—a day which saw the lives of 343 firemen lost.

••••••

I can't remember the last time I didn't go to Mass on Sunday. It's been at least 25 years. Lorraine will tell you I always find a way, even on the road, to attend church.

Father Mychal Judge. I met him at East Rutherford High School—he was a very special priest. Years later, as a chaplain with the New York City Fire Department, Father Judge died in the shadows of the World Trade Center on September 11, 2001, praying for the victims.

My argument is if I can't find one hour a week to thank the man upstairs for all the blessings I've been given, then there's something wrong with me.

But you never hear me on TV pushing religion. It is, above all, a personal matter. It's how you live your life. How you treat others the way you'd want to be treated. My faith provides me with a guide on how to live. I got my faith from my parents—who saw religion as essential to their lives. They set me a wonderful example of how to live a good life. How to believe in God. How to be strong, to be kind. How to care for others.

My belief doesn't make me right, doesn't make me wrong. It just makes me, me.

OVAL OFFICE ROUNDBALL

Hail to the Chief! I get fired up every time I hear that song.

Whether you are a Democrat or a Republican, the president is the president. These men have reached a certain level where you must respect them. Period.

I've been lucky enough to have met with three presidents over my career. Bill Clinton and Barack Obama were in office when I met them. George W. Bush was the owner of the Texas Rangers when our paths crossed.

What's really neat though is that President Clinton and President Obama are both really big basketball fans, so we had something to talk about from the beginning—Never underestimate the power of hoops as an icebreaker, man.

I got to meet President Obama back in 2012 when ESPN decided to celebrate Veterans Day on November 12 by opening the college basketball season with a game between North Carolina and Michigan State on the deck of the aircraft carrier USS Carl Vinson, which was docked at the Naval Air Station North Island on San Diego Bay.

The "Carrier Classic" idea originally came from Michigan State's AD Mark Hollis, who is one of the most creative ADs in college sports. He is the guy who put the idea together for the 2003 basketball game between Kentucky and the Spartans that drew a record crowd of just over 78,000 to Ford Field in Detroit. With just 7,000 fans, including many from the armed services, this one was a little more intimate. The guest list also included President and First Lady Barack and Michelle Obama.

It was an awesome scene, both teams wearing camouflage-patterned uniforms with USA on the back, battling on the deck of an aircraft carrier in front of a crowd of American servicemen and women. At one point, they paused the game for a moment while they lowered the American flag. I was so caught up in the patriotism I suggested if this was going to be a tradition, they should add a game between Army and Navy and make it a doubleheader.

The president, who showed up wearing a brown bomber jacket, is a huge college basketball fan. He picks his bracket every year for ESPN with Andy Katz in the White House. In fact, President Obama and I have something in common—we both picked Michigan State in the 2014 tournament and both came up empty.

And he's more than a fan. He loves to play hoops, too. The president treated himself to an unusual 49th birthday present back in

What an honor it was for Dan Shulman, Jay Bilas, and I to talk hoops with President Obama, who is an enthusiastic and knowledgeable fan of basketball.

2010 when he invited a group of NBA stars to participate in a pickup game over at a gym at Ft. McNair in the district. It was like a Who's Who. Check this roster: Grant Hill, Shane Battier, Carmelo Anthony, Chauncey Billups, Derek Fisher, LeBron James, Magic Johnson, Alonzo Mourning, Chris Paul, Derrick Rose, Bill Russell, Etan Thomas, Dwyane Wade, and David West. He even invited Maya Moore, the star of UConn's women's national championship team, just for a little diversity. I only wish I could have been there. Would I call the president a PTPer or would I say "I'm sorry, Mr. President. You were all-Airport, baby. You look good at the airport, but you can't play."

We had a little chatter on the big ship. It was funny as heck because Dan Shulman, Jay Bilas, and I are sitting there doing the game and during a timeout I said, "Hey guys, I'm going to go over there and ask the president to stop by and take a picture with us."

And my buddies began to laugh.

Well, I got up, and as soon as I did, there were all these secret service guys jumping in front of me. I was lucky. The president spotted me, came over, we shook hands, and pictures were taken. I wanted a picture for myself, so I asked my wife Lorraine to take a picture of me with the president for Twitter, and he says to me, "Hey, Dickie V, man, you've overachieved in marriage!"

I said, "Mr. President, you haven't done too badly either. You've flat-out overachieved with Michelle."

Well, midway through the game, Jay was talking about basketball being a family affair for the Obamas, and I told a tale about sending a question out to my Twitter followers, asking them who they thought was the best coach in college basketball. Most of the replies came back, "Hall of Famer, Coach K." Well, I told the listeners I got a tweet from President Obama that said, "I disagree with you. I'm biased. I think the best guy is up at Oregon State. And his name is Craig Robinson."

I found out later the tweet was a phony. But it made for a nice story. Robinson, the now former Oregon State coach, is President Obama's brother-in-law.

Hey, President Obama knows the game, and I'm sure he had to be happy when his alma mater Harvard, the home of Tommy Amaker, got a couple of big W's in NCAA games the past few years, beating New Mexico and Cincinnati. He's been to games at Howard and Maryland. And look at his cabinet: Arne Duncan, the Secretary of Education, was a big star at Harvard. In fact, he just played on the winning 3x3 team that represented our country in the 2014 FIBA World Championship in Moscow, Russia.

The president is pretty busy these days, but he found time to write a congratulatory-signed letter to Michigan basketball player Jordan Morgan on his graduation. Morgan stepped in at center after starter Mitch McGary needed back surgery and helped lead the Wolverines to the 2014 NCAA Elite Eight against Kentucky. He even gave Morgan and a couple of other basketball players shout-outs when he spoke at the university.

And this wasn't the first time I'd had an exchange with a sitting president.

Back in 1995, Arkansas was playing UCLA for the national championship in Seattle. President Clinton is a huge Arkansas fan. He was at the '94 Final Four in Charlotte to watch the Hogs and Nolan Richardson beat Duke in the finals, and his motorcade created quite a traffic jam near the stadium—cars everywhere, baby!

Anyway, in 1995, ESPN set up an interview with President Clinton, Digger Phelps, and me at a local Arkansas restaurant. We were shooting the breeze and the president says to us, "What do you guys think about the game tonight? Who's going to win?"

Well, I'm not that dumb, man. I'm talking to a president from the state of Arkansas in a big Arkansas restaurant, but I did feel the Razorbacks would be too strong for UCLA, who was playing without their dynamite starting guard, Tyus Edney.

I said, "Mr. President, your Razorbacks are in good shape."

And he yelled to everybody in the restaurant, "Hey, Dickie V says we're home free. We're going to beat them and win the national title!"

"So, Mr. President, who's going to win?" Brad Nessler and I interviewed President Clinton, who is also a big college hoops fan, especially when it comes to cheering for the Arkansas Razorbacks.

Well, sorry, Mr. President, I was wrong. Can't be right all the time. Cameron Dollar stepped in and sparked Jimmy Harrick's Bruins to the national title.

But it was a lot of fun, just like it was when I met President Clinton's wife Hillary. I was doing a book signing in Louisville, and the store called and said, "Look, we just got a call from Hillary's PR staff. She's coming here to sign her book, *It Takes a Village*, on the same day we're promoting yours. You have a choice. You can cancel and do it the following week, or you can go to another room and let her have that room."

I said I'll go to the other room because I want to be there when the President's wife is in town. Well, we went and had a big book signing, and they arranged a meeting with Hillary and me. It was 1996, and I had just done a game between Massachusetts and Kentucky out in Auburn Hills, Michigan. I was totally stunned as Marcus Camby and John Calipari gave the Wildcats a big L.

The first thing Hillary said to me was, "Is Massachusetts really that good?"

We exchanged books, took some pictures, and I said, "Wow, this is special. This family knows their hoops."

Oh yeah, I also had a chance to meet George W. Bush before he was the commander-in-chief. He was the owner of the Texas Rangers, and I got to sit with him and his wife, Laura, at a baseball game. We also had a chance to have dinner in the pressroom. The whole deal was set up by Richie Adubato, the coach of the Dallas Mavericks. Richie knew I was a big baseball fan and arranged for me to meet Bobby Valentine, the manager of the Rangers, as well.

Little did I know when I was sitting with George W. Bush that he would later become the President of the United States.

CHAPTER 4
WAKING UP THE ECHOES

When I was growing up in New Jersey, my favorite sports were football, baseball, and basketball. I really wasn't into tennis until my daughters began to play. I remember watching Notre Dame games on Saturdays or highlights every Sunday with Lindsey Nelson. It was a family affair. My father, uncles, and I would gather around the black-and-white TV and wait for the action to start. Listening to the fight song gave me the shivers: "Cheer, cheer for old Notre Dame." I followed them religiously, from the days of Johnny Lujack and Leon Hart to those of Joe Theismann—who was also from Jersey—and, of course, Joe Montana.

Football really got me going.

In high school, I didn't have the best academic record. As I was starting to make applications to colleges my senior year, my parents—God bless them—knew nothing about schools and their academic requirements. But they knew about Notre Dame because of their visibility on television.

"Richie, why don't you try to go to that school, Notre Dame, the one with the football?" my mother asked me.

"Are you kidding me? I have no chance, Mom. With my grades, the closest I'm going to get to Notre Dame is watching them on TV."

Fast forward several decades later to when my daughter was attending the school, and there I was, taking my father to South Bend for a football weekend. It was one of the biggest thrills of my life to do that for him and my uncle Mike. They were both diehard fans. I remember we walked the campus before the game and, afterward, had dinner with my daughter.

It soon became a ritual—and then one of the highlights of my life. For the six years my daughters were in undergraduate and grad school there, I just closed my calendar. I told the Washington Speakers Bureau: "Here are the Notre Dame home football dates. Don't book me any speeches then."

Every weekend, I'd take someone who'd been good to me in my life—people from East Rutherford, people in business—as my guest. We'd go for three days, starting on Friday afternoon with the Quarterback Club luncheon, followed by the pep rally that night. We'd walk the campus, go the bookstore, buy t-shirts, and go to Parisi's. Then, we'd attend the game on Saturday. After the game, we'd go to dinner with my girls and their friends at local restaurants. Many times, Digger Phelps joined us. Tom

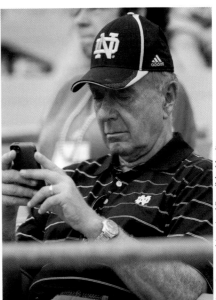

Photo Courtesy of Associated Press/John Mersits

I love Notre Dame, and I love Notre Dame football. But man, being at a game AND being able to Tweet, well, let's just say I always make sure the echoes are awake.

I love mixing with the students on game day. Let me say it again, ND is one special place.

Longo, a friend of mine who played for Notre Dame and whose son went to school with my daughters, and I would split the bill.

Today, my family and I still attend Notre Dame home games about three times a year. Going there has become a cherished part of my life.

I have developed such a love for the school. I am so proud my daughters were student-athletes at the Golden Dome. I guess you can say I was living vicariously through them. Originally, I'd thought they were a lock for either Duke or Carolina, where they had been offered full scholarships for their academic and tennis success. And then Notre Dame came out of the blue to recruit Terri. She said, "I have to tell you, Dad. I know everybody thinks I'm going to Duke, but I love the Golden Dome."

In 2014, she was the vice president of the popular Monogram Club—a group composed of all the letter winners there. She was the keynote speaker when the freshmen athletes came to campus for freshman orientation, telling them what it's like to be a student-athlete at such a fine university like Notre Dame.

Sherri followed in her footsteps.

Who's a proud dad?

They loved it so much, they both went back and got their Masters degree in business at the university.

Then, how about this? I was awarded an honorary degree from the university in 1997. It was such a surprise. We were at a pep rally before the Michigan State game. It was outside in the stadium. Bob Davie was the coach at that time. For some reason, that was the one Friday I had other plans and wasn't going to go. But my daughter insisted I come. She convinced me this was a special pep rally and that I had to be there. So, I pushed the other appointment back and went.

I was in the crowd. Everybody was cheering and singing—a typical Notre Dame pep rally. All of a sudden, the head of the alumni association appeared on the stage and said, "We'd like Dick Vitale to come up to the stage."

The crowd started chanting my name: "Dickie V! Dickie V!"

What was going on?

"Dick, the university has bestowed only a small number of honorary alumni degrees. Today, we are proud to announce we are giving one to you."

Needless to say, I got choked up.

Lorraine and I try to give back to the school. We started the Dick Vitale Family Scholarship Awards. We've given a certain amount of money over the years to the school. They invest it, and the dividends supply financial aid for various students with scholarships. The school picks the recipients, but we made a rule: To be eligible, students must participate in activities without scholarship aid. Over the years, we've been able to help many youngsters, including cheerleaders, band members—even the leprechaun.

You should see the letters I get from these students telling me that without the scholarship they might not have been able to get their degree.

I'm not sure who feels more grateful—the kids or yours truly.

To me, Notre Dame represents greatness. Everybody thinks about Notre Dame football, but the students who you meet there are all achievers. They all chase their dreams. There are many fantastic universities in this country, but this school really fit my daughters. Both of my sons-in-law are Notre Dame graduates, too.

Chris Sforzo, Terri's husband, played lacrosse. Sherri's husband, Thomas Krug, played football.

We are a Notre Dame family. We have memorabilia all over the house.

....

I was really close to Lou Holtz when he coached football there. In fact, Lou had me speak several times at pep rallies, which was always a blast.

My daughters loved hearing him speak. When they were being recruited, the tennis coaches took them to meet Lou, who told them, "Why are you thinking about Duke? You're a Notre Dame girl. I can see it all over you."

They heard Lou speaking about having passion and pride in life. They came home and were so excited about Lou speaking about subjects I spoke about on a regular basis.

"Excuse me," I said, "Excuse me. I talk about that all the time. But you have to hear it from an outsider to believe it?"

My son-in-law Thomas raves about Lou, too.

He played for him before an injury stopped his football career. Thomas had been a backup quarterback to Ron Powlus. After Powlus was injured, Thomas threw three touchdowns in a heartbreaking loss to Florida State in the 1996 Orange Bowl. At that time, a lot of people were telling him maybe he could have started. But Thomas never wavered in his respect for Lou. He never questioned Lou's judgment. "I learned so much from Lou," he told me.

When Thomas became the youngest Circuit Judge in the state of Florida, he received one of the most fantastic letters of his life—from Lou Holtz.

"I want this to be read by your children," the letter said. Lou praised him for his love for the team and the school.

On a recent trip to South Bend, as we were circling the campus, I looked over at Thomas, who had tears streaming from his eyes as he was looking down at the stadium.

Irish eyes make me smile, baby!

Hey, how could I enjoy Notre Dame without Lorraine? Whenever we're on campus, we have a great time.

"People who don't play here don't get it," he said. "Once you come out of that locker room and run out onto that field and feel the adrenaline and the Notre Dame spirit, it's something you never, ever forget."

CHAPTER 5
YOU CAN GO HOME AGAIN, BABY

I know I'm emotional. I can cry at the drop of a hat…and often do.

But I surprised even myself at how quickly I choked up at the press conference before the dedication of the Dick Vitale Court at Calihan Hall at the University of Detroit–Mercy.

It was a special moment in my life—December 5, 2011—the first time I'd been back in Detroit for a while. The memories overwhelmed me, and I lost it—big time.

I couldn't help it. I walked in there crying. I didn't cry when I was enshrined in the Naismith Hall of Fame or when I was inducted into the College Hall of Fame. I don't know what hit me that day… And I suddenly remembered how good Detroit had been to my family and me.

When I got off the plane for my interview, I'll be honest with you: My heart was still in New Jersey. My whole life, I'd known nothing but Jersey. My whole family—parents, siblings, uncles, aunts, cousins— were all there. The same was true for Lorraine.

There I was, in 1973, going off to somewhere I knew very little about. I was greeted with stories about how the University of Detroit (as it was known then) job belonged to another coach, not to me. And I knew nobody wanted to go to their games. I asked myself, "What am I doing here?"

But those people embraced me. The citizens of the Motor City treated me like an unbelievable hero, like royalty.

To this day, when we're in a restaurant, people still come up to me and say, "Man, I'll never forget those Titans."

I'd tell local athletes, "If you want grass, if you want trees, you don't want us. But, if you want to play in front of executives from the leading car companies like GM and Ford and Chrysler, play for us. Get name identity in *The Detroit News* and *Detroit Free Press* on a regular basis. We can give you that visibility." That's what I was selling and selling like you cannot believe.

These people are salt-of-the-earth blue-collar workers—just like my family was. They love their sports teams. If you give them everything you have, they take you to their hearts. You're in—for life.

When the AD, Keri Gaither, told me they'd be dedicating the floor to me, I told her I didn't deserve it. I was there only five years, four as a coach and one as an AD. But she simply said, "I want you to rethink this. I'm going to call you back. We're not naming the court after you because you simply coached here but because of all the visibility you've given to the university. Every time you're on TV, and whenever you speak at various functions, you are associated with the Titans."

When they made a pitch again, I said, "Let's do it."

I pulled back the curtain…and there it was—The Dick Vitale Court. What an honor! The University of Detroit named their court after me, and baby, I can't fully express just how special that is to me.

At the floor dedication, I got about two sentences out before the waterworks started. Maybe it was seeing my former coaches and players again. There they were: Dave "Smokey" Gaines, natty as ever in his white hat; John "Rock Steady Eddie" Long; Terry Tyler; and Dennis Boyd, who hit the buzzer-beating winning shot for our victory against Marquette—still considered the biggest win in school history.

But it was more than that. I realized without getting that head-coaching job at Detroit so long ago, there would be no Dickie V, no ESPN, no Halls of Fame, no financial security. Everything that's happened in my life would not have existed without the U of D. I was a nobody, and they gave me the opportunity I had been looking for.

It was a sobering thought.

I remember my first team meeting. There was lots of apprehension when I was hired. People wanted to know, "Who is this Dick Vitale guy?"

I walked in, took a look around, and said, "I'm Coach Vitale, and we're starting a new program today. If you don't want to be part of it, goodbye. I want players who will play with pride and passion, and I will go out and find 12 young guys who will play their hearts out."

Thank God they stayed.

I shared my goals with them. My dream was to walk into the arena and see, in big letters on the door, "Sold Out. SRO." I was laughed at. They thought I was crazy. Even though Jim Harding, the previous coach, was winning games, they were getting few fans in the arena—Calihan Hall holds a little more than 9,000. I had my work cut out for me, but we succeeded because we were dedicated 24/7 to marketing the program.

For example, we had Titan Toddlers, elementary school kids who participated in a clinic on weekends and received a free ticket for the youngster to attend our games. We had roundball luncheons, where we would honor someone from the pro teams—the Pistons, Tigers, Red Wings; they brought attention to our program. We had a 24-hour Hoops Hysteria marathon, where every two hours a new game took place, like police vs. fire departments and other local match-ups, culminating in our Red-White game.

Do you think Hall of Fame coach Roy Williams needed a 24-hour basketball marathon to generate interest in Tar Heel country?

Do you think John Calipari, Coach K, Rick Pitino, or Roy Williams had to do any of that to get people in the arena? I don't think so, baby!

I was fortunate enough, however, to have outstanding basketball people on my staff, like Brendan Suhr from New Jersey. He came highly recommended from Howard Garfinkel. Also joining my staff was Jim Boyce, an excellent ex-Titan player who was recommended by his former coach and then AD Bob Calihan. A key member of my staff was "Smokey" Gaines, a former Harlem Globetrotter. He took a substantial pay cut to join me, and I'm grateful to him for that. Smokey knew everybody in town. He

Holding court on my court! It was great to see so many of my former players when the U of D named their court after me. It's all about the team, baby.

was Mr. Popularity. He would bring many of the stars from the Lions, Pistons, and Tigers to our practices.

But my favorite place to see great players was St. Cecilia's. I would spend every Saturday morning there. It was run by Sam Washington, who was a legend in the city and a very good friend of mine. He used to tell people, "I'm going to get a cot for Dick," so I could sleep there. I would hang for hours watching all these gifted young players. I saw Campy Russell, George Gervin—so much terrific local talent.

Then, I got familiar with this young coach Mike Brunker, who was working with Sam. I loved his energy and enthusiasm. I watched the way he was coaching many of the superstars there and offered Mike a job with the Titans.

When I entered Titan Territory that night, it brought back so many memories. These people welcomed me, poured out their hearts to me. That's why I was so emotional. Ray McCallum, the current coach, asked if I would talk to his team. I did. I talked about how so many people write down goals, but few really have the commitment to make them a reality. I asked the team if they knew how to make good decisions and if they were selfish because it's only when you have unselfish people who play with a sense of pride that you have a chance to win.

I was warmly welcomed by Matt Terry, the voice of the Titans on radio, and the school's president, Dr. Antoine Garibaldi. Governor Rick Snyder had prepared a proclamation in my honor as well. It was all extremely flattering and much more than I deserved.

Then, there was the dedication of the state-of-the art floor.

I uncovered it, and it read "Dick Vitale Court" along the side with my signature below.

After that came what was for me the best part: the video. It was grainy, but it was wonderful. Of course, my favorite segment was watching our win over Marquette. They were ranked No. 8 at the time. There I was, on February 16, 1977, wearing blue pants and a red tie, pacing the sidelines opposite Al McGuire—one of my idols. Seven seconds, six seconds, five, four, three…then that fabulous shot by Boyd. The arena erupted. I danced, as promised, with the cheerleaders, around the players—Disco Dick at his finest.

When it was my turn to speak, Keri said she'd asked the clock operator to turn the shot clock on. I had five minutes.

Are you serious? I can't say hello in that amount of time.

I expressed my gratitude to everyone involved, of course. "I can't run. I can't jump. I can't shoot. I have a body by linguine. But I'm in 12 Halls of Fame. None of this would have happened if this school hadn't hired me."

Detroit beat St. John's that night. ESPN carried the game. I was interviewed on TV by John Saunders and Fran Fraschilla. Speaking of the media, I still keep in touch with Mike O'Hara, one of the first guys who covered me. Man, those were the days. *The Detroit News* and *Detroit Free Press* treated me in such a special way.

I remember where it all started because, without the Titans and without that opportunity, there wouldn't be a Dickie V.

CHAPTER 6

A DALLAS COWBOY

Let's face it: There's nothing like being part of a college basketball environment. I love going to a college campus and being part of a game that is so special—the fans, the atmosphere, the cheerleaders, the band. The whole scene is absolutely Awesome with a capital A!

I've also been blessed working in a studio with guys like Bob Ley, who taught me how to make a statement on camera quickly and to be concise. OK, OK, I can hear everyone laughing—you can stop now.

But, to me, there is nothing like the adrenaline you get sitting at courtside as you feel the electricity and the energy that is all around you.

In 2013 and 2014, I've had the thrill of sitting and calling the NCAA Final Four for *ESPN International*. Years ago, I learned from broadcasting giant Jim Simpson that you should treat every game and every moment as if it's the biggest game in a kid's life, so it's been a thrill to be part of a game where every shot, every pass, every turnover is so big. I try to treat every game like an NCAA tournament game anyway; so, to me, it's not much different. The stakes are just higher.

Now, I have calling the NCAA Final Four on my resume. It's been wonderful being a part of a broadcast team airing the game to over 80 countries around the world. I was just thrilled to sit courtside for the games.

Now, here I am, calling the games that lead to the big, big trophy.

Now, all my buddies in Italy get to hear me.

So, from Canada to New Zealand, you can't escape Dickie V, Baby!

Initially, I felt an emptiness when ESPN didn't get the Final Four contract. I know our network really tried like heck to obtain the rights, but I've learned in life there are a lot of things we wish we could have that we don't ever get. CBS and TBS have the rights in America, but ESPN has become a player in the NCAA regardless with our pre-game shows, highlight shows, and appearances on *SportsCenter.*

So, we have been part of it—for many years.

When ESPN got the international rights, my boss, John Wildhack, told me it was one of the things he was proudest of, and he wanted to make sure I got a chance to participate in a tournament game. Before 2013, I'd never had the luxury of being part of the visibility and game exposure in the Final Four. My first was with Brad Nessler in 2013, and the second was with Dan Shulman in 2014.

The funny part is Shulman and I did the first college basketball game ever held at "Jerry's House" (AT&T Stadium in Arlington, Texas, nicknamed for Dallas Cowboys owner Jerry Jones), North Carolina vs. Texas back in 2009, so I had a little familiarity with the place when he and I called the 2014 Final Four. And let me just say this: It's huge! A $1.3 billion stadium built for football, which can seat up to 80,000 fans, with a video board that's 72 feet high by 180 feet wide and weighs about 1.2 tons.

I didn't know I was posing with Seattle's Super Bowl-winning QB Russell Wilson. My bad. But he's a champ and laughed off my mistake, gladly accepting my apology.

At that championship, Dallas showed everyone that the Final Four is approaching Super Bowl status in this country. For the games, Jerry Jones hosted former presidents Bill Clinton and George W. Bush in his suite. Quarterbacks Johnny Manziel and Tony Romo were there, too. Bruce Springsteen did a free concert downtown—he rocked Dallas. Drake, the Canadian rapper who's a big Kentucky fan, was in attendance as well as racecar driver Danica Patrick. Former college basketball superstars and NBA players Christian Laettner and Grant Hill were also present.

It was Celebrity City, man.

I had one embarrassing moment during the games though. Sitting near me was a good-looking guy and somebody told me to go take a picture with him. So I did it. When I came back, my people at courtside said, "Dick, we don't think you know who you were just taking a picture with." They told me it was Russell Wilson, the starting quarterback of the Seattle Seahawks, 2014 Super Bowl champions.

I said, "Oh, well. My bad." I went over to apologize to him later.

• •

I was a huge fan of the original *Dallas* when it was on TV years ago. In fact, Audrey Landers, who was a big star on that show, came to my 2014 gala with her sister Judy since Judy is married to my good friend, former Dodgers closer Tom Niedenfuer.

Anyway, this trip, I got to channel my inner J. R. Ewing.

One day, the ESPN producer and I were standing around talking, and I said, "We're in Dallas, man, and I'm going to the stockyards. It would be awesome to jump on a horse with a 10-gallon hat and ride through the streets."

He said, "What a great idea," grabbed one of the assistants and ordered, "Track down a horse, put Dickie on it, get a camera, and go!"

I got my cowboy hat on (thank you, Larry Hagman), got up on the horse, and rode down the streets of Fort Worth.

I just wanted to make sure it was a slow horse, the slowest in the world. Don't get me California Chrome, man. Get me a horse that can't run!

Horsing around at the 2014 Final Four in Dallas. I think the horse took a real liking to me.

And they did.

I've often read that it is when you stop being a kid, that you begin to age. Trust me, I don't feel my age. I'm a kid at heart. OK, I'll be honest. I know my age when I look in the mirror, but that day, on that horse, I felt twelve years old again!

Which brings me to "Joel the Longhorn," a 1,795-pound Texas longhorn that crossed my path during the tournament. As a part of their March Mayhem Challenge, Allstate challenged me to put my basketball knowledge on the line against Joel, so from inside the Fort Worth Steer Pen, I went head-to-head in a bracket contest… with a longhorn. I had to reveal my picks before

I'm good, baby. I beat Joel the Steer in the Allstate Challenge at the 2014 Final Four in Dallas.

Joel made his selections. If I'd lost, I would have had to work as Joel's personal ranch hand, helping to prep him and the rest of his herd for their daily cattle drive down Exchange Avenue.

It was a total M & Mer, a complete mismatch. But, when he picked his final to be Manhattan vs. VCU, I knew I was in the clear. Which was a good thing because I didn't want to come back there to sweep up, muck the stables, wash him—the things I would have had to do if I'd lost. (For the sake of transparency, I will admit, though, when Joel had to put his nose toward one of the teams, I would make sure his food was placed near the team I *wanted* him to pick. After all, there was a lot at stake!)

As a kind of thank you, Allstate contributed to the V Foundation, like they did it the year before when they had me do battle with some dolphins at the Atlanta Aquarium. I was able to win that, too, baby! We were throwing balls in the water, and the ball the dolphin would go for would be his pick. So, I made sure, I'd throw the ball I wanted the dolphin to pick close to him. It's the psychological aspect of coaching—aren't you taught to look for an edge vs. your competition?!

As for the games themselves, Connecticut was just awesome, baby!

Kudos to Kevin Ollie and his Huskies. Talk about a coach whose stock is on the rise. Ollie was able to get a multi-million dollar new deal for bringing home the gold trophy to Storrs, Connecticut. Congrats to the 2014 Champs!

MY JOURNEY

It sure has been a winding road that I've traveled on my awesome 75-year journey, learning about myself, basketball, love, failure, success, loss, family, fatherhood, and everything else in between. Some of the rough spots were tough, and, man, it was never really smooth, but I honestly can't complain. In the end, I think I've become a pretty good "PTPer" in my own right and have gotten a W in the game of life!

That's right, baby, I'm a pretty good PTPer myself. Here I am, signing autographs for the crowd before a game.

CHAPTER 7
A JERSEY GUY

I'm from Jersey, man—born, bred, and proud of it.

Just look at the roster of college basketball coaches the state has produced: Hubie Brown, Richie Adubato, Lou Campanelli, Rollie Massimino, Bill Raftery, and Mike Fratello. We all grew up with a dream—the dream to coach on the collegiate level. It took just one door to open for all of us. Brown, who is in the Hall of Fame, set the tone, moving up from Fair Lawn High School to become an assistant at Duke and then going on to coach in the ABA and, later, the NBA. He hired Fratello as his assistant when he was head coach of the Atlanta Hawks, then Mike became an NBA head coach. It was a domino effect.

Jersey, man. The Sopranos. Jersey Boys—I saw it five times on Broadway. Jon Bon Jovi. Bruce Springsteen. And, most of all, Sinatra—The Chairman of the Board, Old Blue Eyes.

My mother's "claim to fame" was that her doctor, our family physician, was Dr. Joseph Latona. Back in the day of house calls, he came to our home because my mom was really sick. She had tuberculosis as a young woman and was told she would never, ever have children. It was a miracle she ended up having three, yours truly included. One of her best stories was that house call. At that time, Dr. Latona was living in Hasbrouck Heights. Staying right near him was Frank Sinatra, who was a guest in someone's house. While Dr. Latona was over tending to my mom, he told her Frank Sinatra was a couple of houses away. And that's all she ever talked about. She'd had a glimpse of him when he was a young teenage idol. And she never forgot it. My way, buddy, my way. Sinatra. I've been lucky enough to see the Chairman of the Board perform at least five times.

Jersey has always been incredibly special to me and my family. Growing up, I knew nothing but Jersey. The only plane trip I ever took as a kid was to the Dapper Dan in Pittsburgh. My second flight was to the University of Detroit for an interview about their head coaching job. Up until that time, everything was Jersey. Our vacations were even to the Jersey shore. There was nothing like going down to Atlantic City or Seaside Heights. It was a big deal in my family. My father worked in factories, pressing coats, and then was a security guard at night. It was a big thrill for him to be able to get the dollars together for us to have a vacation each summer. We'd get in the car and go down there for a couple of days. It was a blast.

My family was Jersey all the way. I had nine uncles and aunts on my father's side and nine uncles and aunts on my mother's side. All 18 of them—it breaks my heart—are gone now. But every one of them was what our nation was about: blue-collar, hard-working factory workers who never took days off with the flu or a headache. It was all about putting meals on the table for their families, hoping and praying their kids would go on and make it in life.

That way of life: It was always about family.

I grew up in Garfield, New Jersey, and lived on Madeline Avenue. I lost my eye because of an accident with a pencil when I was a kid, but that didn't deter me from getting involved in sports. Across the street from our house was a brick wall, and when I was ten or eleven, my

With my mom and dad. I'll tell you, our family had a doctorate of love. I was a lucky kid.

cousin Johnny Scarpa—who is a dentist, still living in Jersey—and I would go out front and play Yankees vs. Red Sox. It was like handball with a baseball twist: one guy would be in the field and the other guy would throw the pink Spalding ball at the wall in all different directions. If you hit it onto the second deck of the house, where my grandmother lived, that was a home run. If you hit it off the wall onto the second deck, that was a triple. The lower deck was a double. Then, you would be in the field, catching the ball three times. Three outs. Next guy got up. And we had the lineups all down. My whole life was about Jersey—and my family. On Sunday mornings, my mother had the coffee and the donuts ready. After church, all my uncles and aunts would come over. Now, my uncles were fanatical sports fans and they would say, "Who do you like? Do you like Mantle, Mays, or Duke Snider?"

I used to laugh as my father would come in and say, "Are you kidding me? Give me Joe D. Joe DiMaggio." Naturally, being a proud paisan, I expected nothing less.

I'll never forget the love and laughter in those conversations, man. It was Jersey. It was home.

Recently, I showed my grandchildren an article with a picture of me that said I came within one out from a perfect game. It said, "Richie (as I was known then) Vitale was working on a perfect game. The last batter got a single." I struck out 15 of 18 batters.

So, I was a pretty good baseball player, pretty good at basketball, too. At the time, we were still living in Garfield. All of a sudden, though, my grandmother lent some money to my father and mother and to my Aunt Lee and Uncle Carl. Our two families used the funds to build two homes next to each other with connecting driveways. My mother and her sister were always inseparable, and now their houses were as well. I was going into high school at Garfield when we moved away. It's amazing that, even in the early days, how much recruiting was a part of it. I was a pretty good young athlete, growing up in Little League Baseball. Just after the move, the high school coach came over to speak with my parents about where I should go to school (more like where I should play). He said, "Look, we can work it out. You have relatives there, so you can go to Garfield." I stayed there for two years.

Then, I developed an awful infection in my left eye. It was brutal, brutal. I must have missed 70-80 days of school. I couldn't go out into the sun. I was constantly tearing up; my eye was always red. I knew I'd have to repeat my junior year, and I didn't want to go back to Garfield since I'd be one year behind. We were living in East Paterson (which is now Elmwood Park), but the sending district, since they had no high school, was East Rutherford.

My vision finally caught up to me, and I never was the athlete I probably should have been in high school. I did play varsity basketball; I started, shot the ball pretty well. But the biggest mistake was when I was a 13-year-old kid learning how to throw a curve ball. It cost me big time as my arm was shot. By my varsity years, I couldn't throw a ball through a glass window even if I wanted to.

I could have been a better student, too. I should have read more books. Instead of paying attention, I'd sit in the back of the classroom at East Rutherford High and read *The New York Daily News* and Dick Young's column. Man, I used to love those dot-dot-dots. One day, my teacher ran to my desk, ripped the paper out of my hands, and said to me, "Richie, you have wasted all that brain matter. You could be such a student. Where are you going? All you care about is sports."

When I was in high school, college was the furthest thing from my mind. Nobody in my family went to college, so I was thinking: get a job, buy a new car, have three-year payments. But God bless my father, he convinced me college was something I needed to consider. One summer, I worked in his factory—like a sweat shop, really—and my job was to bring him the coats to be pressed. And he would press those coats, then we'd get in the car and drive home. And he asked me, "Richie, do you want to do this? Go to school, son."

I wanted to play a little college basketball. But nobody wanted me. I wasn't recruited by anybody. I always felt in my heart that I could play with somebody though. There was a team that used to always come to the East as a cupcake and get blown out by NYU. This team was from Virginia—Roanoke College.

I told my buddies I was going to play there, that I was going to go to school at Roanoke. And I got accepted.

I went to Roanoke. I was there no more than three weeks and got totally homesick.

I went to see the coach who told me, "Why don't you come to the gym and play with the guys?" So I did, and I realized I wasn't good enough. In the back of your mind, you always think you are. I called home, and my mother was crushed.

I don't know how many dollars she scraped together for me to go to Roanoke—tuition, room and board. It was tough. I was so worried I was hurting my mom and dad by coming home because they would lose all the money they put down. But I just couldn't make it at Roanoke. I was homesick, so I went back to Jersey.

At the time, my mother was working as a seamstress. She knew how hard it was to earn money without a college degree and was absolutely determined that I be one of the first in our family to go to college. And I knew better than to argue with her. The next week, there was an ad in the paper about Seton Hall-Paterson. We drove over there. Classes had already started, but late registration was still on. I applied, and they accepted me.

Seton Hall-Paterson had its own basketball team, too. I played my first year although I had no scholarship and had to work. To get through school, I worked produce at Modell's Shopping Center; I used to sell, bananas and tomatoes, can you believe it? Then, I became a member of the sales staff at their clothing store. I was always trying to make a few dollars to help

I always knew how to handle the Rock! While I was a pretty good basketball player in high school, I was no Diaper Dandy.

out my family and offset the cost of my education.

Even though it wasn't high-level Division I, I can say I was a college player and had a lot of fun. We were competitive on the level we played. I played just one year (I got maybe 10 minutes on varsity), but that year allowed me to feel important.

Some of the stars on our team were Johnny Ebner and Al Pogorelec. They were local high school players from North Jersey who I followed when they played on the scholastic level. They were solid players, but not talented enough to play for Seton Hall's main campus. Seton Hall had very good teams in the 50's under Honey Russell. I remember going up to the main campus to see guys like Golden "Sonny" Sunkett and Melvin Knight, whose sons became outstanding players at Stanford and Pitt. I used to go see them play every weekend at Walsh gymnasium in South Orange.

I graduated from Seton Hall-Paterson in 1962 with a BS degree in Business. My college experience wasn't the same as what my daughters had at Notre Dame because I was a commuting student. They each enjoyed a full life as students on campus while, in my case, it was simply a means to getting a degree. But getting that degree, no matter how I went about it, made all the hard work worth it.

I was honored by my alma mater, Seton Hall, with its 2014 Many Are One Humanitarian Award. But I told them I didn't deserve the honor because I didn't go to the main campus. They pointed out that my degree came from Seton Hall, end of story. They said, "You are our Humanitarian and Man of the Year." And that was that. I was certainly flattered.

My buddy, Larry Cirignano, who was the basketball coach at Passaic High School, came up with a phrase I use all the time: "A boy with a ball and a dream." Chasing that dream, hoping to catch that dream. Having now accomplished so much, I'm still that same boy with a ball and a dream. And I have my Jersey roots to thank for a solid foundation.

CHAPTER 8
MY STORY

Everybody has a story.

Mine is about my left eye.

When I was four, I lost the vision in my left eye in an accident. My eye was poked with a pencil, irreparably damaging the cornea. I've had to wear a glass eye ever since.

When I give speeches today, I talk about my journey from being a sixth-grade teacher to the Hall of Fame—all the ups and downs of my career. I talk about how you don't get to the top of the mountain without getting some bumps and bruises along the way. It's not a smooth path. I talk about how it's the way you respond to and battle your setbacks that makes you stronger. How you handle adversity that makes you who you are.

But, for me, it was a long, tough journey that I want to share with you, a journey that started long before I ever became a coach.

When I was young, my good eye would drift; I had no control where it was going. I never could look anyone straight in the eye. I turned my head left or right, trying to compensate for it, but that didn't really work either. Try as I might, I couldn't make eye contact.

As a result, I was bullied a lot as a kid, although I didn't realize it was bullying. I guess I just thought it was just a way of life—or simply put, teasing. As a kid, you just take it. Even though I wanted the name-calling to stop, I was afraid to complain about it to a teacher or a coach because I didn't want to be labeled as soft or weak. I also didn't want anyone to feel sorry for me.

My peers didn't make it any easier.

The other kids would tease me: "Hey, one eye."

"How you doing, one eye?"

Jokes at my expense were the norm. The other kids never realized, or seemed to care about, the pain they caused me when they made these nasty comments to me. I was deeply hurt.

When I pitched in Little League, opposing players—and even parents—would shout, "Can you even see the plate?"

They thought they were being so cool, but their words cut me like a knife.

Even so, I went out there, sucked it up, and played.

Afterward, though, I went home, looked in the mirror, and cried because I had no control over it. It was out of my hands.

The ridicule I endured definitely impacted my confidence.

As a teenager, I even became so shy about approaching girls to ask them out on a date because I was embarrassed about my eye.

As an adult, I've found some people think my eye problem is the reason for my upbeat personality, energy, and enthusiasm. They've said I was trying to compensate by being overly energetic. Maybe it's true.

Here I am, young Richie Vitale. Man, look at that beautiful hair!

All I know is, the world of television allows for a kind of bullying all its own.

One time, in the 1980s, I came out of the studio and asked the switchboard operator how everything was going. I was told everything was great except for this one fan who kept calling in and saying, "ESPN should get rid of that one-eyed guy. His eye is going all over the place."

I was devastated.

It was like a knife going through me all over again, like I was back on the pitcher's mound in Little League so long ago.

If he'd said he didn't like what I was saying, that would have been one thing. Or if he didn't agree with what I was saying, I could have dealt with that. But this was something totally different, and it was really hurtful.

After that conversation, I called up my boss, Steve Anderson, then vice president in charge of production. I said maybe I should get out of the TV business. I told him the story and that I didn't want to embarrass the network. Anderson put me at ease by explaining that I was hired for my basketball knowledge and enthusiasm. It meant the world to me to have his support.

So, I kept on doing my thing.

A while later, my wife took my daughters to Dr. Conrad Giles for an eye test in Birmingham, Michigan; Giles was a pediatric eye specialist and a big basketball fan. During the appointment, he asked Lorraine, "Are you any relation to Dick Vitale." She naturally said yes, that I was her husband. Then, he said, "Even though I deal with kids, I would be willing to help him with his eye problem. I can eliminate the drifting in his eye, but I cannot restore vision."

Lorraine came home and told me I should go see him, and I did.

He looked at my eye, "Dick, we can take care of that for you. I need you to cooperate with me. But I have to tell you I can't operate on your bad eye. I have to operate on your good eye to get it to function properly. I have to explain this to you before you agree to surgery because there's always a chance of losing vision. But I want you to know I have never lost a patient's vision in surgery in all my years of practice. I understand your fear because that's your only good eye, and I have to operate on it. I just need you to trust me."

It was a tough decision for me. The teasing had really bothered me for longer than I'd like to admit. I had felt miserable for years, decades even. I called Steve Anderson and told him what I was going to do. He told me not to worry about getting surgery and to continue doing my job. "Let me tell you something. We didn't hire you to be Robert Redford. We hired you for your basketball opinions. Don't let people like that bother you." Despite Anderson's encouragement, he was a fantastic boss, I decided to have the surgery. I decided to have it for me.

And I'm so glad I did. The procedure alleviated the problem of my eye drifting. Dr. Giles also fitted me for contacts so I didn't have to wear my thick, Coke-bottle glasses any longer. It absolutely gave me the confidence I'd been lacking; it changed everything.

•••

The world would be a much better place if people treated one another with decency and respect. There is no reason to be cruel to someone who is down or has any sort of problem, physical or otherwise.

Trust me, man. I know.

And today, if you're being bullied, you do not have to just suck it up. If you have or your child has a problem, tell someone in authority and talk about the pain. There are a lot of people out there who provide helpful guidance and support, like counselors, spiritual leaders, teachers, coaches, etc., all you need to do is reach out. Bullying is a problem that has really left its mark on our society, and I know there is more we can all do to stop it. I feel so strongly about the issue that I recorded a piece for an anti-bullying campaign for *YouTube*.

I'm 75 years old and have been so lucky, so blessed. Television definitely gave me a different life. But my message here is simple: I thought I was just being teased when I was getting ridiculed about my eye even though I knew deep down it was really bullying; those words caused me considerable pain which could have been avoided. Please, I beg you from the bottom of my heart, don't be a BULLY and don't put up with one either.

CHAPTER 9
MAKING THE RIGHT CHOICE

A lot of people don't know this, but I almost dropped out of high school.

When I was a "senior," I came back to East Rutherford and was ready to have a big year—because I'd missed a whole year with an eye infection, it would actually be my fifth year. Everybody, including me, thought I'd be eligible to play basketball since I lost a year due to the medical problem. I had letters from doctors about my eye, so I didn't think there would be any issue. I was prepared and more than ready to play.

Well, I got a letter from the state saying that since this was my fifth year and because I'd played in a couple of games as a sophomore on the varsity level at Garfield High School, the clock had run out on my eligibility.

I went ballistic.

I told the principal I didn't want to go to school if I couldn't play basketball.

In short, I was quitting.

I know now I acted like a little spoiled brat. My mother and father called the school. My mother was crying. My father was upset. So, the principal called Ken Sinofsky, the head football coach, to come in and talk to me, knowing the respect I had for him. He came into that office and, let me tell you, in no uncertain words, he ripped into me. He pushed me up against the wall. He had that look in his eye when he spoke to me, you know, that look adults have when they're about to tell you something you really need to hear but don't really want to stomach.

"You're breaking your parents' hearts. You're not what I thought you were. I thought you were special, but you're not. You're a baby. You can't get your way—so what you're going to do is quit and hurt everybody. And you're only going to hurt yourself. I'm telling you now, I want you in my office today at three o'clock, and you'd better be there."

Today, if a teacher or a coach grabbed you by the throat and pushed you against the wall like he did to me, he'd be fired immediately. But it was the greatest thing that ever happened to me. He cared. He gave a darn. Sometimes, I think about how so much has changed, how all the rules and laws in place have actually taken away authority from people who genuinely care. I'm not condoning abuse by any means. But I'm telling you, what he did, he did out of love and respect. And I'm so grateful for it.

So, I went to his office at three o'clock. He said, "I know you can't play, but I want you to be with us at practice every day. Come to practice." After that meeting, I became the student assistant of the team. There were days when I ran practice. He gave me leadership responsibilities. Back then, I had no idea—but I was getting valuable on-the-job training about how to be a coach.

Look, he wasn't a basketball guy. He'd be the first to tell you: He was the football coach. He coached basketball just to keep his football guys in

Coach Ken Sinofsky—I owe him so much. He gave me a chance when I needed it most.

shape. But he had certain qualities I really admired. I learned so much about coaching from him: The way he had the respect of his players, the way he had an organized plan for what he wanted them to achieve every day, the way he executed his plan.

When I was roasted at Seton Hall, I made sure they brought him to the front because I wanted him to hear exactly what I thought about him. He commanded such respect. When I was a student and he was coaching football, I used to say to myself, "Man, I'd give anything in my life to get that kind of respect when I walked through the halls." Everybody just looked up to him like you wouldn't believe.

Coach Sinofsky was way ahead of his time.

He reminded me of Bill Parcells—both Jersey guys. I saw a lot of Sinofsky in Parcells when he was coaching the Giants.

There is no doubt in my mind—and I mean this—Sinofsky would have been a giant in coaching had he gotten an opportunity on the college level. In fact, they wanted him so badly to switch over and take the head coaching job at Wayne Valley High that they made him the principal and head coach in football. He was a flat-out winner. He could have won anytime, anywhere.

But the door just never opened for him. As it was, he won five state championships at East Rutherford and Wayne Valley.

There are some coaches out there, put them in any sport, and they can win. You talk about the Krzyzewskis, the Pitinos. Those guys can win in anything.

They just have that way of getting people to buy into their philosophy and their concepts.

Ken Sinofsky was one of those coaches.

Every day at practice, Coach Sinofsky opened up with a talk to the team. It could be about anything. It could be about anyone. When I became a high school coach at East Rutherford, I was thrilled beyond words to share an office with him. I absorbed everything he said to me. "Look. When you run practice, come up with a plan for the day."

Every day, I started practice with a talk to my team, just like he did. One talk in particular stands out in my mind. Remember Rick Leach, who played quarterback for Michigan? He made the cover of *Sports Illustrated* in the mid-70s. I remember coming to practice, walking into the locker room, and saying, "See this guy who's on the cover here? Rick Leach. Know what he did this week throwing the football?" (At that time, his passing numbers were minute.) "You know why he's on the cover? Because he's a winner. Michigan wins. He's the catalyst who makes them win. People want winners."

I talked to my team every day. About anything. About anyone. Some tragedy happened. Somebody was on drugs. That's why one of the biggest heartbreaks for me in my career was Les Cason. I kept talking. But he

I loved teaching and coaching at the high school level.

just didn't listen. I'll have more on that later.

A long-time Jersey buddy, Lou Ravettine, who ultimately coached with me as an assistant at East Rutherford, was a terrific college basketball player at Fairleigh Dickinson. He was so good that one day when I was up at Kutsher's Country Club in the Catskills for a clinic and ended up sitting with Ike Richman, who was the owner of the Philadelphia 76ers, I begged him to give Lou a tryout. We were then notified that he would be given a shot to make the team. But Lou didn't go because he felt his chances were slim anyway, and he didn't want to have to give up a chance to teach and coach.

But listen to this: It was 1956 and Lou was an outstanding freshman player, good enough he was getting ink in Augie Leo's Cracker Barrel column in the hometown paper, the *Clifton-Passaic Herald News*. Leo played semi-pro ball with Sinofsky. Lou's name had just appeared in "The Cracker Barrel," and, trust me, that was big in our area. Well, I arrived at one of his games and went up to him and I've got this big stick that I was holding it like a mic. "Hey," I said, "I'm Richie Vitale and I'm here with Lou Ravettiine, the outstanding freshman player. Lou, tell us how it feels to be a star?"

Man, I even had a shtick back then in 1956.

It was almost like I was auditioning for ESPN.

Considering all I've been able to do since I graduated high school, I have nothing but gratitude for Coach Sinofsky. He helped me make the right choice back then, so I could make all kinds of choices later. Thanks, Coach.

CHAPTER 10
FIRST STEPS

I graduated from Seton Hall in 1962, receiving a newly minted bachelor's degree in business management.

Later on, I pursued a master's degree in elementary education. I sat in my car every night, ate a tuna fish or ham sandwich, and drove to Paterson State—which is now William Paterson—with Mike Fratello and Richie Adubato. We all got our degrees, which we wanted to have in case we didn't become college coaches.

It never hurts to have a Plan B, man.

My first job was working in accounting, if you can imagine that. I worked for the McBride Company in Paterson—nice job, making good money with good people. But I was so bored, man—sitting there doing trial balances, looking at the people around me, looking at the clock.

Dickie V was not meant for office work.

At that time, I coached a baseball team called the Garfield Benignos, an amateur team for kids between the ages of 16 and 19. It was there I got my first taste of recruiting— going after and getting all the Blue Chip kids in the North Jersey area. We had a terrific team, too. A team so good, we won the state championship and represented the area in the national tournament in Johnstown, Pennsylvania.

One of our fans turned out to be an administrator in education for Garfield Public schools in New Jersey, who later asked me if I'd ever thought about teaching. I said, "I'd love to teach, but I have a business degree."

He said, "No problem with that. We can get you a job in elementary school with a provisional certificate." That means I had to go get additional credits in education to get a permanent certificate, which I was willing do.

I'd been at McBride's only three months, but that was long enough, so I quit.

I took a big cut in pay and reported to Mark Twain School No. 3 in the fall. Basically, I taught seventh and eighth grade self-contained classes. My first contract was for a whopping $4,500. Wow, how does that compare to some of the deals NBA coaches like Steve Kerr, Derek Fisher, and Stan Van Gundy are getting today, raking in millions coaching a game we all love?

But the best thing the school gave me was a coaching job—junior high football and basketball.

I had a blast. I fell in love with coaching. I didn't care about the money. Every day, it was exciting to go to work.

I loved being around young kids. I loved motivating them, loved inspiring them.

Then, I got my big break. In 1964, I was hired by my alma mater, East Rutherford, as a sixth grade teacher and high school basketball coach.

I've never forgotten my interview with the superintendent.

He said, "The reason you're getting the job? Nobody else wants it."

Basketball there was so bad. To make matters worse, we only had a 65-foot by 40-foot gym to practice in. Way smaller than regulation.

But I was on my way, baby.

In my seven years there, we won four state sectional championships, two consecutive state championships, not to mention 35 consecutive victories. I was very blessed to have an assistant coach named Bob Stolarz. Bob was a gym rat who absolutely loved the game and had a strong rapport with the kids.

It was a wonderful feeling to have turned that program around.

Being a teacher taught me how to be organized, to have a game plan in English, History, Math. The same discipline carried over into coaching.

If you are an efficient and effective coach, you start off every day with a plan. You don't just walk in there and roll out the ball. You've organized what you are going to do. You break down your offenses, your defenses, your individual skills.

Plus, you are standing in front of people and communicating. To me, coaching is the art of communicating your concepts, your theories. In essence, you are teaching.

I didn't love the paycheck, but I loved teaching.

I owe a lot to my early teaching experience in Jersey.

I still get letters from people who told their kids I was their former teacher, but the kids don't believe them. So I write 'em back.

One of my former students is now a principal.

I'm also indebted to another facet of Jersey life: the diner culture.

Growing up, the night didn't end for me without going to Ross' Diner on Route 46 in Elmwood Park. We would sit there for hours, talking. Sometimes, it would be Adubato. Sometimes, it would be Tommy Ramsden, a buddy I'd met at Seton Hall-Paterson. We sat there all night, drawing up plays using napkins and salt and pepper shakers.

It was on one such night that we decided to drive to the Final Four—which was in Louisville. It was 1969, the first Final Four I'd ever attended. What was it about that year that was so wonderful for me? We had no tickets but were able to buy some on the street. I don't remember what we paid, but it was worth it. UCLA beat Drake and Purdue.

One night in Garfield, New Jersey, we almost got into trouble with the cops. I was in a bar at two in the morning drinking my traditional cranberry juice—with Adubato, Fratello, and Jerry Tarkanian, who was at Long Beach State at the time and was scouting my best player, Les Cason, a 6-foot-10 center. The topic of conversation was how do you get over the top of a screen? We went outside and put these garbage cans in the street, using them as x's and o's to demonstrate our different theories.

Then, the cops came asking, "What the heck are you doing? You're making a racket and the neighbors are complaining."

"We're working on basketball."

They thought we were nuts. But they didn't arrest us. They just started laughing hysterically.

I will never forget one time when Hubie Brown and I set up a scrimmage between our two teams. We were in the gym, screaming, going crazy at our players as we were stopping the action on every play, making corrections.

"Stop any time you want."

The referee was Bill Kunkel, a former NBA ref who'd pitched for the Yankees.

I went to the men's room. There were two guys standing in the corner, and—I'll never forget this—they said to each other, "Man, we just got back from Camp LeJeune. That's not half as tough as these guys are."

One time, Hubie Brown and I went over to see Adubato, who was coaching at Our Lady of the Valley. They were playing St. Peter's of New Brunswick. Their star was John Somogyi, who was the leading high school scorer in the country, averaging like 45 a game. And Richie is coaching against him. The place is packed, standing room only.

So, Richie sneaked us in the back way. We had to come through a window to get into the place.

Here I am giving my guys a pep talk with Bob Stolarz (standing right). They always listened—and they won, which made me look pretty good.

And Richie shuts Somogyi down. Holds him to like 25 (ha, ha).

Back then, North Jersey was a cradle for coaches.

Ramsden and I formed the Garden State Coaches' Clinic. We brought in successful area coaches to speak. We charged admission and got the junior high and high school coaches to join us at the Saddle Brook Marriott. Each year, we would bring in star coaches, like Lou Carnesecca of St. John's, Lefty Driesell of Maryland, and I even got a commitment from Bob Knight of West Point. I'd heard him speak and said we had to get him.

Once the day arrived, everybody was at the clinic, waiting. All of a sudden, this young guy walked in and said, "Coach, I'm here from West Point. Coach Knight had an emergency he had to take care of. I'm here to replace him."

Replace Knight? His name was Don DeVoe, and he went on to coach at Tennessee, Virginia Tech, Wyoming, and Navy.

We also ran a summer camp and would bring in guys like Wes Unseld, the rebounding machine from the Washington Bullets, and many of the stars from coaching and the NBA. Also working for us were Fratello and Abubato. I remember in those days, you'd get $25 and a baloney sandwich to speak. Well, we also bought Hubie Brown in. Gave him $50 and a cheese sandwich.

I remember talking to Bob Hurley Sr., the Hall of Fame coach from St. Anthony's of Jersey City. He said, "Dickie V, I remember inviting you to speak at my camp when you were an assistant at Rutgers. I gave you $25, a sandwich, and a soft drink, and you were in hoops heaven. I know, Dick, you get more than $25 dollars today."

All of us have never forgotten where we came from.

CHAPTER 11

SWEET LORRAINE

My wife, Lorraine, was my best recruit—ever. She was absolutely drop-dead gorgeous. And still is, if I do say so myself. If Bo Derek was a 10, Lorraine was a 15.

I will never forget the night I met her in July 1970—the year after the Miracle Mets won it all. I was at the Blue Swan Inn in Roselle Park, New Jersey, with Richie Adubato and a bunch of coaches. We went there after summer league games to talk basketball, shoot the breeze. Just a bunch of guys at a big table, having fun. And, all of a sudden, these two girls walked in. Lorraine had red hair, white boots, hot pants—all the guys around the table were saying, "Oh my god! Who is that?"

I said, "Guys, don't even think about it. She's mine."

So, I went over and asked her to dance.

She said no. It was the loneliest feeling in the world having to walk back to that table where the guys were giving high fives, teasing me. They were busting on me. Finally, the competitor in me came out. "Guys," I said, "I'm going back over there."

I went over and told her, "These guys are putting me down. They are mocking me. All I want is a dance."

But she shot me down, again. "I'm not in the mood to dance," she said. "I'm with my girlfriend, relaxing, having a good time."

One more time—the walk of shame.

Finally, I said, "Guys, you know I never bet. I'm not a betting guy. I work hard for my money. Put your money on this table, and I guarantee I will get her to dance."

They were laughing. They threw $5, $10, $20 on the table.

I went over a third time and told her, "Look, I asked you to dance. I don't want anything else. But, please, I'm begging you—please dance with me. I bet my buddies I could dance with you. I'll tell you what I'll do: I'll give you the money I win from these guys if you dance with me."

She started laughing and said, "You really want to dance that bad? Come on."

And we danced.

Well, I came back to the table to collect my winnings. I saw her look over at me, and I saw that she was leaving with her girlfriend.

What happened next I owe to the fact that I have always been a fanatic for music and cars. And I've always had a new car. That night, I had just bought a brand-new, shiny, lime-green Pontiac convertible. It was a beautiful night, so I had put the top down. Now, I didn't want anybody to park next to me because I was afraid of getting it scratched, so I parked the car horizontally right next to the front door. I didn't know this until later, but Lorraine told me that when she and her girlfriend walked in, she had said to her friend, "Man, I'd like to meet the guy who owns this car."

See, sometimes the planets do align.

So, now, here I was, walking her out. She was going to her car. I said, "Look, can I walk you to your car? Let me ask you this: Can you wait just a minute? I want to put my jacket in my car." And I threw my jacket into the car not realizing she'd noticed the car earlier. Then, she and her girlfriend hit each other with their elbows.

"Oh, look who owns this car," her girlfriend said.

I turned around and said to her, "Can I have your phone number?"

She said, "I don't give my phone number out when I meet people for the first time."

As I started walking away, she said, "If you really want my number, it's in the phone book. My name is McGrath. M-c-G-r-a-t-h. Lodi, New Jersey."

I thought she was playing games. That was Friday night. Sunday, I looked in the phone book and called the operator. And, sure enough, it was there—McGrath, Lodi, New Jersey.

I called her up. I knew I had her right away because the first thing she said on the phone was, "I can't believe you called, but I'm really happy you did."

"Look," I said. "I've got tickets for tomorrow night for Dionne Warwick at the Garden State Arts Center. I'd love to take you."

She said fine. We went to the concert and got married 10 months later—May 22, 1971—with a reception following at my parents' house.

Imagine if I had taken no for an answer.

That's being a recruiter. It got me the best recruit I ever signed.

One more thing: Lorraine and I renewed our vows in the spring of 1996 in front of family and friends. It was a memorable weekend as we celebrated our special day with coaches from all over the nation, including Rick Pitino, Jimmy Boeheim, Adubato, Mike Fratello, the late Rick Majerus, and many of my friends at ESPN.

Hope I can have another on the 50th.

Our priest, Father Gerald from Sarasota, came to our celebration and had us repeat our vows. He said, "For better or worse, richer or poorer," and my beautiful bride whispered softly with a smile, "Richer is better."

That brought down the house.

Lorraine has been my rock these past 43 years. She is very even-keeled emotionally—almost reserved. The very opposite of me. I'm emotional. But our values are very much the same.

My wife is a Hall of Famer. She's been the heart and soul of our family. I'm so glad my girls take after their mother, that they turned out so well is a true testament to her.

We went to see Dionne Warwick, and 43 years later, we're still dancing, baby.

Me and the real rock of my life, my beautiful wife, Lorraine. She is absolutely the best thing that ever happened to me.

CHAPTER 12

LOST POTENTIAL

Willis Reed was the toast of Manhattan in 1970 when the Knicks won their first NBA championship.

The 6-foot-9 big man became the first player in league history to be named the NBA All-Star Game MVP, the NBA Regular Season MVP, and the NBA Finals MVP—all in the same season. He also was elected to the All-NBA first team and NBA All-Defensive first team.

But Willis' most memorable performance occurred on May 8, 1970 in Game 7 of the NBA Finals. The Knicks were playing the Lakers with Wilt Chamberlain and Jerry West in the Garden. Willis was considered doubtful because he was nursing a bad thigh injury—a torn muscle that had kept him from playing in Game 6.

When he limped onto the court for pre-game warm ups, the place went bonkers. Reed started and scored the Knicks' first two field goals, his only points of the game. But his determination was inspirational. His buddy Clyde Frazier took over from there, and the Knicks won, 113-99, in the biggest game in franchise history.

That magic moment was voted the greatest moment in the history of Madison Square Garden.

It's hard to disagree.

Around that time, Willis and I had become very good friends. A lot of people don't know this, but we ran a charity basketball game in North Jersey to benefit a little boy, Sammy Davis who'd had both his legs amputated after a train accident. After reading about Sammy in the local papers, I got together with my buddies and said, "Let's get a game together to raise money for the youngster to help defray some of his medical expenses."

I called up Willis, and through him, we were able to get superstars galore. It was a Who's Who of basketball. The game was played at Paul VI High School in Clifton. The lineup? Would you believe Billy Cunningham, Rick Barry, Wes Unseld, Dr. J, and, of course, Willis Reed?

And introducing all those players? The one, the only Howard Garfinkel of Five-Star fame. It was classic Garf. The intros he gave to these guys were off the charts.

The players played in the game free of charge. We raised a lot of money as well as Sammy's spirits.

When I think of Willis Reed, I'm reminded of Leslie Cason, the best player I've ever coached.

Photo Courtesy of Manny Rubio/USA TODAY

Willis Reed was the toast of New York when the Knicks won the NBA title in 1970. Barely able to walk, Willis inspired his teammates by starting Game 7 of the NBA Finals at Madison Square Garden, and the Knicks cruised to an easy win for the title.

A happy time with Leslie Cason as we celebrate winning the state championship. He was as good as any player I've ever seen or coached. His is a tragic story—he was never able to overcome his addictions or accept the right kind of help.

He was a 6-foot-10 multi-talented, versatile big man who played for me at East Rutherford High School. He was *so* talented. I remember Willis watched him play and then later worked with him to sharpen his skills.

"My God," Willis told me, "I can't believe his skill for a big kid playing on the perimeter."

At that time, Leslie was so good that some people were calling him a young Willis. He scored over 3,000 points in four years and led us to two Group I state championships. He was recruited by 200 schools.

But his life turned out so differently.

I worked out with him like you can't believe, and I still remember the very first time I saw him in the gym. He was just 12 years old and he was already 6-foot-5. Even though his favorite sport was baseball, I remember teaching him how to make a right-hand and a left-hand layup. Hours and hours, I would work with him. That's something you don't forget.

Today, when I'm watching Kevin Durant play, I still think of Leslie and say to myself, "Should have been, could have been, would have been—had he listened."

Unfortunately, he didn't. He took the wrong turn. And it just broke my heart.

There is no one who goes out and lectures about staying away from the drug and alcohol scene more than I do. Speech after speech after speech—and I did it back in the day, too.

But my words fell on deaf ears. He just wouldn't—or couldn't—listen. I can't tell you how many hours I sat with him, but I just couldn't get my message across. I was unable to connect. Peer pressure got the best of him. He got involved with the wrong people.

Leslie was a terrific talent as a sophomore and junior. We went 29-0 his senior year in 1971. But it was all a mirage. His abilities started to diminish. One day, he came into my office and said I was just a white coach using a black kid to get a college job. Man, we got into a heated exchange.

"Leslie, I've known you since the sixth grade," I said. "Where have all these characters been in your life? How come they are coming around now? Did you ever ask them that question?" I could see what was happening. "Can't you see what you're doing with your life right now?" I told him. "You're getting with the wrong guys, they're pulling you down. They don't care about you. They will be gone tomorrow. We care about you."

"You're using me," he said. "My friends told me you're using me to get a college job."

I blew up:

> You know what? I'm going to tell you something right now, and I want you to understand it. No way, shape, or form am I going to take any college job because of you. Let me make this as clear as I can: Leslie, I'm going to make it someday. And I'm going to make it on my own because I have the drive and the desire. And I'm

doing things the right way. There is nobody in the world—other than maybe your mom and your step-dad—who want you to succeed more than I do. I want you to make it so bad.

I'm going to tell you something else you don't want to hear. Yeah, we went undefeated, but you are nowhere near the player you were in your sophomore and junior years. You lost your hands. Balls are bouncing off your hands. You don't have the hand-eye coordination you once had. The quickness. I don't see the touch you had.

And I know why, Leslie. You can absolutely give me all the excuses you want. I know what it is. You're messing with that stuff. You're messing.

I was cursing up and down.

"No, I'm not. No, I'm not," was all he could say.

It's amazing how they look you in the eye and flat out lie to you.

Because of his talent, Leslie was invited to play in the Dapper Dan game, a showcase in Pittsburgh for all the great ones that was put on by Sonny Vaccaro, who played a vital role in helping coaches make zillions through shoe deals. Many people did not realize that Sonny and his wife Pam helped many a kid get opportunities to go to college.

The Dapper Dan should have been Leslie's opportunity to showcase his skills against the best high school talent in America. He bombed. I felt very embarrassed for him—and for me.

Leslie signed to play for Jerry Tarkanian at Long Beach State, but since his academics were so bad from skipping class, he couldn't get accepted. He wound up playing at San Jacinto Junior College, which produced future NBA players like Tom Henderson of Hawaii and Ray Williams of Minnesota. I thought it would be the place for him to grow his skills and get his academics together. Tom Young of Rutgers even offered to give Leslie another chance and was going to take him as a transfer. Leslie enrolled at Rutgers but was never anything more than a reserve, just playing in parts of two seasons.

Then, when I was coaching the Detroit Pistons, Leslie called me again and pleaded for me to get him a shot at the NBA. In fact, he said to me, "Coach, I'm working out. I'm really getting my act together. I know I can play."

I said, "Leslie. I'm going to give you one last chance."

I called a buddy of mine, Joe Mullaney, who was coaching the new Baltimore Claws of the ABA and got Leslie a tryout. He went to their rookie camp and lasted 48 hours—he couldn't cut it. Wasted potential.

Leslie wasn't a bad kid, but he was easily influenced. We had a reunion of my former players from our East Rutherford High School's state championship teams. Bob Stolarz got all the guys together and invited me back to Jersey; we were there celebrating all the memories of those days. And it brought us to tears when we thought about all our successes and how the guy who was really the key to it all wasn't with us.

Then came the really sad part—Leslie got himself totally hooked on the drug scene.

I will never forget the 1996 Final Four, which was held in East Rutherford. I was working for ESPN and had just done a Top 10 list for David Letterman and went to sleep early. The phone rings at 6:30 in the morning, and the guy on the other end says to me, "Have you seen the back page of *The Daily News*?"

"What's on the back page?" I asked.

"It's all about Leslie Cason, a big story by Ian O'Connor. Here's his high school coach, on top of the world with ESPN, and here's Leslie, pictures and all, sleeping on park benches in the Bowery, where he was arrested multiple times for drugs."

I got the picture right away. They were trying to show a coach who forgets about his kid. But, when I read his quotes, I was absolutely touched. He said, "I wish I would have listened to my coach. He basically wanted me to do everything right and he's not at fault for what happened to me in my life."

Well, I immediately tried to get in contact with the people involved in the Bowery. I was able to connect with Pastor Ibach from the lower West side and told him I would love to help Leslie with anything he needed in the way of shirts, toiletries, and anything else. I told him I wanted all the money to be sent to him and not be given to Leslie personally.

Leslie found out about the plan and got in touch with me through the mail. The first letters were touching: They told me how much he cared about me, how he was really sad that he had let me down. "Coach," he said, "I wish I would have listened."

Then, he started to get a little defiant in his the last letter: He had gone to see the pastor and asked for some of the money and the pastor said. "No. You want to get a new bed, a new alarm clock, toiletries, it's one thing. But Coach said not to give you the money."

Well, he wrote me a letter saying, "You don't trust me. You're going to send the money to the priests. They're going to steal the money. You've got to send me the money."

But I knew where the cash would go: right into his arm.

That was really the last time we had contact.

I read in the news that Leslie Cason had passed on April 27, 1997, from complications of AIDS. He was 43.

I was devastated.

It all haunts me to this day. I have a major emptiness inside because I couldn't do more to save his career—let alone his life. You want to be proud of what your players accomplish. But, in Leslie's case, I can't say I was proud. I only wish I could have reached him and saved him from a life on the streets. For me, Cason will always be the true definition of could have, would have, should have been.

CHAPTER 13
PILGRIMAGE TO THE POCONOS

Five-Star was the legendary invitational basketball camp, run each summer in Honesdale, Pennsylvania. It was owned by Will Klein and run by the equally legendary Howard Garfinkel.

In its prime, his camp was the most influential, most prestigious showcase for the best college prospects in this country. It was the place to be seen if you had any role in college basketball—or wanted one. When I first started going, it was held in August at Camp Bryn Mawr in the Poconos. The kids lived in cabins; they played on outdoor courts in orange and white Five-Star t-shirts with no numbers on the back, so you had to pay attention.

Five-Star was the camp people talked about and others went out and tried to emulate. The place was always crawling with coaches, there to recruit the campers.

Garf always had the best lecturers speak before the afternoon session—stars like Hubie Brown, Chuck Daly, Jimmy Lynam, and Bob Knight. And there were great counselors: college assistants like Rick Pitino, John Calipari, and Mike Fratello, who ran the stations and made Five-Star the best teaching camp in America.

Garf grew up on Park Avenue. He came from money. At one point, his family owned the largest textile company in New York. He tells wonderful stories about meeting cafe society, including one about my favorite, Mr. Sinatra, who told his bodyguard "Let the kid use the phone," when Garf needed to use the telephone in the backroom. Priceless and 100% Garf, man.

He also claims that *A Star Is Born*, with Judy Garland, was his inspiration.

Garf turned Five-Star into Broadway with high major impact players and street legends like Patrick Ewing, Chris Mullin, Isiah Thomas, Lloyd Daniels, Alonzo Mourning, Christian Laetttner, Grant Hill, and Bobby Hurley. Even LeBron James came when he was in the ninth grade to play in the developmental league.

But those days are gone. Today, shoe companies run their own camps, and competition is fierce. After all, there are only so many "best" players to go around, and everyone wants them.

Garf got most of them. And I was in awe, man.

You might wonder how I found myself in such exalted company. Garf put me in there. He'd heard me speak at a banquet. I guess he was impressed. Anyway, he helped me get a job at Rutgers and, afterward, told me he was going to bring me in to

Me and Howard Garfinkel. His support was crucial when I wanted to move up and advance my career in coaching. A great guy!

speak. So, I became one of the first assistants to address the campers. While I was speaking, across from me were guys like Moses Malone and Michael Jordan—all the great ones over the years.

I spoke there several times: as an assistant at Rutgers, as the head coach at the University of Detroit, and after I'd taken the job with the Pistons. I recently went back there to be inducted into the camp's Hall of Fame and gave a speech on chasing your dreams.

Five-Star was a very special place; Garf earned his place in the College Basketball Hall of Fame as a contributor. He was honored for having given so many coaches their start and for his efforts on behalf of grass-roots basketball when his camp was thriving.

In fact, I credit Five-Star for helping me develop the strong voice I use in broadcasting today.

One day, it was pouring outside, but I kept on speaking. Later, Garf said, "The only guy who could have pulled it off was Dickie V. His voice was so strong, coming through the rain and the lightning. He didn't miss a beat. He went on for one hour straight, and he had the kids in the palm of his hand. And he's going on about 'A Ball, A Boy, and a Dream.'"

It was a storm like you couldn't believe, but the kids loved it.

It's also where I started what some people refer to as "Vitale-ese."

Words like "PTPers," "Diaper Dandies," "Glass Eater," and "Surf and Turfer" just came naturally when you saw the caliber of the kids who were there. Case in point: Patrick Ewing and Chris Mullin played there as high schoolers, long before their Dream Team days.

I still remember the year Michael Jordan showed up for the first time. Nobody knew who he was—at first. By the end of the week, Garf was on the phone with Dave Krider of *Street and Smith's*, screaming, "Stop the presses. We got a kid here who's better than all those guys you have on your *Street and Smith's* All-American team. He's from Wilmington, North Carolina. His name: Michael Jordan."

But it was too late; the magazine had already gone to press, so the rest of America didn't find out about Michael until the next season.

Garf prided himself on teaching, as opposed to just rolling the balls out—like you see at so many camps today. He was making the campers work. That camp inspired and motivated kids to leave there and think to themselves, "You know, I'm not as good as maybe I thought I was in my little area. I've got to go out and work if I want to be a good player and compete at this level."

One time, I remember there was this high school junior from Petersburg, Virginia, who was there. His name was Moses Malone. I was one of a long list of coaches who tried to recruit him when he was in high school. After his senior year, he was invited to play in the Dapper Dan Roundball Classic in Pittsburgh; I can remember when I was at the University of Detroit, sitting in the lobby of a local hotel late at night, waiting for him to come in. My assistant, David "Smokey" Gaines, had formed a relationship with Moses as well as his family and friends. They were really tight. I was waiting in the lobby to meet him so I could share a few words; he got in a little later. Then, all I know is the next day it didn't affect him as he went for like 35 points.

Anyway, it was raining cats and dogs in Honesdale one day and everybody was trying to get something to eat, and here's this kid—all alone—throwing the ball against the backboard. He's grabbing rebounds. He flips the ball and grabs it again. And he's doing a tap drill 20 times with the right hand, 20 times with the left hand. Nobody is there supervising him. He's all by himself.

That's why he became one of the greatest rebounders ever in the game. He went after every rebound like it was his last meal.

Garf always said Moses was the only camper in the history of Five-Star who was too good for the camp.

When I was coaching the Pistons, Bob Lanier was our All-Star center, All-Pro. And Moses was playing for Houston. Our game was at eight o'clock at night, and around 3:30 p.m., Bob is already there in the whirlpool. He's doing all kinds of ice and heat on his knees.

I asked him what he was doing there so early.

"Dick, are you kidding me? This guy is so relentless, the most tenacious rebounder I have ever seen. Do me a favor. Please have Leon Douglas ready to give me a break. Spare me some minutes because this guy never stops."

Moses went on to become an All-Pro and won an NBA title with the Sixers in 1983.

I'll say this to all you kids out there: You want to be special? You just can't dream it. It's great to chase your dreams, but you've got to go out there and make a commitment to make your dreams come true. I saw it that day when Moses was working out all by himself at Five-Star.

Photo Courtesy of Malcolm Emmons/USA TODAY

Moses Malone is a great example of someone who had extraordinary talent who also understood that, to succeed, a lot of hard work had to be done. He was an All-Pro with the Sixers and helped them win the NBA title in 1983.

CHAPTER 14
PUTTING RUTGERS ON THE MAP

Howard Garfinkel changed my life.

He heard me speaking at my high school awards banquet. Afterward, he came up and introduced himself.

As I've pointed out earlier, I knew who he was. The famous Garf.

He, Lorraine, and I went to the Candlewyck Diner in East Rutherford. We sat there talking until two in the morning. What Garf said made me very happy. He told me I didn't belong in high school; I belonged in college. And he was going to do everything in his power to get me a job there.

I wondered what he could do. I'd been writing letters all over the place, asking—practically begging—colleges to let me be an assistant coach. And I kept getting just as many rejections back.

To be a successful coach, you need an aggressive personality. Head coaches have that trait. Well, I had that trait. And I really believe if you are successful on the high school level and you have a strong personality, some college coaches just don't feel secure enough bringing somebody in with that trait.

Garfinkel, through his contacts and with his influence, got me an interview with Dick Lloyd, the head coach at Rutgers. And I'll always be indebted to him for that.

I was 30 years old when I took the Rutgers assistant job. And we made recruiting history.

There is no way I get a Phil Sellers, a Mike Dabney to commit with the rules we have today. The rules favor the elite, all the super schools. If you are an excellent player and I wanted to recruit you, I would have needed so many hours just to get you to look up when I walked in. When Duke walks in, Carolina walks in, Kentucky walks in, you lift your head high; your eyes are as big as half-dollars. But Rutgers, then? Not so much.

I don't have the magic formula for what makes a good recruiter, but I do know that product, exposure, and visibility all play a vital part in signing a prospect. Well, we didn't have that at Rutgers in the early 70s, so I had to make up for that with persistence. Lorraine will tell you I spent almost every day starting in my car in New Brunswick and driving to

I needed help to make that big jump into the college ranks of coaching. College Hall of Famer Howard Garfinkel made things happen and helped me get the assistant job at Rutgers.

Brooklyn, New York, to Thomas Jefferson High School, hanging out, getting to know Sellers, his mother, his girlfriend, his coaches, his people.

You can't do that now, and I feel it limits the coach. I understand the reason for the no-contact rule: Kids start to feel hassled. But I'm not sure I buy that either. A good coach can handle contact in a professional manner. Besides, I was a man with a mission: Get Phil Sellers to sign with Rutgers.

He was the No. 1 prospect in the country. MVP of the Dapper Dan. And I wanted him, no matter that he was being actively recruited by 200 or so other schools.

The first time I went to see him, it was a Who's Who of coaches lined up against the wall of the gym. I wanted to get my autograph book.

Anyway, I've always had the ability to relate to young athletes. The key is to be honest with them, and I was very honest with Phil. I told him that all of these schools had had many others like him. But Rutgers had never, ever had a Phil Sellers. He could be so special, playing in New York at Madison Square Garden.

I gave it my best shot.

But Phil committed to Notre Dame.

When he called to tell me, he said, "Coach, it kills me to tell you this because I really loved everything you said about Rutgers. All the time we spent together—I loved it. Nobody recruited me better than you. But there's something about Notre Dame, and I have to go there."

I swallowed hard and told him I wished him all the luck in the world, and that I was absolutely flattered, that I felt, in my heart, that he genuinely had considered us. Many people felt he was playing us for a game. But I also let him know that I could tell, by the sound of his voice, he didn't really want Notre Dame but was caught up in the magic of the name. All his friends were urging him to sign with Notre Dame, asking him, "Rutgers? What is Rutgers?"

It was an ego thing. And it still is today.

Later, I was at a post-season high school All-Star game. I was recruiting Jeff Kleinbaum. Phil was playing in the game. He came over and told me he needed to talk to me after the game. I was talking to Garf, and neither of us could figure out what he wanted to talk about.

Then, he told me that night that I was right, that his friends and his peers influenced him about the power of the name of Notre Dame. Plus, he'd begun to worry about academics because Notre Dame has such strong requirements. "To be honest with you," he said. "I really wanted to stay home and go to Rutgers."

I jumped with joy.

But, before I could celebrate, I had to take care of the paperwork.

I called Dick Lloyd, who told me that since Rutgers wasn't on the national letter of intent, it didn't mean anything that he'd signed with Notre Dame. We weren't in violation if we took him.

When he announced for Rutgers, he set off our recruiting.

Mike Dabney was the best player in New Jersey. Jeff Kleinbaum was a big star on Long Island. Mike Palko was a New Jersey star. And Ronnie Williams was out of Washington, D.C., and they all said, "Yes."

And we were on our way, baby.

And with Phil and Mike as a tandem, the rest was history.

Phil's nickname was "Phil the Thrill." Fans adored watching him work both ends of the court at the Barn, our noisy gym on College Avenue. Rutgers went to the NIT in both his freshman and sophomore seasons. Then, the school made back-to-back appearances in the NCAA tournament in his junior and senior years.

Rutgers' best season came in the 1975-76 campaign. The team was 31-0 in the regular season and finished 31-2. Their only losses were to Michigan and UCLA in the tournament.

For his efforts, Phil was the Haggerty Award winner as the best player in the city and was a Top 10 selection on the All-American teams. His jersey, number 12, was retired, putting him in a select group of Scarlet Knights to be so honored. He was a phenomenal collegiate player.

But the NBA was a real challenge because he was known as a 'tweener. At 6-foot-5, he dominated on the college level, but now he had to make the transition to play on the perimeter. When I got the Pistons job, he was playing in Europe; he called me and asked for a chance. There was no way I was going to say no to somebody who played a vital part in my becoming a head coach on the collegiate level. Recruiting him certainly opened doors for me.

Phil came down and started working out with all the players like Lanier. Then, we had a rookie camp and the battle for that last small forward spot was coming down to a choice between him and John Long, who starred for me at the University of Detroit. John had superb skills from the perimeter and could really shoot the rock.

Well, I think he knew it was going to be tough for him to survive and that John was a step ahead of him.

Phil went on and became an assistant coach at Rutgers for three years before settling into a job with a mortgage-banking firm in New Jersey.

He is still the all-time leading scorer and rebounder in Rutgers history.

What makes me particularly proud is that—even though I had left by then—Tom Young did such a brilliant job utilizing him on that Rutgers team. Their talent was unbelievable with Sellers and Dabney, and Young was able to recruit point guard Eddie Jordan, James Bailey (a big shot blocker), and Hollis Copeland. They were dynamite.

I am so happy for the role Phil played on that team at Rutgers. Talk about mid-majors. Rutgers was just like George Mason and Butler in that respect. Wow, Rutgers in the Final Four, with that lightning quick combination of Sellers and Dabney.

MOTOR CITY MADNESS

To this day, I believe Dave DeBusschere, the starting forward on the two championship Knicks teams, played a vital role in my getting the head-coaching job at the University of Detroit, his alma mater.

He claimed he hadn't done anything, that I'd gotten the job on my own—but still.

In the spring of 1973, Dick Lloyd was leaving to move into administration at Rutgers. He recommended me to be the next head coach. He said he felt that all of my contacts in New Jersey from my high school days would be a big plus in recruiting. But the Athletic Director at the time, Fred Gruninger, was new on the block and he told me, "I'm interviewing a lot of big names for the position." He told me he would recommend me as an assistant to the new coach, so I could stay on. But I wasn't interested in staying on those terms alone. If I wasn't good enough to be the head coach there, I'd be an assistant somewhere else.

One night, I was in the Knicks locker room talking to Willis Reed. DeBusschere walked by, and I told Willis that I'd love to meet him since he was one of my favorite players.

Boom! Willis brought him over. We exchanged small talk: "What do you do for a living now?"

"I'm looking for a head coaching job," I told him.

"What about my alma mater, the University of Detroit?"

Jim Harding had just gotten fired. Willis told Dave I had a really good rapport with kids. He then asked Dave to call for me, told him that I'd be terrific.

I'd never thought about it, hadn't even applied to Detroit. I thought it had just been idle chatter.

Then, my phone rang.

It was Bob Calihan, the AD at Detroit, telling me the school wanted to talk to me about the job. Could I fly out for an interview in two days?

I told him I could but asked if they could send me a plane ticket since I wasn't making any cash.

He told me to fly in, and they'd reimburse me when I got there.

I was stunned.

In fact, I thought it was a joke, so I called back, and Calihan answered. I asked him if he recently called me and he said yes, and that he was looking forward to my coming out for an interview.

I flew to Detroit—it was only the second flight I had ever taken—and when I got off the plane, I picked up copies of the local papers. There was a big headline

Photo Courtesy of Manny Rubio/USA TODAY

Thanks to New York Knick Dave DeBusschere, I ended up at the University of Detroit—it was one of the best moves I ever made.

Chalking it up for my team at the U of D. The guys listened, learned, and excelled on the court. They made me look pretty good.

which basically said, "Detroit to Name a Coach Tomorrow. Tom Villemure is Front Runner." Villemure was a former Titan player who played with Dave DeBusschere and was experiencing coaching success at Grand Valley State.

"So, what was I doing here?" I asked myself. I also asked the hiring committee the same thing when I went in for my interview.

"But," I said, "since I came all this way, I'm going to spend the next 30 minutes telling you that somebody is going to give me a chance. And when they do, I won't let them down."

I proceeded to tell them my plans for the school.

I told them about our recruitment of #1 prospect Phil Sellers to Rutgers and said I'd go after Tom LaGarde, the high school sensation from Detroit Central Catholic—We ultimately tried to recruit him when I eventually got the job, but he was set on going to North Carolina with Dean Smith. Can you blame him?

Anyway, that night they called and told me I had the job.

I felt good about all this, but here's the thing: I didn't really want the job. I wanted to stay home, coach in New Jersey, in my comfort zone.

I talked things over with Lloyd, who told me not to do anything rash. From not being considered as a candidate, I suddenly had an interview with Gruninger on Monday.

Detroit called me and said that I was using them for leverage for the Rutgers job. They gave me 24 hours to decide, or they'd pull the offer.

I was forced to make a decision.

Howard Garfinkel convinced me Detroit wanted me. I was an afterthought at Rutgers.

I accepted Detroit's offer and went on to start the next chapter of my life. Lorraine and I were really sad about leaving Jersey, saying good-bye to family and friends, but we embraced the change and made the move.

There were some difficulties in the beginning. *Time* Magazine had listed Detroit as the murder capital of the U.S., which certainly didn't help recruiting. Other recruiters took glee in sending that piece to prospects. I couldn't believe how vicious coaches could be. But I just kept plugging away. I busted my gut to get U of D good players and put people in the seats.

And the program started to turn around…slowly.

Even though we were 17-and-9 my first year, I felt we were building something. We signed two local stars, forwards John Long and Terry Tyler. My second year, we won 17 again, but we finished strong, winning 13 of our last 17 games. My third year, we won 19 straight games at home until that streak was broken by North Carolina, which was ranked third at the time. The Tar Heels were led by the incomparable Phil Ford. Then came our big game—against Marquette, coached by the legendary Al McGuire. I can't tell you how in awe I was of Al. He had that real New York way about him. He was so authentic, so genuine, and don't believe he was a guy who would just show up for the games. He had a masterful way of communicating with his athletes. A near-record crowd at Calihan Hall saw us play them tough, but we lost at the buzzer. After the heartbreaker, I made a vow that by the time Long and Tyler were upperclassmen, they would somehow pay them back. We lost only one more game and finished 19-8.

It all came together my final year coaching at the University of Detroit.

We had won 20 straight games, and I was feeling pretty good about our chances to make the NCAA tournament. Then, I was talking to my good friend Larry Donald of *Basketball Times*, and he told me we were one of three teams in contention for two independent spots in the NCAA tournament, along with Marquette and Notre Dame. Our final regular season game was against Marquette in Milwaukee.

We won baby, we won! I throw down some disco moves with my team following our upset of Marquette—on their floor—in 1977. The U of D still considers it the biggest win in school history.

"I'm sorry to tell you this, Dick," he said. "If you don't win, you're out."

What? You've got to be kidding me.

I felt like reaching for the Maalox. We had an outstanding team that year with Tyler, Long, and Terry Duerod, who all went on to play in the NBA. But Marquette did, too, with Butch Lee and all those New York guys who would eventually upset North Carolina and win the national championship. I could feel the tension before the game. So, I told my team in the locker room, "Guys, I'm so confident that we are going to beat them tonight, I'm going to go out to center court after we win and dance with the cheerleaders. Get in a circle in front of all those Marquette fans and do 'The Disco Dick.'"

It was upset city. We beat Marquette, 65-64, when Dennis Boyd dribbled down the clock and hit a shot at the buzzer. It was a magical moment, beating one of my favorite coaches. It was being called the biggest win in school history.

Boyd was mobbed by the players at the other end of the court. It wasn't long before my players began chanting, "Dance, dance, dance." So, I stormed the court by myself and started putting down steps. Hey, I was imitating John Travolta in *Saturday Night Fever*. The story became the lead of the 11 o'clock newscasts back in Detroit. If that happened today with all the cable stations, ESPN, and the internet, I'm sure I would have gone viral.

Now the NCAA had to recognize we were the better team. They couldn't deny us anymore. And they didn't. We got into the 32-team tournament.

The top-ranked team in the country was Michigan—only 60 miles away. But they wouldn't schedule us during the regular season. Maybe because in my first year at Detroit, we upset a nationally-ranked Michigan team with Campanella "Campy" Russell. Trust me, it is tough to schedule a big-time, elite program when you are a mid-major seeking name recognition. My players kept screaming, "Why can't we play Michigan? We work out with those guys. They're good, but we're good, too. We can play with those guys."

When we saw the brackets, I called a team meeting. "You guys have been talking about playing Michigan all year. Well, get to the Sweet 16, you'll get your chance."

We did. Lexington, the home of Rupp Arena where Adolph Rupp and Joe B. Hall had strolled the sidelines, was in a frenzy. We were David, man, playing Goliath. Their phone budget was more than our entire recruiting budget.

They were ranked first in the country and had future NBA players like Rickey Green and Phil Hubbard. We were ranked around 20th in the nation, but believe me, we weren't intimidated.

Our kids played their hearts out, but we lost, 86-81. And I maintain—and I told this to the late Johnny Orr during a visit to Iowa State that "We cost you guys a national title." We took so much out of them, physically and emotionally, that they had nothing left since they were upset 36 hours later by UNC-Charlotte and Cornbread Maxwell in the Regional finals.

By the way, superstar broadcaster Curt Gowdy and Hall of Famer John Wooden were the commentators for our game for NBC. I was in awe.

Had we beaten Michigan, we might have won it all. And just think how good we could have been if Earl Cureton, a 6-foot-10 center from the Motor City was eligible. He was practicing with us every day, but he had to sit the year out as a transfer. I was eating my heart out watching him going against Long and Tyler every day, dreaming about what it would be like having him in our lineup. Think about it. We won 21 straight without him. We won at Marquette. With him, we would have been a monster. Who knows? We could have been a mid-major that won a national championship.

Cureton wanted to come to Detroit originally, but he needed a little academic help so he went to Robert Morris Junior College in Pittsburgh with the understanding he was going to stay there for a year and then transfer to play for his hometown team. Well, Robert Morris went Division I while he was there, so he was subject to the transfer rule where he had to sit out for a season once he got to Detroit. We battled with the NCAA over that one, but we lost the case.

Man, I felt like it was first class all the way at the U of D. I loved this car, and believe it or not, I loved the white shoes, too.

CHAPTER 16

TAKING A WRONG TURN

I made a major, major mistake when I accepted the head-coaching job for the Detroit Pistons.

As usual, Jimmy V put it best.

When I was coaching the University of Detroit, I used to tease Jimmy that I would put Iona on the schedule because we needed a cupcake game. I can say I never lost to Jimmy V. We had more talent than he had. When it was rumored I might be going to the pros, he called and said, "Dick, you're a college coach. You have spirit, enthusiasm. And you're young." He added, "I'm going from Iona to somewhere big. You could go from Detroit to somewhere big because you're winning. You can relate to kids. You don't mess with happiness."

But I did. Big time.

When I resigned from U of D and moved upstairs to the athletic director's office, I appointed Gaines as the head coach. Our record over two years was 48-10. I was proud of the fact that we'd built a winner, a team that created excitement in the Motor City. But I was looking for another challenge.

And when owner Bill Davidson approached me about taking the Pistons job, I was absolutely ecstatic.

I made a decision, one that really didn't fit my personality or my style of coaching. I let my ego dictate and got carried away by three major letters: NBA. But think about it. In 1970, I'm a sixth-grade teacher. Seven years later, I have the Pistons owner sitting with me, offering me a six-figure job.

So I jumped to the pros. Anybody would have.

I wasn't really cut out for the job, though, because I couldn't handle losing. I'm the one who had to go to the sidelines at the U of D because of my bleeding ulcers. And now I'm about to coach in an 82-game, regular-season league where losing is just a part of the deal. But I went ahead anyway.

Back then, the team was an also-ran in the city. Baseball was king, followed by football. Then there was hockey—the Red Wings and Gordie Howe. The Pistons had very little to offer fans in terms of identity and history.

Nonetheless, they'd moved to the Pontiac Silverdome during my first season. A big arena in the suburbs with many seats to fill… That's where I came in.

I had faced similar problems at the U of D. But rather than sitting back and accepting them, I went full-throttle ahead. I did a lot of radio. I launched a one-man PR campaign, determined to get the school's name out there. I felt that once people saw us, saw how

Photo Courtesy of Associated Press/JHC

Not a good day. My tears flowed when I resigned as the head basketball coach at the U of D because of my bleeding ulcers. I moved upstairs as the school's AD, but I wanted to stay courtside.

much fun the games could be, they'd want to attend. And they did. It all worked. We created an exciting situation. And we filled the stands.

My reputation had preceded me, and the Pistons wanted me to duplicate my success. Get their name out there, get people in the seats. I tried to create excitement.

My favorite ploy was a bumper sticker that read, "Re-VITALE-ized." It symbolized the new energy and excitement that I hoped to infuse into the team as their new coach. I even put it on my own car. A real act of love, baby.

But we had just one major problem: We were limited in depth and talent. You cannot win in the NBA on a regular basis without those two things. Also, I was weighed down with injuries on my frontcourt. Knee injury to Bob Lanier. Blood clot to John Shumate. You just aren't going to beat the likes of Moses and Kareem playing with players who are just excited to put on an NBA uniform. You've gotta have the talent and the depth to win on that level.

And I was losing. It was tearing me to pieces.

I admired the way guys like Chuck Daly and Red Holzman handled losing: When they lost a game, they would move on to the next one, shake it off. That was not me. I couldn't handle those L's; they just tore at my insides. Let's face reality. In the collegiate game, it's all about the coaches. They are the backbone, the rocks of the college game. In the NBA, it's all about the name on the back of that jersey. Man, you'd better have players. Look at it this way: I love Phil Jackson. What he did with Chicago and Los Angeles was magical—winning all those championships—but let's face it, Phil would be the first to tell you having Hall of Famers like Michael Jordan, Scottie Pippen, and Dennis Rodman in Chicago helped. So did going to L.A. and having the likes of Kobe and Shaquille.

Now, in defense of Phil, he also had the magic touch of being able to blend those egos and talents together into a team, like Red Auerbach did. That is what a NBA championship coach is all about.

But the Pistons were in need of major rebuilding.

Having played sports all my life, I knew that players are going to play hard if they respect you. Unfortunately, I had been a head coach in college for only four years before I took the Pistons job, which was a bit of a problem. Not too many players were enthusiastic about my "Let's win it for the Gipper" style of coaching.

I also found out that the level of play was unbelievable. I sat in amazement on the sidelines. The weakest guy on the roster was probably better than most of the players in college. Developing match-ups, having the personnel to offset the skills of opposing players became very difficult for me to manage.

Through it all, Davidson was so good to me. He kept telling me to be patient. He told me even though you want to get it done in one year, you can't, so relax. But I couldn't. It wasn't in my nature. Three days into my NBA career, I was in the hospital for five days. My old problem, ulcers, had resurfaced.

I got the Pistons baby, or did they get me? In the end, which came quickly, I found out that I wasn't a good fit for the NBA.

Not a great start.

But it wasn't all bad. Lanier, a future Hall of Famer, was our center, but he was dealing with knee problems. M. L. Carr was our swingman. But best of all, I had two of my former U of D players—Tyler and Long, known in the Motor City as Thunder and Lightning. They almost made it feel like Old Home Week. We scored, but, unfortunately, we couldn't stop the opposing teams from scoring as well. We lost our first five games.

But I still remember my first NBA win. It was October 25, 1978, against the Cleveland Cavaliers. And it felt good.

What felt even better was our one-sided win against the Celtics—yes, the CELTICS—on March 9, 1979. We scored 160 points in a late-season blowout, baby, at the Silverdome!

By the end of my first season, with Lanier, Carr, Kevin Porter, and Long setting the pace, we had seven players who were averaging more than 11 points per game. At least I'd accomplished one of my goals: We were exciting to watch.

We just couldn't stop anybody, and that doesn't bring home trophies.

We finished fourth in our division with an overall record of 30-52.

Remember the Celtics? They finished last in the league, and when the season ended, Mr. Davidson wanted Bob McAdoo. The Celtics signed Carr as a free agent. I hated to lose him; he was the consummate team player. Davidson demanded compensation in McAdoo, a terrific shooter who had led the league in scoring for three years. Word was we wouldn't get McAdoo straight up for Carr.

To finish the deal, the Celtics asked for the Pistons' 1980 first-round draft pick, and Davidson complied with Auerbach's request, which completed the trade. Since they now had two first-round draft picks, Boston then used one of them to trade for center Robert Parish from Golden State, and selected forward Kevin McHale in the 1980 draft with the other first-round pick. Those two players, along with Larry Bird, were the core parts in the Celtics return to glory in the '80s. And we ended up with McAdoo, who really deep down never wanted to be in the Motor City. He wanted to be part of a team where he could just blend in. He was tired of being a guy who had to score big or else his team would suffer. Well, he finally got his way and went to the Lakers, where he helped them win some championships. I later told Auerbach at a banquet that I never received my championship ring for helping the Celtics back to glory (ha, ha).

The next year, after we got off to a 4-8 start, I had the worst day of my professional life—Nov. 8, 1979. I was sitting at home when Lorraine came in and told me she had just gotten a phone call from the secretary at the team's office. "Mr. Davidson's coming over to see you," she said.

Then she told me something I didn't see coming.

"You're going to get fired," she said.

I said to her, "You can't be serious. There's no way. We're bringing in fans." But she heard me on the phone with Mr. Davidson, going off and telling him, "Mr. D, we need a general manager. We need someone who I can report to, someone I can talk to about players and personnel."

My wife said to me when I got done, "You just can't express yourself like that to ownership. They're going to be upset."

Well, she was right again. Always listen to your bride.

She just wanted to prepare me. Then, she left because she didn't want to see the ax fall.

It did. There was a knock at my door. Davidson and I sat down at the kitchen table, and he said, "I made a coaching change."

I said, "What does that mean?"

He said, "Well, basically, we'd like to move you to an administrative role."

And I said, "No way. If I'm not coaching, I'm moving on."

That was the end of my NBA career. I was devastated. I cried and cried. But part of me felt relieved, too, because I wouldn't have to deal with the pressure of coaching a pro team any more.

My owner was good. He didn't want to fire me. I fired myself. He kept saying to me, "Be patient." But I moaned and groaned to him all the time; I'd brought him to a point where he didn't have a choice.

In the NBA, the number of games wears you out. Still, coaching a winning NBA team is the one thing that's missing from my resume. Sometimes, I think I didn't give myself enough time to accomplish it; I wish I hadn't been so tough on myself. I think about what I should or could have done was control my emotions a lot more. Coulda, shoulda, woulda.

But time had run out for me.

I got the ziggy, baby. It was time to move on.

CHAPTER 17
A NEW OPPORTUNITY

So there it was—the ziggy. I got the ziggy, baby.

I went from teaching grade school in New Jersey to the head coach of the Pistons; my career had just exploded. In less than two decades, what had happened to me was unbelievable. I was flying. Then, all of a sudden, the balloon burst.

I was as depressed as can be.

I didn't want to leave the house. I retreated to my room, listening for the phone to ring, waiting for someone to call and offer me a job. But it didn't happen. I was embarrassed to go out—trying to avoid eye contact with caring friends and neighbors who didn't know what to say or how to act. I had been a popular figure in Detroit—very visible. Now—in my eyes, at least—I felt like a nobody. I became obsessed with watching soap operas on TV; I got addicted to the Luke and Laura saga of *General Hospital*.

And that's when Lorraine stepped in.

She lit into me, man. She ripped me from top to bottom: "You are acting like a spoiled little brat. So you got fired. All of a sudden instead of picking up the pieces and fighting on, you're quitting. You are violating everything you believe in. You're not the first person to be fired. You won't be the last one. You've got to get on with your life."

And that's why I love her because she has always provided me with encouragement and, most of all, love.

Then, I got a phone call from Scotty Connal, an executive from ESPN in the middle of November of 1979 that would change my life forever.

He said he'd like me to do a game for ESPN.

ESPN? You kidding me? Sounds like a disease, man. I had never even heard of it.

Scotty told me that when he was the executive producer at NBC Sports and they televised our game against Michigan in the Sweet 16 in Lexington, he was impressed when I called my team over to give them a speech after practice. Curt Gowdy and John Wooden were the broadcasters and they were in the stands with Scotty. I told the team that Gowdy and Wooden represent everything you hear about the word "Greatness."

Later, Scotty told me Gowdy and Wooden said after the game that they thought my enthusiasm and passion for the game might be good on TV some day.

Scotty said he wrote my name down. When he'd seen I'd gotten fired by the Pistons, he decided to invite me to do the very first major college basketball game on his new network.

I told him initially: "No way, I'm not interested. I'm not a TV guy. I want to get back to where I belong and coach. Thanks so much, Mr. Connal, but I'm really not interested."

Well, lucky for me, he called back. Lorraine practically kicked me out of the house: "Do the game," she said. "Go there and have some fun. Get out of the house."

Funny how life works out. Had we not gone to the Sweet 16, Connal wouldn't have ever thought to call me, and I probably would have never, ever had a career in television. It's amazing how things happen.

I had no idea of what I was getting myself into.

December 5, 1979: I went to Chicago to do the DePaul-Wisconsin game. It was being played at Alumni Hall on the DePaul campus.

Since Chicago was not a place I often visited, I walked around the streets all day, taking in the beauty, going to restaurants, enjoying myself. It was the first time I'd been out of the house for any length of time. I was still a mess mentally. When bad things happen, people forget your number. They don't return your calls, except for your friends. I'd learned a lot about people then. Lorraine told me "Rich, a lot of people who you think are your friends, they're associates. I found out you can count your friends on one hand when your back is against the wall."

Anyway, when I got to Chicago, I had no idea of how TV worked, knew nothing about production meetings. The game was scheduled for eight o'clock, so I walked in about an hour and twenty minutes before tip-off. Plenty of time, I thought.

The producer was going wild. "Where have you been? We've been looking for you all over."

"I've been walking the streets. What's the problem?"

"Dick, we've got a game."

"I know. We've got about an hour to go."

"An hour to go? We've got to talk about production."

"They told me to do a game. And that's what I'm going to do. I'm going to talk hoops."

And that was exactly what I did.

For two straight minutes during the opening of the telecast—on both teams, top to bottom. DePaul was No. 1 in the nation. Ray Meyer, Mark Aguirre. Wisconsin had a great player in Wes Matthews. All that Joe Boyle, my play-by-play guy, got to say was, "Hi. Tonight we're here with Dick Vitale, and we're doing DePaul-Wisconsin." I hope he didn't get paid by the word because he didn't get another one in until it was time to go to commercial.

I talked while the producer was talking in my ear. I even spoke during commercials.

My first words? "It should be a classic match-up. College basketball excitement and enthusiasm."

It was. De Paul won, 90-77.

Photo Courtesy of ESPN

The new adventure. It's December 5, 1979, and I'm doing my first game with ESPN. Joe Boyle, the play-by-play man, was terrific, putting up with my constant talking.

When I got home after the game, Scotty called me and said, "Look. You have three things we can't teach: your enthusiasm, your knowledge, your candid nature. But you have no clue how to get in and out. I'm going to assign a pro's pro to work with you—Jim Simpson, formerly of NBC, a Hall of Famer." I owe Jim so much for being a positive influence on me in doing remotes and so much to Bob Ley—for teaching me how to get in and out during studio assignments.

I still don't know if I completely get it, the whole TV thing. But I guess that's good. Today, we're getting too technical, too structured, getting away from the free and easy, just letting it flow. Those early days, they were the best.

Back then, I made about $350 for my first game. I worked on a game-by-game basis for ESPN because I really wanted to get back to where I belonged: coaching in college.

And I didn't know where ESPN was going. Remember this was the late seventies. ESPN was trying out a new, groundbreaking format: Sports—24 hours a day. And it was in only 100,000 homes in this country.

And questions kept creeping into my mind: Did I belong there? Was TV for me?

Working with legendary broadcaster Jim Simpson. I have to say, he was terrific, helping smooth out a few rough spots as I found my way doing the games.

Scotty told me, "Dick, you have something that's really rare. You connect with people—whether they agree with you or not. You make a statement, and they're going to the water cooler the next day to talk about it. People react. 'Did you hear what Vitale said last night?' Don't give this up. You can make a heck of a living doing this."

I decided to give it a year before I made up my mind, so I did some more games for them. I admit I had fun. But, in the back of my mind, I felt college was where I belonged. I was still applying for coaching jobs.

At the end of the year, I told Scotty I still had reservations about the job. Again, he convinced me to stay.

In the beginning, I had no idea of how popular ESPN would become, but as I kept seeing more attention coming my way, I knew we were growing as a network, and I was part of that.

In 1983, my whole concept of college basketball changed.

That year, I went to my first Final Four for ESPN. I was doing studio work for them, appearing on *SportsCenter*.

That was the year Jimmy V cut down the nets when NC State upset Houston. I couldn't believe the number of people coming up to me for pictures, asking for autographs, questioning a statement I'd made. I'd said you can't win a national title with a freshman point guard. And Houston had Alvin Franklin, the point guard in question, and all those other fantastic players—Clyde Drexler, Michael Young, and Hakeem Olajuwon. All those superstars. Reid Gettys, one of their guards, told *Sports Illustrated*, "Opinions are like a-holes. Everybody has them."

And everyone reacted.

Scotty said, "I told you. You connect."

It was around that time I realized maybe this was the way to go. I didn't feel the tension, the pressure of coaching. In TV, you don't get the same highs and the same lows you get from coaching, but there is still a rush. I have a ritual I do after every game I cover: I never watch the winning coach. I take a look at the coach and the players on the losing team, watch them walk out of the arena, and I tell myself that I am lucky. I don't have to deal with the media, unhappy players, parents upset that their kids aren't playing.

I've said it many times, and I still believe it to this day. If I'd stayed in coaching, I'd have been dead by 50.

CHAPTER 18

MICHAEL

Michael Jordan is the greatest of all time, no question about it. I base my judgment on what he achieved throughout his NBA career, not so much what he did as a college player at North Carolina even though he was pretty good there. Michael was a freshman on Dean Smith's first NCAA championship team in 1982, the star of the U.S. 1984 Olympic gold medal team, and the biggest name on the 1992 Dream Team that struck gold in the Olympics in Barcelona. He was the total package, the most sensational, competitive winner I've ever seen when he played for the NBA Chicago Bulls when they had two three-peats in the NBA playoffs—one in 1991, 1992, and 1993; and the other in 1996, 1997, and 1998.

Along the way, he collected loads of hardware during a remarkable Hall of Fame career, including five MVP awards, 10 All-NBA first-team selections. He participated in 14 All-Star games, winning three MVPs and leading the league in scoring 10 times. Jordan won six NBA Finals MVP awards and holds the league records for highest career season scoring average, with 30.12 points per game. He upped that to 33.45 points in the playoffs.

Jordan was voted the greatest North American athlete of the 20th century by ESPN, ahead of Babe Ruth.

Michael's game belonged in the stratosphere, up in that rarified air. He was a high flier who entertained crowds by taking off from the foul line and slamming home dunks when he participated in slam dunk contests at the All-Star game. There was a reason fans called him "Air Jordan." Nike even named a sneaker "Air Jordan" after him. Simply put, he became the face of global basketball, and his face was everywhere. At his height, he was the most recognized athlete in the world since the Champ, Muhammad Ali.

I found out how good Michael was early. I saw him play at Five-Star on the outdoor courts up in Honesdale, Pennsylvania. Nobody knew who he was when he arrived. But everybody knew who he was by the end of the week. Jordan was just a Diaper Dandy when he made the game-winning shot for Carolina against Georgetown in the 1982 national championship game. Down one, Dean Smith called a timeout with less than a half minute to play. Think about the stars he had on the floor—James Worthy, Sam Perkins. But who steps up and makes the big shot? A freshman, Michael the Magnificent. And his career was off and running, big time, after that clutch shot that gave Dean Smith his first national championship.

Michael had no problem taking on responsibility.

I remember when he was a sophomore in college. I was doing one of his games and this woman comes down to the court. I had no idea who she was. She says to me, "You don't know me. I'm Michael Jordan's mother, and I wanted to thank you for all the nice things you've said about Michael." Then, I got a big kiss from her.

Michael played in the greatest game I ever broadcast for ESPN. The date was Feb. 10, 1983. Virginia vs. Carolina at Carmichael Auditorium in Chapel Hill in an unforgettable ACC

Photo Courtesy of ESPN/Kevin Mazur

I knew how special Michael Jordan was when he was at North Carolina. Hands down, I thought he was the best.

showdown. Carolina was ranked No. 1. Virginia was No. 2. Virginia's 7-foot-4 center Ralph Sampson was the national Player of the Year.

Carolina had won the first game between these two Goliaths, but Virginia looked like it was going to win the revenge match. Ralph was going off, giving Virginia a 63-53 lead with 4:12 left to play before Michelangelo, Dean Smith, went to work. The Heels scored the last 11 points of the game—Michael was right in the middle of the action. He went off. Jordan cut Virginia's lead to 63-62 when he tipped in a missed three pointer by Jimmy Braddock with 1:07 left. Then, he stripped Rick Carlisle as he attempted to bring the ball up on the next possession and went coast to coast for a monster dunk to give Carolina the lead.

Virginia still had a chance to win, but Michael rose over Sampson for a rebound to prevent a game-winning tip-in with just one second to play. Immediately afterward, I went off, saying, "Forget Ralph Sampson. The best player in the nation is Michael 'the Magnificent' Jordan."

The story played great everywhere but in Charlottesville. I had to go up there to do a Virginia game the next week, and as soon as I arrived, I saw headlines in the local paper. "Dickie V says Jordan is the best." Then, who do I happen to run into walking down the hallway at University Hall before the game? It's Ralph.

He came up to me and said, "Here comes Michael Jordan's PR agent."

I said to him, "Ralph, I love you, but Michael is special."

Funny thing is that Ralph and I have talked about it since. A few years back, I was a speaker at a luncheon to honor the ACC Legends before the conference's annual tournament in Greensboro; Ralph was there. I remember standing next to him and Ralph's saying to me. "Hey, you were right about Michael."

Michael thought he could do anything he wanted to do as an athlete—golf, baseball, anything. Back in 1993, after the Olympics and the death of his father, he announced his retirement. It was the lead story in every paper in the world. Jordan then pulled another surprise when he signed a minor league baseball contract with the Chicago White Sox on February 7, 1994. I remember running into him in spring training that year because the White Sox worked out in Sarasota, right in my backyard. We were sitting, talking in the trainer's room, and I said, "Michael, have you touched a ball recently?"

"No," he said, "I haven't."

Then, I said, "Let me guess. If you had to play a game tomorrow, do you think you could?"

He said, "Are you kidding me? I know I could get 20."

Michael doing his thing for the Tar Heels in 1983. What a player!

This is how the super players think. "You're going to tell me I couldn't get two baskets and a foul shot a quarter? That I couldn't get a basket on a run out or a little jump shot or that I couldn't grab an offensive rebound and score on a put back? It's just two baskets and a foul shot. I couldn't do that every quarter?"

Then, Michael came back to the NBA the following year, and we saw instantly the 25's, the 30's, the 35's. You couldn't stop him. You literally couldn't stop him. All you could do was hope to contain him, as Dan Patrick would say. If you were playing against him, you had to hope he had a sub-par night shooting the rock because he was impossible to defend. Michael was the ultimate, solid-gold PTPer.

CHAPTER 19
TERRI AND SHERRI

Like any dad, I've always been about my family.

I know a lot of people look at me and think I'm a 24/7 hoops junkie, but anyone who really knows me knows how much of a family man I am. Lorraine and I can't do enough for and with our family. We share a lot of time together.

I have two daughters: Terri and Sherri. They are two years apart in age, though some people mistake them for twins because they resemble each other so much. They were very close growing up and still are today.

Terri and Sherri are the spitting image of my wife, physically and emotionally—thank God. They're not emotional like me. They're more even-keeled, rational. I couldn't be prouder of my daughters because I see so much of Lorraine in them.

I remember when they were born.

I was coaching at Rutgers when the call came: "Your wife has been rushed to the hospital in New Brunswick." We were playing Pittsburgh, and I was on the bench. When the game finally ended, I got myself to the hospital. A few hours later, I had a daughter, Terri.

Then came Sherri. This time, I was at practice at the University of Detroit when I got the call: "Your wife is having a baby." I rushed to the hospital and saw my second daughter, Sherri, come into the world.

Like any other dad, it was love at first sight for me with both of them.

It's only later that you realize the enormous responsibility you have when you are a parent. Throughout their lives, I've tried to steer them in the right direction. I've tried to raise them with the same values my parents instilled in me. And I've tried to do things that make them proud of me. All my honors, my inductions into various Halls of Fame, are for my family. I've found that honors don't mean a thing unless you have someone to share them with.

After I got fired from the Pistons, I had a lot of free time on my hands—too much, if you must know. I decided to teach my daughters basketball. We had a basket out back. Every day when they came home from school, I'd put my coaching hat on in the backyard, ready to work with them on their lefty and righty layups. And no less than the master of the game, the big guy, Bob Lanier, would stop by and introduce them to the fine art of shooting because the Big Dobber was as good as it gets.

We enrolled them in the local CYO, Catholic Youth Organization. When they were doing their layup drills, they were very good. They could shoot the Rock.

Me and my gals. Let me tell you, I'm the luckiest guy around. My wonderful wife, Lorraine, and my daughters, Terri and Sherri, have made my life fabulous.

But they weren't so good in game situations. They were unable to get free and had problems with other players guarding them. I used to laugh hysterically when they said, "It's so different, Dad. When we're in the yard, it's one thing, but it's tougher playing five-on-five."

Terri was about ten; Sherri was around eight at the time.

I was a little broken-hearted when my wife finally told me. She said, "Rich, Terri and Sherri don't really have a desire to play hoops."

I looked at my wife for a minute, swallowed hard, and finally accepted the fact that she was right. Their hearts weren't in it, and there was nothing I could do to change that. I always believed that, to be successful, you have to have a passion and a desire in your heart to do what you love to achieve success. I just wanted them to find something they loved—swimming, dancing, music, softball, tennis, anything—and attack it to the best of their ability.

So Sherri and Terri decided to try swimming.

My girls were outstanding swimmers between the ages of 6 and 10. They were winning medals at the local swim club in breaststroke, freestyle, and backstroke; then, they went on to the next level, joining an AAU swimming program. That's when they swam against the best of the best. And I'm telling you, that was tough.

But, one day, they came home, crying.

"What are you crying about? What's wrong?"

"We don't really enjoy swimming."

"To be honest with you, Dad," they said, "we really want to play tennis."

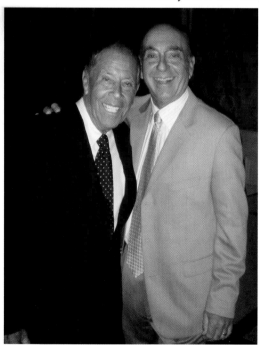

Here I am with Nick Bollettieri whose tennis camp helped my girls hone their tennis skills. Both Terri and Sherri went on to play tennis in college.

At the time, they were taking tennis lessons twice a week. And they fell in love with it. They also played a little softball, which they seemed to like. Then, they asked, "Can we put all the time we were doing in swimming and transfer it to tennis?" I said, "If that's what you want."

We entered them in some local tournaments. They were everybody's favorites to play because it was Love City. Zero and Zero. They were getting blitzed by all the kids in the neighborhood, but they kept competing. I told them, "Just have fun and keep competing."

Then, it all changed.

I had to go to a game—there was snow and ice—cars were stranded. And I couldn't get to the airport. I called my wife: "What are we doing? Why do we live here? We have no relatives here. I'm here only because I coached here. I like the people here, they treat you like royalty, but the winter months are too tough to deal with."

So, we went on a little vacation to the Sarasota-Bradenton area in Florida. We rented an apartment, and I put the girls in Nick Bollettieri's tennis camp for a week. The sun was shining. We went to the beaches--It was beautiful. We loved it there.

Terri and Sherri fell in love, too—with the camp. They saw all the pros working out—Jimmy Arias, Aaron Krickstein, Kathy Horvath, Lisa Bonder, Susan Sloan—all the people who played on the tour, who they'd seen on the TV. There were also some young stars starting out, too. You've heard of them. Their names? Andre Agassi, Monica Seles, Jim Courier, David Wheaton. It was unreal, the intensity and passion.

When the girls finally came to me and asked, "Dad, why can't we live here and go to the academy all the time?" I could find no reason why not.

At the time, we lived at Pebble Creek North in West Bloomfield and were fortunate to get a buyer really fast.

A year later, my daughters asked if they could go and play in some tournaments in Michigan. Again, why not?

We went up there. Everybody just figured, here come those Vitale girls; this will be cupcake city.

They were shocked out of their minds: "What has happened to their game?" was the cry from many of them. "Look, those are not the same kids we watched a couple of years ago."

When Terri was 15 and Sherri was 13, I could see they were going to play at the collegiate level. The academics were there, too. In fact, Bolletierri said to me, "Dick, I'll be very honest. Pros? I doubt it, but your girls are going to able to pick almost any school in the country and play tennis." They played in all the national tournaments. They won multiple state championships—in singles and doubles—against tough competition. If you are in the top 40, you can go to many of the schools on scholarship. Terri got her national ranking as high as the 40's; Sherri made it to the top 15 in the nation.

When they were young, I would take them out of school so they could go to Duke-Carolina games with me. They toured both campuses, felt the incredible spirit both schools had. Terri particularly liked Duke, and I was convinced she would go there.

Then, she had a visit to Notre Dame that changed her world—and mine. She flat-out fell in love with the place—the physical beauty of its campus, its strong academics, its storied athletic past. But, more than that, she was attracted to its strong sense of giving back, of paying your good fortune forward.

I tested her resolve by having her visit the school in the winter—plenty of snow, ice. But she stayed true to her choice. She had a tennis scholarship and matriculated.

All was not smooth sailing at first. Terri had been a straight-A student in high school but got a C+ on her first term paper at Notre Dame. She was on the phone, devastated. She was in tears even talking about how Notre Dame might not be the right place for her; I told her to get a grip on life, man. If I'd gotten a C+ in college, I'd have celebrated for a week. I told her to look in the mirror every day—something I try to do every day—and tell herself that she was as good as anyone at Notre Dame. Beyond academics, she felt intimidated by her teammates, too. But, as I reminded her, she was on a full scholarship. They wouldn't have given it to her if she couldn't play.

Four years later, she was the recipient of the Knute Rockne Tennis Athlete of the Year Award. At graduation, she told me, "Dad, I want to tell you how much I love you."

Like I said—a lot of responsibility. But so much joy, too.

The transition to college was easier for Sherri because she had her sister. Bollettieri was very honest with her. He felt that, with her power and strength, Sherri had a shot at professional tennis. But she'd have had to go to tournaments in Europe to qualify for points. That would take time—and take her away from our family.

I told her she'd have to do that if she wanted to be a pro. She looked me straight in the eye and said, "Dad, I have no desire to be a pro. I want to go to a great college like Terri did. I want to be a student-athlete and go on from there."

Sherri was being heavily recruited. She'd had a phenomenal high school record. I told the Notre Dame coach that it shouldn't be hard to recruit Sherri because she'd been coming to football weekends for two years. When it came time to make a decision, she tried to play the "I've got to look at this school and that school" game—Duke, Indiana, UCLA. But I knew where she was going: Notre Dame. Terri and Sherri were teammates for two years at the Golden Dome. They both graduated, got their Masters degrees in business from the school, and married fellow Domers.

Today, I see my girls doing the same thing with their kids, telling them the same things they heard over the dinner table about making good decisions, about doing the right thing. They have both grown up to be beautiful, accomplished, caring women.

They still work for me today. They handle my fan mail, my website, my requests for charities. They coordinate my life with IMG, my management company. In short, they handle my life outside ESPN.

They are invaluable. I couldn't imagine my life without them.

But that shouldn't come as any surprise since I knew that when I first held them as babies.

Who loves the Rock? My daughters know what basketball means to me, and while they didn't play, they both enjoy how much I love the game.

CHAPTER 20
GROWING UP WITH ESPN

I started with ESPN in December 1979.

Initially, my daughters thought it was a fraud. They asked Lorraine, "Where does Dad go to do games? We never see him on TV." In West Bloomfield, Michigan, where we lived, we didn't have cable, so they didn't have a chance to see me on TV for several years.

In the years since, ESPN's reach has grown exponentially. It's funny looking back to the days when the girls couldn't find me on TV.

Now, I'm going to throw some facts at you, courtesy of the ESPN website.

ESPN was launched on September 7, 1979, a cable and satellite TV network, broadcasting from Bristol, Connecticut. When it started, it reached around 100,000 homes in this country. As of this writing, it reaches approximately 95,300,000 households. It is a joint venture, now owned by Disney, which has 80%, and the Hearst Corporation, which owns 20%.

It was founded by Bill Rasmussen, his son, Scott, and Ed Egan, an Aetna insurance agent. Its first president was Chet Simmons, who had been the Commissioner of the U.S. Football League. John Skipper took the help as ESPN President in 2012. George Bodenheimer, former president, rose to be the Executive Chairman of ESPN, Inc. in 2012 until leaving the company in 2014.

ESPN was originally founded to promote sports at the University of Connecticut, the NHL's Hartford Whalers, and the Bristol Red Sox.

The company paid $30,000 for a transponder to broadcast sports 24 hours a day, seven days a week. They hired sportscasters and trucks to travel around the country, covering various events. The land in Bristol cost $18,000. The campus was built on a dump.

Early on, the company knew it would be difficult to secure rights for professional sports but also knew they could negotiate terms with the NCAA for college sports. And that's what they did. They felt if they rebroadcast college games, they could attract new viewers. They covered 18 different sports for two years, including many championship games, except for basketball.

An estimated 30,000 viewers watched the launch of the station in 1979.

The first score the network announced was for tennis: Chris Evert beat Billie Jean King.

The station struggled in its early years. Anheuser Busch was vital to its survival, giving them $1,000,000 in 1979 and $5,000,000 in 1981 to keep them afloat.

I loved working with Robin Roberts and Jimmy Valvano. Here we are at the Final Four in 1992.

As one of the early cable broadcasters, ESPN paid the NBA $2.4 billion in 1982 for a six-year contract. Then, the station obtained the U.S. Football League. In 1987, it gained partial rights to the NFL. It agreed to simulcast the games on local TV affiliates. Its Sunday Night Football program spurred its rise to legitimacy. Its programs on the NFL Draft, the Pre-Game Show, and Post-Game Highlights brought the network to a new level.

In 1990, ESPN added Major League Baseball to its line-up.

Today, ESPN broadcasts 65 sports, 24 hours a day, to 61 countries. There are more than 32 networks on TV, a magazine, and a website.

One more thing: The music lead-in to ESPN's *SportsCenter* is famous—six notes in particular: "Da Da Da, Da Da Da." The theme was written by John Colby, a Grammy winner for his music in the film *The Civil War,* by Ken Burns.

ESPN has become a giant, and I'm proud to have been a little spoke in this giant wheel. I'll also admit I'm addicted to it. I love all sports. I follow baseball, basketball, football. I'm even getting into ice hockey, following the Tampa Bay Lightning. I am absolutely lost without *SportsCenter.*

Today, the campus is 123 acres. I remember when we had one little trailer where I'd go to get my assignments. Now, it's like a college campus: mailroom, libraries, studios, dining halls. It's become an incredible place.

I've watched the people grow, too. In 1981, my driver was George Bodenheimer. He'd take me back and forth, and we'd talk. He also worked in the mailroom. He rose up to be president of ESPN. I watched another of my drivers, Freddie Gaudelli, go on to become an award-winning executive producer for Sunday Night Football on NBC. I watched people like John Wildhack, who had been one of my producers early on, become second in command to John Skipper. It's been amazing to watch guys like Mo Davenport, an assistant producer who became the head of ESPN radio, and Steve Anderson, one of my producers who has risen to executive VP.

The list goes on and on. It has been amazing to watch them and the network grow.

But I've grown a little, too.

TV was foreign to me when I took the job at ESPN. Even today, when we're talking about what we're going to do, talking about the videos, the graphics, the producers still tease me: "Why are you doing this? You're going to go off and do your own thing anyway."

And they're right.

My strength has been that I'm spontaneous, off the cuff. I try to have fun at what I do. I'm not the most polished of announcers. I'm not as smooth as some guys. But then I think about Chris

I was thrilled that former ESPN president George Bodenheimer spoke on my behalf when I was inducted into the National Sportscasters Hall of Fame.

Berman, John Madden, Terry Bradshaw—a little bit off the wall. I think people appreciate it when you're enthusiastic and energetic and have obvious passion for what you do.

I remember last year doing an interview with Seth Davis of CBS. He said, "When you first started, you received a lot of criticism for being loud, talking too much. But now, I notice that 90% of what people write is positive."

What I realize most now is just how much love and passion I've always had for what I do. I love the game of basketball, but I also care about what people think. People who say they don't care about others' opinions don't have a sense of pride in what they do. Look, you can rip me. That's your opinion, your right, as long as it's not personal. But I always want people to think I did a good job, gave it my all. And it's my love and passion that got me through when fans didn't respond nicely to my analysis.

In 2014, I celebrated my 35th year at ESPN. There was a compilation tape made that was just hilarious. ESPN had 35 of their personalities impersonate me, one in honor of each year I'd been there. And, I have to admit, some of them they were better than me. When I saw the opening of my very first show on YouTube, I couldn't stop laughing. I had no clue back then; I went two minutes straight, all about DePaul and Wisconsin. Unbelievable!

In my defense, I have to say that now I usually go 15 seconds, in and out. But, just in case I go over, I discovered the producers have invented the Dickie V Rule: They signal me that I have 15 seconds when I really have 20. Hey, whatever works, baby.

Because I watch a lot of TV, I know what it takes to keep people interested. I've seen a lot of former coaches and players come on the air and play to their peers. They want to show the world how much they know. They get so technical that they bore the hell out of 90% of the audience. Because the 90% are just like my mom and dad, my uncles, my Jersey people. They grew up with Mel Allen, Red Barber, Vin Scully, Joe Garagiola telling stories. I watch baseball now, and every pitch is dissected; you're in Z'sville, bored out of your mind by the third inning.

Hey, I coached. I can x and o just as well as the next guy. I can talk about the shuffle cut, the flex cuts, and coming off the curls, defensive rotation. But you have to make it simple so the majority of people know what you're talking about and want to keep listening. When I look at that red light, it's like I'm sitting and talking to my buddies.

And I think it's worked for me.

I get such a thrill when fans come up to me saying, "Man, I love what you said about that PTPer or the Diaper Dandy."

It just makes me smile and say, "Well, I must have made a connection." Just like Scotty used to say

To me, that's what it's all about. The game belongs to the people. And I do my thing for them.

CHAPTER 21
BUILDING MY BRAND

Is there anyone out there who hasn't imitated me, for good or for bad? I don't think I can go a day anymore without somebody saying, "Hey, am I a PTPer?" or "Give me a T.O., Baby!" or "It's Awesome, Baby!"

I hear it when we go out to eat, go to a sporting event, go to a concert. People always ask me "Where did you get those terms from?" They came from the locker room or from my buddies when we were sitting around in the diner, watching games. These days, you hear it from kids on the playground. One of my biggest kicks is stopping by a playground to watch a pick-up game, and the kids go: "Dickie V! We can't believe it! Call our games, Dickie V!"

My style has given me an identity, a brand. And that brand has allowed me to do other things, TV commercials and speaking events, for many major corporate groups.

And I've received some recognition along the way.

I'm a season ticket holder at the Tampa Bay Rays home games, and one night, Evan Longoria hits a home run. I'm looking up at the scoreboard, and all of a sudden, they're flashing a giant picture of me, yelling, "Awesome, Baby!"

You know, we are all entertainers in some way. TV is a medium where you are there to entertain and educate. That is something I learned from Scotty Connal—Remember, you're not out there searching for a cure for cancer or looking to solve the problems of the Middle East; you're there to talk about basketball, a game you love.

I just try to be myself. I think John Madden did it for years in football. Al McGuire did it in hoops. Let's face reality: Most guys who coached know a little about the x's and o's or the game. But the bottom line is you want to keep in tune with what is happening, and you can't forget you are in the business of entertainment, not just stats and facts.

When I first started at ESPN, I brought most of the lingo I use on air with me. It actually came from the locker room. I just picked it up from the players. Guys would come up to me and say, "Coach, give me some more PT. This guy just won't give me the Rock," things like that. And I transferred it over the TV. I have a whole glossary of phrases I used.

Now guys are sending me letters, asking me to use phrases they invented on the tube.

Bobbleheads, baby, bobbleheads!

Photo Courtesy of ESPN/Robert Smith

During the 1987 NCAA tournament, I said I would stand on my head if Austin Peay upset Illinois. Well, Austin Peay won, 68-67, and I lived up to my word at the school's sports banquet.

Hey, people were calling me Mr. Enthusiasm long before I ever got into television. In fact, they labeled me that when I was in the Motor City coaching the Titans. Writers like Mike O'Hara, Jerry Greene, and the late Joe Falls used to come up to me and say, "You're mild today compared to how enthusiastic you were when you were here with us." It wasn't something that was manufactured for TV. That's who I am. When that red light goes on, I'm absolutely myself.

I can remember one time in 1987 when an Illini team led by Ken Norman and Doug Altenberger received the No. 3 seed in the NCAA tournament and I predicted that they would reach the Final Four. In the first round, Illinois faced Austin Peay, the champions of the Ohio Valley Conference who got most of their fame with the chant they developed for 1970's star player James "Fly" Williams, a scoring machine who was recruited out of Brooklyn by Leonard Hamilton: "The Fly Is Open ... Let's Go Peay!" Back then, early rounds of the NCAA tournament were shown on ESPN, and in the second half, with Peay down to the Illini by only three points, I figured I'd have a little fun. So, I said coming out of the break, "There is no way Illinois loses this game! If Illinois loses, I'll stand on my head."

Sure enough, Austin Peay pulled off a 68-67 upset, and months later, I was invited to Austin Peay to be the keynote speaker at their annual banquet. And, yes, I stood on my head for the kids.

Two years later, Princeton was playing the Big East champion, Georgetown, in a No. 1 vs. No. 16 matchup in the first round of the NCAA tournament. I figured it would be a blowout. I guess I forget Pete Carril was coaching the Ivy League champions.

Before the game, I said to John Saunders, "This was supposed to be a total mismatch. An M and M'er. You know what I'll do if Princeton wins? I will hitchhike from Bristol to Providence for the second-round game, put on a Princeton cheerleading outfit, and cheer with the Princeton cheerleaders."

They came to us at halftime and Princeton was winning. John Saunders and I are sitting there, and he turns to the camera and says, "Dick Vitale, I hope you're ready to put on your tutu and go out and dance with the Princeton cheerleaders!"

But it wasn't meant to be. I got saved by a no-call at the end.

I probably saved some bids for the mid-majors in the process.

Things really got wild when Jimmy V joined us in the studio. He was the funniest guy I had ever been around. One time, John, Jimmy V, and I were in the studio, talking about Michigan. During a commercial, we decided to do a little Motown, singing the Four Tops, etc. When we were getting ready to go back on air, all three of us agreed to stand up and sing. When the red light went on, they fooled me—I was the only one standing and singing. Those two guys were laughing hysterically.

I love interacting with the fans the same way when we go to the campuses.

ESPN does Midnight Madness at campuses all over the country. I was at Cincinnati in 1994, doing the festivities with the fantastic Robin Roberts, who has since gone on to have an excellent career at *Good Morning America* and is also a member of the Board of Directors with the V Foundation—she was always one of my favorites to work with at ESPN. There was never any doubt in my mind that she, Ley, Mike Tirico, Chris Fowler, Dan Shulman, and Saunders were going to become mega stars.

Anyway, I wanted to get an up-close and personal look at their Diaper Dandies—Danny Fortson and LaZelle Durden. They had a contest, a half court shot to win tuition for the year. They picked a senior named Cory Clouse to attempt the shot before thousands of people and a national TV audience.

The cameras were rolling, and I tossed the ball to him, adding, "And, Cory, I'll throw in the books if the shot goes in."

Then, I told him, "Let it fly, Cory."

He did, and the ball went in. Pandemonium. I jumped into his arms. I still have people asking me about the shot. It was such a moment of spontaneity that you couldn't have possibly scripted it for TV.

Whenever I go to the Carolina-Duke game at Cameron, I let the Cameron Crazies pass me up the stands. My wife gets nervous. It keeps me young, keeps me vibrant. When I go to Notre Dame football games, I always sit in the stands with my family, wearing my Irish sweatshirt. I'm not there as a broadcaster; I'm there as a fan. And my daughters are always asking me, "When are you going to start acting your age?"

I tell them, "When I start acting my age, the party's over. Right now, I'm just young at heart, as Sinatra used to sing, 'Fairy tales can come true…'"

I still go out and shoot free throws before the games I broadcast. This year, Kentucky really struggled from the line in

I flew in to welcome everyone to the 2001 ESPYS dressed as Elvis. Do you think I could pass for The King?

Photo Courtesy of ESPN/Kevin Mazur

101

the national championship game. Shooting brick after brick. I'm in my shirt and tie and shoes and will still make seven-of-10. I could always shoot the Rock, baby!

Even though I've calmed down a little from the start of my career, I'll still try almost anything once. One year at the ESPYS (2001), I was a Flying Elvis during the opening. It was scary. I'm up there at the top of the ceiling looking down—I hate heights. They put a harness on me, and as I'm flying down, I throw my wig into the crowd, and Cybil Shepherd catches it. Michael Jordan is sitting down there, laughing like crazy. Then, I get up and say, "Welcome to the ESPYS." It was nuts!

Needless to say, it doesn't take much for me to get started. I'm up for just about anything as long as I get to do it my way.

CHAPTER 22
LATE NIGHT ENTERTAINMENT

I'm no stranger to late night TV, baby.

I made a guest appearance on the *Conan O'Brien Show* when TBS brought his show to Atlanta for the Final Four in 2013.

Charles Barkley was there, too. He has been campaigning for years for us to do a sporting event together on TV, and once Conan got wind of it, it became of a reality. He had Charles, who works for TBS doing NBA games, and I do color commentary on a slam-dunk contest involving weird dunking mascots. Man, I don't know where they came up with some of those characters. They assembled a morbidly obese Colonel Sanders, a Superman with his cape stuck in a toilet, BL Mr.T, and, of course, the sagging Peachtree Towers with Erectile Dysfunction—don't ask—and let them do their thing.

Man, the lines were just flowing.

Charles is a funny guy; he didn't take any prisoners, first ripping into one of his best friends, Michael Jordan, and his co-host on TBS NBA telecasts, Shaquille O'Neal. Among other things, Charles talked about the fact Michael hasn't done a good job as a GM. "I love Michael, but people tell me he's good looking. He's not good looking. Listen, every man who's got $500 million dollars is good looking. If he was a plumber, people wouldn't be saying he's good looking. No way."

Next, Sir Charles, a spokesman for Weight Watchers, took on Shaq. "You know, Shaquille gives me a hard time, but these are my real arms, unlike him. He doesn't even use his own body in his lotion commercial. I've seen his Fat <bleep> body. He's using a stunt double."

Then came the main event.

When Colonel Sanders came out, Charles immediately defended him. "We should never say anything bad about the Colonel," he said, reflecting on his taste for fried chicken.

I couldn't resist taking a shot at my buddy. "He looks wide-bodied like you when you played," The amazing thing was that Colonel Sanders somehow put the ball into the basket despite jumping off a trampoline while wearing a big oversized fat suit. Sign him to a 10-day contract.

"He's lacking hang time," Charles said. "He's not a PTPer."

Next, they brought out "Superman with His Cape Stuck in a Toilet," and Charles said, "He reminds me of Shaq during his last couple of years."

When Conan O'Brien brought his show to Atlanta for the Final Four in 2013, I had a great time with him, Hank Aaron, and, of course, Charles Barkley. The one-liners flowed freely and often.

I immediately turned to Charles and said, "Hey, Charles, I thought he was going to flush it, baby."

I know Charles's favorite mascot had to be "BL Mr. T," who had the head of Mr. T combined with a BLT sandwich body. On a side note, I once saw Kentucky fans deliver a pizza to Charles when he played for Auburn and was sitting on the bench, waiting for tipoff.

"Be careful, Dick," Charles said. "I've met Mr. T before, and I don't think you really want to tick him off."

"It's the Baconator," I said.

"A good effort, but lack of hang time," Charles said.

"Charles likes hang time," I said, "because Michael used to hang on him and jam in his face."

The craziest mascot came last—"Peachtree Towers with Erectile Dysfunction," or as Conan said, "An iconic part of the Atlanta skyline with an embarrassing personal problem." When Charles saw the building was slumped over, he immediately cracked a joke about his lack of spring and issues with ED.

"That explains why he can't get up," Charles said. (ha, ha)

We had a blast with Conan. Can you imagine Charles and me on camera, doing a college game or an NBA game? Now, that would be fun.

I always thought Charles could be special, a real standout if he put his mind to it more. I remember when he was at Auburn and the coach there, Sonny Smith, had me come in to talk to him because he wasn't really working hard. I got in his face and told him what I thought. "Son, let me tell you something. You know you have a chance to make a lot of money and to be special. Don't let it slip away. Get in there early; work on your game."

He has always thanked me for that.

Eventually, he became a PTPer in everything he did and was a natural for the 1992 Olympic Dream team and the Naismith Hall of Fame.

Being with him on Conan was a special night for me. I walked into the green room before the show and sitting there on the couch was Hank Aaron, one of the all-time leaders in home runs. I said, "Mr. Aaron, I'm such a fan, but more than that, my father, who's up in heaven, would be going nuts. He loved you. He loved your quick wrists and your consistency—you were one of his favorite players." My wife and I sat there with him for 40 minutes, just talking baseball. Wow. My dad would have been in baseball heaven to know I was sitting there with Hammerin' Hank.

Photo Courtesy of ESPN

I've done some wacky promos over the years for ESPN.

••••••••••••••••••••••

My life has always been about spontaneity. I never know what's going to happen next. Back in 1996, when the Final Four was at the Meadowlands, David Letterman invited me to the Big Apple to do a Top Ten list on his late night show.

His writers came up with "Top Ten Reasons Dick Vitale is Nuts," and they had me read it on the air…and here they are:

10. I like to run though the locker room wearing nothing but a referee's whistle and yelling, "Baby!"
9. I keep repainting the roof of my house to match Dennis Rodman's hair.
8. Five minutes after my first child was born, I dumped Gatorade on my wife.
7. I'm on a strict diet of shoelaces and floor wax.
6. I've invited David Letterman to host the next ESPY awards.
5. For a cheap rush, I take hits of stale air from an old basketball.
4. My project, ESPN3, is a new channel devoted to coverage of my Rogaine treatment.
3. When I make love to my wife, I always go for the three-pointer, baby.
2. I've referred to everything as "baby" except for my real baby.

And the No. 1 reason why Dick Vitale is nuts? Right now, I think I'm whispering!

Funny.

I have always been amazed how these late night talk show hosts like Conan, David Letterman, Jay Leno, Jimmy Fallon, and Jimmy Kimmel can be so consistently funny day after day. I guess that's why they're making mega-bucks.

Hey, baby! I'll talk hoops with anyone.

CHAPTER 23
GOING TO THE MOVIES

I have always loved sports movies with a message, and one of my all-time favorites is *Remember the Titans*, a film based loosely on the true story of Herman Boone, an African-American who was hired as the new head football coach in 1971 at the newly integrated T.C. Williams High in Northern Virginia. Boone took over from the then-current and quite popular white coach, Bill Yoast, who had been nominated for the Virginia High School Hall of Fame.

As a show of respect, Boone—who is played by my favorite actor, Denzel Washington—offers the position of defensive coordinator to Yoast, who at first refuses but then relents because he's afraid the players he coached the previous year would lose out on their chances at scholarships.

Well, Boone first integrates the buses when the team goes up to Gettysburg for summer camp. Black and white team members frequently get into racially motivated conflicts that week of the pre-season, including some between the leaders of both sides, returning captain Gerry Bertier and new emerging leader Julius Campbell. But, after some forceful lectures and tough coaching, the team finally starts to bond big-time, and Bertier and Campbell not only become friends but also co-leaders of the team. When the team returns from camp, things get ugly. Boone gets told by the school board that if he loses even a single game, he will be fired. Talk about pressure.

The Titans wind up going through the season undefeated and overcoming racial prejudice from opposing coaches, players, and even referees to win the state championship. At one point in the state semi-finals, it becomes apparent the referees are biased against the Titans. Yoast warns the head official he will go to the press and expose the scandal unless the game is officiated fairly. The Titans win, but Yoast is told his behavior had cost him any chance he had of making the Hall of Fame. While celebrating the victory, Bertier—a high school All-American lineman—was in an automobile accident. He was paralyzed. Obviously, Bertier could not play due to injury, but the team goes on to win the title anyway. Ten years later, Bertier dies after winning the gold medal in the Shot Put in the Paralympics. The team, coaches, and athletes all reunite to attend his funeral.

Boone coached the Titans for five more years until he retired.

Now, let me tell you why I'm bringing this up.

During the credits, it comes out that Boone still lives in Alexandria, Virginia. After seeing the movie, I decided I would really like to talk to him. So, I dialed information and got the number. When I made the call, a young lady answers the phone. I say, "Hi, is this where Herman Boone lives?"

She says, "Who's calling?"

I say, "Dick Vitale."

She was stunned. She must have been a

After I saw the movie Remember the Titans, *I found the real Herman Boone, the coach portrayed by Denzel Washington in the movie. What a fantastic guy. In this photo, Herman takes time out during his 1971 training camp to talk with one of his players.*

Photo Courtesy of Associated Press

basketball fan. She said, "Dick Vitale from ESPN? Are you kidding?"

I say, "No, I just saw the movie and was so touched, I wanted to tell him how much I enjoyed it."

So, she yells, "Dad, Dick Vitale's on the line!"

He comes on the telephone. Well, we talk, stay in touch, and one weekend, I fly him out to Notre Dame as my guest and get him to speak at the pep rally. The crowd went crazy.

That's the effect movies can have to people. My favorite actors are Robert DeNiro, Al Pacino, Denzel, and Dustin Hoffman. Yeah, that's my Final Four. And Julia Roberts has to be my favorite female actress.

Hey, I got a taste of acting in Hollywood. I did some cameos in movies like *Blue Chips*, *Love and Basketball*, *He Got Game*, and *Hoop Dreams*. I even did a bit as a baseball color commentator in *The Naked Gun: From the Files of Police Squad*, a comedy starring Leslie Nielsen. I shared the broadcast booth with Curt Gowdy, Tim McCarver, Mel Allen, Jim Palmer, Dick Enberg, Billy Crystal, and Dr. Joyce Brothers. I remember we all went for lunch one day and got to hear a lot of stories from Crystal, who is a big Yankees fan. Man, he knows his sports.

I had a line in the movie where I was supposed to go crazy over a relief pitcher. And Dr. Brothers was supposed to say, "Richard, Richard. Calm down. It's only a game. Do you need some help?"

Well, my wife was sitting in the back near the directors, and she told me later in the car, "That will never make the movie."

I said, "Why?"

"They said, 'Cut it.'" It wound up on the cutting room floor.

Blue Chips is a story about the evils in the world of recruiting and the pressure to win in the big time. Nick Nolte starred as the coach; they filmed it in Indiana. They had a lot of people I knew like Shaquille O'Neal, Penny Hardaway, Bobby Hurley, Calbert Cheaney, Steve Alford, and even The General, Robert Montgomery Knight, playing roles.

People probably don't realize this, but I was once offered a chance to do my own TV sitcom. Oh yeah. That's right, baby. 1999. I had been featured in a few promos for ESPN called, "Hoops Malone," which promoted a made-up TV show. It featured me, George Gervin, and a sock puppet named "O'Hoolix." Well, all of a sudden, Disney is talking to me about making a sitcom with yours truly as the coach. They contacted my agents at IMG about writing a script for me. We went to Hollywood twice. They told me, "Look, a lot of announcers like Bob Uecker and Alex Karras have made the crossover."

They even said they would shoot episodes in Orlando, so I wouldn't have to leave Florida. They also told me, "This is a different world financially from where you're at." But I guess I must have learned my lessons from making the journey to the NBA and thought about Jimmy V's line, "Never mess with happy." I was happy calling games at ESPN, and I never pursued the big or small screen again.

We were a fictional family in the Hoops Malone *promos for ESPN. It almost turned into a real series.*

Photo Courtesy of ESPN

CHAPTER 24
GROWING OUR FAMILY

And now we are 11.

My family.

It started out as just Lorraine and me. We had Terri and Sherri. Then, we added Chris and Tom. One by one came Sydney, Ryan, then Connor and Jake, and finally Ava.

I love them all.

And what better place to celebrate family than at Disney World. For a 2014 campaign that started its run during March Madness, Disney filmed my family enjoying a trip to Disney World. The 30-second spot starts with us all in a huddle. Then, I say, "Break!" We all separate, and the ad shows vignettes of us interacting with different Disney characters. I tell the genie he has to box out. My granddaughter

Photo Courtesy of ESPN

Let me tell you, there IS magic at Disney! My family had a blast as we were filmed walking around, checking everything out at Disney World for a commercial. The Kingdom is the place to be, baby!

meets Cinderella, and my grandson sword-fights with Darth Vader while I intone, "Hey, Vader, this kid is a Diaper Dandy!"

The cameras followed us onto the different rides. The spot ends with all of us together and a shot of Sleeping Beauty's castle is in the background.

I think I had a better time seeing the smiles on the faces of my grandkids than anyone else.

Anyway, it got me thinking about how lucky I am to have such a wonderful clan.

I have two high-quality sons-in-law. To me, they are two awesome guys who had a purpose and a goal they wanted to achieve when they got out of Notre Dame. They used sports in a positive way. They didn't allow sports to use them.

Dr. Chris Sforzo, Terri's husband, grew up on Long Island. He was a lacrosse player at Notre Dame. He and Terri met in their freshman year and dated as a two-sport couple—when they had the time, of course. When they graduated, Terri got a job in advertising at Leo Burnett in Chicago while Chris went to Loyola-Chicago medical school. He didn't choose an easy path. After he got his M.D., he was accepted for his residency at Shand's Hospital at the University of Florida. After completing his residency, he wasn't finished. He received a fellowship to complete his Hand and Microsurgery training under the tutelage of Dr. Paul Dell, Dr. Larry Chidgey, and Dr. Tom Wright. Since completing his fellowship, Chris has established a very successful practice in Sarasota, FL.

He started a local lacrosse league, the Lakewood Ranch Lightning, with two other former Division I players who now coach. Their sons are among the players on the field. The team was one of two youth lacrosse teams who were recently invited to participate in the seventh annual U.S. Lacrosse's Champion Challenge at the Disney Wide World of Sports Complex in Orlando. Chris also coaches the only youth travel lacrosse team in the area, the Manasota Monsters.

And he has stayed involved with Notre Dame lacrosse after he graduated. He has also done some commentary on the sport on TV.

Thomas Krug, who's married to Sherri, grew up in Los Gatos, California. He lived 15 minutes from the beach and once climbed Mt. Whitney. Tom was a three-sport star in high school, so good he was inducted into the Los Gatos High School Hall of Fame.

Obviously, football was his first love since he had a scholarship to Notre Dame in that sport. But he was no slouch at basketball or baseball, either. When he was in college, Tom was 6-foot-5 and threw a ball like a rifle. He had played all of seven minutes before he replaced Ron Powlus in Notre Dame's defeat of Navy. Anyone who watched his Orange Bowl performance might have thought we'd see him on Sundays. But a neck injury put an end to his football-playing days.

After college, Thomas went to New York and worked two years in sports management. Then, he decided to pursue his dream. He attended the Stetson University School of Law. He had been a long-time attorney with the Sarasota State Attorney's Office before deciding to run for a judgeship. He is now one of the youngest judges in the state of Florida, presiding over all types of criminal cases.

Not too many people know this, but when I was young, I was really fascinated by the law. I went to the Bergen County Court House to watch criminal cases all the time. Unfortunately, I never had the patience to do the studying to prepare for a law degree. In a way, and I've never told Thomas this, I am envious of his role as a judge in the United States Circuit Court. But, in an alternate universe, who knows?

Richie Vitale, appearing for the prosecution, your honor. All rise for the Honorable Judge Rich Vitale.

Ah, the road not taken.

··········

It's hard to believe, but I have five (!) grandchildren.

The oldest, Sydney, is the daughter of Terri and Chris. She played on the varsity high school tennis team team at Out of Door Academy in Lakewood Ranch as a sixth grader. Her brother, Ryan, plays travel lacrosse and baseball as well as some football. His father coaches his teams. Ryan

Five! And, man, are they growing up fast! Baby, I love my grandchildren—there's nothing better in the world than being the grandpa!

shows a lot of potential in lacrosse.

Sherri's twins, Connor and Jake, are both very similar to their dad. They play multiple sports and have a great love of tennis, baseball, and basketball. In fact, they play baseball on an 11-and-under travel team, the Tampa Spartans, who qualified to play in the World Series at Disney World in their age group.

Ava, Sherri's youngest, has a love for tennis. She's a bundle of energy—I see a lot of her mother in her. She also plays soccer, which helps with her mobility and agility.

We are fortunate that all of our grandkids are solid academically and have followed in the footsteps of their moms and dads and not their Papa.

Our families live within five minutes of each other, which makes it very helpful in that we have one another to lean on without needing to travel far.

We are blessed that Lorraine played a major role with my daughters as they were climbing the tennis ladder. She is so even keeled. To her, all the youngsters are winners because they are trying their best.

Because of my contact with so many young athletes, I'm often asked what it takes to raise talented young athletes.

I have some ideas I'd like to share that might help a youngster to pursue his or her dreams.

1. **You have to balance your life.**

   I think sometimes parents are unrealistic.

   I remember when my daughters were playing junior tennis, there were other players who were just as good, or maybe even a little better, but their parents didn't convince them of the importance of a college education. Everything was pro-oriented. Now, being around sports all my life gave me a little edge in understanding the reality of the situation. My girls, good as they were, could play anywhere in college. But the pros were another story. Being a professional athlete is very tough and doesn't happen for everyone; those types of athletes are unique to say the least. I've seen kids who didn't go to college, who tried to play the pro tour and didn't get anywhere. Today, they are struggling big time.

   So go to college. Have fun. And prepare for the biggest game of all, the game of life.

2. **Be realistic.**

   Know your talent—and your limitations.

   I think there's a tendency for kids who are playing well to think winning a big tournament is the greatest thing in the world. Obviously, you want to develop a competitive sense of pride, but you do not want it to dictate the self-esteem of a child. I've seen kids who felt like losers in life after a loss, not just on the court or field.

3. **Don't let your sport become your identity.**

   I told each of my girls many times that tennis does not define you. The game does not dictate the person you are. Tennis doesn't tell me whether you are a good person or a bad person. Don't think you are a great person just because you are a star in a given sport and win all the time because the next time, you may lose—and the time after that.

   Unfortunately, there are a lot of athletes out there who think they are good people just because they have success in the game. Well, that isn't necessarily true. Just because you can hit a baseball, throw a football, or shoot a jump shot doesn't make you a better person than the guy sitting in the stands. It may make you better as an individual athlete, but that's it.

4. **Be a total person.**

That's what kids forget. Too many youngsters who participate in travel tournaments, whether it is AAU or national tennis and golf events, allow their personalities to be dictated by whether they are number one.

There is nothing wrong in trying to be the best. But you must be realistic along the way. Many times, if youngsters don't live up to the expectations placed on them, they get depressed. That type of thinking can ultimately lead to bad decisions, which many times involved drugs and alcohol.

There has to be a separation between your life and your athletic ability.

5. **Control your effort.**

Effort is all you can control. You should always have a plan that you want to complete that will prepare you in the best possible way to reach your maximum potential.

6. **Feel good about yourself.**

For parents, that means praise the good things your child has done and offer constructive feedback on things that need to be improved. It is very important that you make your child feel good. Nick Bollettieri, the No. 1 tennis guru and Hall of Famer who has produced 10 number ones, told me he has one rule of thumb: Whenever he is coaching youngsters, he finds something positive to tell them whether they've won or lost; then, he points out what they could do to make themselves better. I agree with Nick; there is nothing greater in the world of coaching than a little hug, a little praise. It goes a long, long way.

7. **Winning.**

I define winning very simply: Winning is the ability of any individual in pursuit of any goal in life to do his or her best. Giving your best doesn't always mean you'll be the victor though. That is often defined by size, strength, quickness—characteristics that are out of your hands.

But, if you can look at yourself in the mirror and know you've given it your best, then you are a winner regardless of the score.

I know all of this works. My family is living proof.

....

I will never forget my 70th birthday when my daughters, Terri and Sherri, threw a party for me at the Beach Club on Lido Beach, which is one magnificent resort. They had many of my friends and family at the party. It really was special to feel the love from everyone who was there.

My daughters both spoke at the party, and they told those at the gathering that they were so proud to be a part of my life. They moved me to tears. I felt so proud that they feel that way. There is nothing greater in life than bringing happiness to your family.

CHAPTER 25
SAVING MY VOICE

I was scared, man. Really scared.

There was something wrong with my voice. My voice was my claim to fame, the source of my joy is talking to people. And, let's face it—my moneymaker.

A lot of people don't realize it, but for about a two-year period, I went to production meetings and wasn't concerned about the game. I could do a game in my sleep, talk about a 2-3 zone and match-ups. I try to go beyond x's and o's, try to get a little more of the inside story about players. I could always tell when a guy wasn't ready to play. Anybody can talk about a zone defense, but what about the kid in the recruiting process? What about some of the things in his life you want to share with the audience?

And then my voice let me down.

It hurt so bad that I called my boss, Dan Steir, and told him my voice was hurting me terribly.

I'd be doing a game, and my throat would be driving me crazy. I wasn't thinking about the game. All I could think about was the pain. I was constantly getting phone calls: "What's wrong? Are you OK? What's wrong with your throat? You really look like you're struggling." It was driving me batty.

I would go to my buddy and partner Dan Shulman every time-out.

"Dan, how do I sound?"

"Relax. Take some more water," he told me.

It was two years of feeling awful. I would sit in my room prior to a game or flying to a contest and have tears rolling down my face because I was scared about how I sounded.

I would ask myself questions constantly. "How am I going to get through this? What am I doing?"

I was so blessed that my bosses really hung in there with me.

I went to several different throat specialists. They all gave me the same analysis. They said, "Over the years, you, like so many coaches, have damaged your vocal cords because you are speaking from the throat instead of from the diaphragm. Really, we don't think it's malignant or anything like that. You're just going to have to live with this."

It was so frustrating because I was always hoarse. I couldn't project like I wanted to.

I thought maybe it was part of the aging process.

One day, my son-in-law Chris came over. He's a hand, shoulder, and elbow surgeon; he said he'd met a terrific ear, nose, and throat specialist who he wanted me to meet. "He's terrific and knows his stuff. I want you to see him, so I'm making an appointment immediately. His name is Dr. Dan Deems in Sarasota."

I agreed and went to see Dr. Deems. After initially examining me, he said, "I'll be honest, Dick. I don't have the equipment here to get right onto your vocal cords. But there is something there that needs further evaluation. I'm going to arrange for you to go to the Moffitt Cancer

Institute in Tampa."

I swallowed hard: "Cancer Institute?"

He said, "Look, he's a throat specialist. He's one of the best."

So, I went to see this throat surgeon at Moffitt Cancer Institute. After his evaluation, he said, "You have had problems with your throat because you basically speak from your vocal cords as opposed to your diaphragm. That obviously causes damage and hoarseness. Just do what you've been doing and you have to live with what you have."

Then, he added, "The one thing I firmly believe is this is a non-malignant issue."

I came back, and I was totally confused. I didn't know what to do because the analysis was no different from the other throat specialists who had seen me. I went back to Dr. Deems, and he asked me how I made out and I told him, "I'm still all confused."

He said, "Look, Dick, I did a little research. The best surgeon—the best throat guy in the world—is Dr. Steven Zeitels in Boston, Mass. He is a genius about the voice box. I will do all I can to get you an appointment with him."

And he did.

We did the Jimmy V Classic in New York City, and then my wife and I got on a plane at 5:30 A.M. and arrived in his office at 7 A.M. He'd made a special appointment just to see me. I walked into his office and found out there was a Who's Who of stars who had seen Dr. Zeitels. He had a Wall of Fame that included Julie Andrews, Cher, Lionel Richie, James Taylor, and Adele— she even thanked him on national TV for saving her career.

And soon I would be part of that wall.

He wasn't a basketball guy; in fact, he had no clue who I was and what I did for a living. He told me, "Look, I don't know who you are, but there's a buzz in my office from people who are big sports fans. They said, 'That is Dickie V from ESPN who you're treating.'"

We laughed.

I then said, "Doctor, I've been to several guys and all of them told me the same thing."

He said, "Dick," and what he said next stopped me in my tracks, "Let's get one thing straight right now. Personally, I don't care what those other people told you. You're here because I'm very good at what I do, and you're going to listen to me. You need me much more than I need you. I want to take care of you, but I will not allow celebrities to tell me how to treat them."

I said, "Aye, Aye, sir." I thought I was in the Marines, talking to the lieutenant in charge.

He immediately ran this tube down my throat. It was attached to a monitor where he was able to get right onto the vocal cords. I was choking up, tearing up, because it was so uncomfortable. Then, he called my wife over and he said, "Take a look at this. This is his dilemma. He has ulcerated lesions on his vocal cords that must be removed immediately. And I will tell you this now—they might be malignant. I will not be able to tell until I do surgery."

My world stopped when I heard the word "malignant."

I'll be honest with you. I walked out of there, shedding tears hysterically like a little baby. The thing that took me to the top of the mountain was my voice, and now it was probably going to take me down.

He scheduled surgery for two weeks later, on December 18, 2007. The waiting was brutal. I can feel for every man and woman who has had to wait for a biopsy to come down to determine whether or not they have cancer.

Just waiting. Thinking about your family, your career, about the journey you've taken. Yes, you get to feel a little sorry for yourself, no doubt about it. But, after all my years on ESPN, I figured it was time to get this thing taken care of.

When I got home, I told Dr. Deems that I was still confused. I didn't know if I should go through with the surgery. That was all put to rest when I called Dr. Zeitels up and said, "Doctor, I decided I don't want the surgery. I'm going to live with what I have and hope and pray for the best."

He stopped me immediately and said, "You're going to do what? Are you serious? You are making a major, major mistake." He said, "Dick, I'll tell you what I'm going to do. I'm going to e-mail my findings from my evaluation to Dr. Deems, and I guarantee you the moment he sees them, he'll call you immediately and tell you to get that surgery."

The man knows what he's talking about. In less than five minutes, Dr. Deems called me and said, "Dick, have the surgery."

I went in to get the surgery at Mass General. It was an incredible moment. There, at six o'clock in the morning, waiting in the lobby to meet me were John Saunders, my buddy from ESPN, and Sandy Montag, who represents me with IMG. I said, "What are you guys doing here?"

They said, "Are you kidding? We heard about your surgery and we wanted to come and offer you some support."

I turned to John and said, "John, just do me a favor. When I come out of surgery— because I'll have been knocked out from all of that anesthesia—give me thumbs up if it's not cancerous. Don't do anything if it's cancerous."

I came out of the surgery after a number of hours. I was all blurry-eyed, and John's got thumbs up. Dr. Zeitels said it was non-cancerous and removed the lesions anyway. But, he said, "You have Dysplasia—pre-cancerous cells that must be monitored regularly."

Now, for another part of the story: When I was going into the operating room, they said, "You can't bring anything in there with you." I said, "Wait a minute, Dr. Zeitels. I'm bringing St. Jude with me to the operating room. I'm Catholic, and my mom gave me a card of St. Jude that I carry in my pocket all the time. He's like a miracle worker in the Catholic faith—the patron saint of lost causes—and he's been with me all the time ever since I lost my eye as a kid. And he is going to be with me in surgery."

Dr. Zeitels had no clue what I was talking about, but he said, "Put it in the pocket of your gown."

After the operation, the first thing he said to me is, "I don't know who's in your pocket, but take it everywhere you go because it seems to work."

Let me make it clear. Dr. Zeitels is the Michael Jordan of throat surgeons. OK, since we were in Boston, make him the Larry Bird of throat surgeons!

By the way, there were only three people other than my wife and immediate family who knew what I was going through on a daily basis. They were Dan Steir, Dan Shulman, and my research guru, Howie Schwab.

I will simply say, "Thanks, guys. You were a terrific support team."

During the period after surgery, the letters I got, the phone calls, were unbelievable.

Of course, for me, after the surgery—after the euphoria of knowing I didn't have cancer subsided—the hard part of recovery began.

I was scared. I didn't know what I'd sound like.

I had to be absolutely silent for three-and-a-half weeks. That's right: 24-25 days.

No sound, no whimper, not a peep. I had a dry-erase white board that I used to communicate. The hardest part for me was that I couldn't write as fast as I wanted to speak—my thoughts came faster than my ability to write them down. It was very frustrating, but somehow I managed.

When I went back to see Dr. Zeitels after three weeks, he looked at me and said, "Now, it's time for you to talk."

I couldn't get the words out. I began to cry. He said, "It's OK." I was so afraid of what was going to come out. He said, "Count to 10."

I began to count. "1…2…"

He said, "A little bit louder." And I did it. Then he said, "Just take it slowly each day. I promise you that you are going to be able to work again." Then, like a coach, he said, "My friend, when I met you, I thought you were going to be a tough patient. But you have been terrific."

After the initial recovery, I had intensive speech therapy. Imagine, if you can, Dickie V singing "My country, 'tis of thee" and "Row, row, row your boat." Awesome, Baby! I think there might be a national anthem performance in my future.

I broke my silence only once. I'd awakened from a dream, muttering a few words and then panicked. Luckily, Lorraine was there, assuring me it was okay, and that what little she'd heard of my voice, it sounded just fine.

Two months later, on February 8, it was comeback city when I did the Duke-Carolina game. What a way to put my voice back in gear.

Photo Courtesy of Bob Donnan/ USA TODAY

I'm back! Following my throat surgery, I took two months off to recover. I returned to action on February 8, 2008, covering the Duke-Carolina game. The fans were just as happy to see me as I was to see them. What a way to return!

CHAPTER 26
CELEBRITY WATCHING

I get a real kick out of going star watching when I am in the Los Angeles area. I could start a new show called *Star Searching* with producer Dick Vitale…it sounds pretty good if you ask me. One of my favorite places to go when I am in the Beverly Hills area is this deli called "Nate and Al's." You can guarantee you will see Larry King every morning, starting his day.

But he's not the only one I see there. There are stars galore. You can walk in there and see them all.

One day, I'm there with Lorraine and ask the waitress, "Who's here?"

"Well," she says to me, "I don't know. There's a guy here who everybody's got a little buzz about. He's in sports. I don't know him. It's Vitolli or Vitali."

I laughed my head off because she had no idea who I was. I remember being there one day with Tim Conway. Another time, Danny DeVito. But the real thrill came when I realized, sitting to my right, was Frank Sinatra Jr., and I didn't have the guts to say anything to him.

My grandchildren have had opportunities galore to meet and mingle with the famous in the world of sports. Isn't that what grandparents are for? I admit it, I spoil them.

Case in point: In 2010, while the entire Vitale family was at the Final Four in Indianapolis, a call came from my IMG agent, Sue Lipton, who said, "Look, IMG represents Peyton Manning. His wife is in town and would like you to come to a surprise birthday party for him on Sunday night."

I said, "Geez, that's the only night I'm free, and I promised to go out with my entire family."

Sue called back, "Look. Bring everybody to the surprise party."

So I did.

Let me tell you: The respect he showed my grandkids was unbelievable, signing pictures and footballs.

His brother Eli was there, as was Troy Aikman. A bunch of guys from the Colts were there, too. A great time was had by all.

We got back home. On Tuesday, my grandkids went to school. Their kindergarten teacher called up my daughter Sherri and said, "I want to talk to you about Connor and Jake. I know your father knows a lot of people in the sports world, but the kids are starting to hallucinate."

Surprise! I was in Indy in 2010 for the Final Four when Peyton Manning's wife reached out and invited me to a surprise party she was throwing for Peyton. I took my entire clan and had a great time. Here, Peyton is on the left, his brother Eli on the right. I mean, how often do you get to have your photo taken with two Super Bowl-winning QBs?

Sherri asked, "What do you mean?"

The teacher responded, "They're telling the other kids they went to Peyton Manning's surprise birthday party."

Sherri replied, "They're not hallucinating. They did go."

The next day, at show and tell, she had her sons bring in pictures of them at the party with Peyton.

Reminds me of the time I took the family to Wimbledon in 2012.

Wimbledon. One of the greatest sporting events in the world. Played at the All-England Club, in London, and arguably the most prestigious. The only one of the Grand Slam tournaments still played on grass. The Ladies and Gentlemen's Singles Final played in late June and early July, on the second Saturday and Sunday respectively.

So, there we were—Lorraine and me, Terri, Sherri, and my five grandchildren.

This was the first time we had been there. We had amazing seats—up close—so we could really see all the great tennis stars: Roger Federer, Novak Djokovic, Serena Williams, the Bryan twins. While I was there, Wimbledon saw the biggest upset in years, when Lukas Rosol stunned Rafael Nadal.

Yes, my friends, there is more to life than basketball. I had a blast visiting England. I saw the Tower of London and got to visit Buckingham Palace, even though the Queen was not in residence.

But I have to say the highlight of the trip, for me, was spending several days at Wimbledon.

It was a thrill to meet lots of fans there. People come from all over the world to Wimbledon. There are fans of all sports, including college basketball there. Needless to say, that added to my enjoyment.

My grandchildren play tennis, just like their mothers did. They have some potential and work hard at it, just like their mothers did. So, it was a pleasure to be with them there and enjoy the fabulous matches that were taking place in front of us.

The only fly in the ointment: Connor and Jake had become infatuated with Roger Federer. They were so determined to meet him they were driving me bananas.

Finally, I said to them, "I don't know Roger Federer. I've never met Roger Federer. So just enjoy the tennis. I'll tell you what I'll do. I'll introduce you to all the ESPN people—Patrick McEnroe, Chris Fowler, Chris Evert, Hannah Storm, Mary Joe Fernandez, Brad Gilbert."

They got their pictures taken with them. But it wasn't enough.

"They're not Roger Federer," they said.

What's a doting grandfather to do?

One afternoon, I ran into Chip Brooks, who was the former coach for my daughters when they started playing tennis at the Nick Bollettieri Tennis Academy. He was there to coach Sabine Lisicki of Germany. Also there to support Lisicki was Dirk Nowitzki, and he was cheering her on big time. A few days later, I ran into Chip again and complimented him on Lisicki's win over Maria Sharapova. He asked how Terri and Sherri were doing.

I told him, "The whole family's here. We're having a blast, but…" I paused.

"What's going on?"

"Is there any way I can get to a practice court to watch Federer?"

He replied, "He just came on the court when we left. And he's getting ready for his match. There's only one problem. When we practiced, there were only 100 people there. Now, there is a mob there ready to watch Federer hit."

I told him that my grandchildren were dying to meet him.

"Well, that's going to be tough."

Then, he saw the ESPN All-Access Pass around my neck.

"Let me look at that thing." He scanned it to see what privileges I had. "Dick, that pass can get you in the locker rooms, on the court—it can get you into any place at Wimbledon."

He added, "Keep them close to you, as you go through the crowds, showing that pass to security, and I'm sure they'll let you in on the court."

Then, he asked me, "Do you know Paul Annacone?"

Yes, I knew him; I met him when he was playing at Bollettieri's when my daughters were there. He was from Long Island.

Well, Annacone was Federer's coach.

Are you kidding me?

We got through the crowd and got on the court, five feet away from where Federer was practicing with Annacone. You could feel the intensity. Annacone is telling Federer how he's going to move the ball right to left. He was preparing Federer to play the next match against Djokovic. I didn't want to bother him. I was just hoping we could make eye contact.

Then, he said, "Roger, you are done and you are ready!"

As Paul started to pick up the balls, we finally made eye contact. He asked, "Dick, how are you doing?" He said, "I really wish I had more time, but I've got to get with Roger and talk with him about this big match."

I asked, "Any chance—any chance at all—he can take a picture with my grandkids?"

"No problem. Roger, come over here."

Federer stood next to us, said, "Oh, man, I've got a real tough match. This Djokovic is tremendous."

I replied, "Let me just tell you this: As a tennis fan—and I know many of my friends feel the same way—win or lose, you are the best to ever have played this game."

And he told me—and I'll never forget his words—"Coming from you, sir, that means a lot."

I thought then that he must have known who I was from TV.

He took six practice balls and autographed them all and gave them to Connor and Jake. No doubt, I'd brought joy to both of them. They were so proud wearing their Roger Federer hats and shirts. And you could see the smiles on their faces from a mile away.

How awesome is this? My grandsons Connor and Jake wanted to meet Roger Federer at Wimbledon, and I actually (luckily!) made it happen. What a great champion he is!

Federer went on to win Wimbledon, defeating the British favorite, Andy Murray.

Yet, amidst the pressure of the tournament, he still took the time to make two boys' day.

Today, that picture hangs proudly on my Wall of Celebrities in my house.

When I think about how hard I tried to get my grandchildren some one-on-one time with Roger Federer, I feel blessed that I could make it happen for them. And I also remember my father and uncles taking me to Yankee Stadium—so I could see my heroes. And I will always be grateful to them for that.

PASSIONS

Throughout my life, there have been many different things that I've enjoyed as much—and at times even more—than basketball. My interests. My hobbies. My passions. I think one of the keys to becoming a "Surf and Turfer" in life is finding what you really love and trying new things. Man, I do love the Rock, but if I only had that one thing, I'd definitely be incomplete.

Photo Courtesy of ESPN/Darren Abate

I can talk about basketball all day, every day—but I never do. I always leave time for other things in my life. Balance baby, balance.

CHAPTER 27
TAKE ME OUT TO THE BALL GAME

When most people think of me, they think basketball—24/7.

But I love baseball, too.

I've been a baseball fanatic since I was a kid. It has a calming effect on me, sitting there, watching the game materialize, watching the teams' strategies play out.

I loved the Yankees. I loved Mel Allen as he gave a great home run call. When I was a young boy, my mom gave me a Yankee uniform for Christmas. It was the greatest gift in the world. I went to bed with my uniform and my glove dreaming of playing for them, being in the Majors—just like every other kid in America back then. I used to hitchhike to Yankee Stadium, begging for nickels and dimes from people to get in.

But, when I moved to Florida, I became loyal to the local team. I fell in love with the Tampa Bay Rays.

I love their former manager Joe Maddon. To me, successful teams start with leadership at the top. And Joe's one of the best. I think he's done an excellent job in getting the players to create a winning environment. And he is one of the best communicators in sports.

I'm a Rays diehard now.

I even briefly considered being a part owner of the team, but I settled for my box, my front-row seats, right by the visitors' dugout. I've had them since the formation of the team in 1998. I have players coming up to me, shaking my hand, wanting my autograph, wanting a photo. I'm happy to oblige. But what they don't realize is that I want their autograph and their photo. I go to spring training, and all the guys want to talk about basketball. But I want to talk baseball.

It's baseball, up-close and personal.

Sometimes, too personal—like the time in 2010 vs. Toronto when I was hit in the chest by a foul ball. This was the first —and, hopefully, the last—time in over a decade that a line drive came into the box. It got me right in the rib cage. Paramedics came to treat me; luckily, I had only bruises on my chest.

Scary, man.

Maddon even offered to send over a glove, but it was a little late for that.

I'm a huge Tampa Bay Rays fan. Here I am, with the help of my grandkids, throwing out the first pitch at a Rays game. Play Ball!

One of the big thrills of my life was throwing out the ceremonial first pitch for the Rays in their pursuit of the American League Championship title in 2008. I said I'd do it if all my grandkids could be on the mound with me. They were all decked out in their Rays stuff. Remember, I was a pretty good pitcher when I was young. Even so, I don't know where the ball went, but it was a pretty good pitch. I got some laughs out of the players.

I also gave them some advice before the series with the Red Sox.

"You don't win championships by being a bunch of individual all-stars," I told them. "You do it by being a team—doing all the intangibles and playing together and really trying to help one another in chasing your goals."

And that's really what they're about.

Now, I won't say it made any difference, but they did beat Boston. Unfortunately, they ended their season with a loss to the Phillies in the World Series. Even though the Rays didn't take the crown, that was a special moment for me as Jamie Moyer, the son-in-law of Digger Phelps, was one of the star pitchers on the Phillies.

I'm proud to be counted as one of the major Rays fans.

But the Yankees were my first love.

Growing up in Jersey, they were my team. I was first taken to a game by my father and my uncles when I was 5-6 years old. We didn't have the best seats by any means, but we were there, in Yankee Stadium, watching Joe DiMaggio, the Yankee Clipper. I remember the Yankees at the time: Vic Raschi, Allie Reynolds. I got my first baseball ever from relief superstar Joe Page. He threw me a ball when I was standing by the railing.

My cousin remained a Yankees fan all his life. But when I was 10-11, I strayed. I became a big Red Sox fan. I can tell you some of the players from that era: Ted Williams, Dom DiMaggio, Vern Stephens, Johnny Pesky, Bobby Doerr, Mel Parnell, Birdie Tebbetts. When

Photo Courtesy of Malcolm Emmons/USA TODAY Sports

the Red Sox kept losing to the Yanks, I switched allegiance to the front-runners and became a big Yankee fan—again. I love winners, what can I say?

Once, when I was 15 or 16, a friend and I sneaked into Yankee Stadium. We went to buy tickets and saw an open door. We went in, running around all the bases, sitting in the dugout.

Hanging out at the stadium, hanging outside the door, waiting to see Mickey Mantle arrive at the park: To me Yankee Stadium was like a cathedral, and I followed the team religiously.

Sundays, we would battle. My uncle Sam. My uncle Frank. My uncle Joe. They were fanatical fans. Some liked the Yankees with Mickey Mantle. Others liked the Dodgers with Duke Snider. And there were those who liked Willie Mays of the Giants.

Then, my father would pipe in: "You don't know nothing. What do you know?" he would say to my uncle Frank. Talking about Snider, Mays, DiMaggio, No. 5.

"No. 5 was the best of them all. He never had to make a great catch. He is the only guy in the Hall of Fame who never had to make a spectacular catch because he was always waiting for the

Willie Mays—maybe the best ever, and man, he has the charisma.

Here I am with the Yankees great, legendary closer Mariano Rivera. What a pitcher!

ball. He had the biggest jump off the ball of anyone who ever played. Give me the Yankee Clipper."

But the Yankee Clipper broke my heart one time.

It was a Sunday night in the early '80s. I was in the Detroit Metro airport, coming back from a game. And I couldn't believe my eyes. The terminal was almost empty, but there was DiMaggio, wearing a raincoat, standing next to the wall.

Oh, my God. Is that Joe DiMaggio?

"Sir, you're not Joe DiMaggio, are you?"

"Please don't bother me. I'm trying to relax."

It was him. I was crushed when I couldn't get an autograph.

I wasn't a kid at this time. I was in my late thirties. And I'm not saying he was a bad guy, but for me, seeing him and knowing there was nobody around, I thought for sure I could get an autograph. But I never got to ask him. His body language told me not to annoy him.

One of the things that turned me off about the Yankees was when free agency came in and the Yankees just started buying this player, that player.

I went for the David: the small payroll. My Rays play their hearts out.

Just like my favorite baseball player of all-time: Mays. He had flair, charisma, the smile. He had ability. He could run, catch, hit with power. He had five tools, plus, he had a magnificent, winning personality.

Now, I really liked Mantle, too. Who wouldn't like a player who had his power from both sides of the plate? His only problem was numerous injuries to his knees. I never got to meet Mickey. The closest I ever got was when we would go to Mantle's restaurant in New York City and look at all his memorabilia.

• •

It's been over 60 years since I put on my first baseball jersey and became a proud member of the Garfield Little League Baseball team. Being a member of Little League helped instill my passion and enthusiasm for sports, teamwork—and for giving back.

And it also made me eligible for induction into the Peter J. McGovern Little League Museum's Hall of Excellence on August 18, 2012.

No one gets inducted into a Hall of Fame by themselves. It's about teamwork.

And I had Team Vitale with me—all 11 of us.

I was honored to be inducted into the Little League Hall of Excellence in 2012.

125

Just hanging out with the Rays mascot, Raymond.

On the night before I was honored, my grandchildren were allowed to play on the same field where the championship game is held. It was awesome for them. And, for me, it had been a dream of mine since I was 12 years old. I played for Mazzo, but we didn't qualify for the Little League World Series. Now, the dream had become a reality—and it was the thrill of thrills to have my grandchildren throw out the ceremonial pitch at the induction ceremony.

I had a chance to share a moment with the teams in the dining hall. I really enjoy speaking to kids—especially those who are living out their dreams, playing their hearts out. It was a memorable day—one I'll always treasure.

And I felt privileged—and humbled—to be among them.

Another humbling moment came when I took the grandkids to the Baseball Hall of Fame in Cooperstown.

So much history, so much athletic excellence on display.

We were taken into the vault, where the most valuable memorabilia is kept, and had to put on special gloves. We saw the bat Babe Ruth used when he hit his 60th home run. That alone is worth hundreds of thousands of dollars. We saw Ted Williams' bat when he hit his last home run. My grandkids were going wild, taking pictures. I admit I was, too.

I can't wait to go back.

My grandsons and I met National League Cy Young-winning pitcher Clayton Kershaw.

CHAPTER
MUSIC

Sports and music: To me, they're a common denominator.

I know most people think that I'm all hoops, all the time. But, really, one of my favorite hobbies is music. I love it. It's a vital part of my life.

It started when I was a young kid. I just loved the sounds. In those days, it was all about Frank Sinatra, Dean Martin, and Sammy Davis, Jr.

Then, when I was a teenager in the '50s, I tuned in to Alan Freed, listened to the Countdown. I grew up with rock 'n roll—heck, I was there at its birth, man. Driving around in my 1955 red convertible, playing that music nice and loud, dreaming my dreams.

Today, I love going to concerts. Elton John, Celine Dion, Beyonce, Mariah Carey, Smokey Robinson, Kenny Chesney, Billy Joel, Barry Manilow, Tina Turner, Tim McGraw, and Faith Hill. I love all kinds of music. Lorraine and I look for all sorts of concerts to go to. I've seen Andrea Bocelli. Josh Groban. Funny story about Josh Groban. I was tweeting that I didn't know anything about him; even though he'd sold 20 million albums in less than 10 years, somehow he wasn't on my radar. Anyway, my family told me we were going to see this guy. "He's unbelievable," they said. I told Lorraine that I wasn't going. So I put on Twitter: "Will you please tell me who is this guy, Josh Groban, my Twit family? I need help. My wife is dragging me to see him."

I got flooded with responses, to say the least.

When he sang, "The Prayer," it gave me chills. Middle of the show, Josh Groban pulled a shock on me. He said, "I understand my guy Dickie V from the world of basketball is in the house. How am I doing, Dickie V?" I guess someone sent him my tweet. After the show, my family and I got to meet him.

Man, he's phenomenal!

One of the joys for me about coaching the University of Detroit Titans was that it was in the heart of Motown. I loved them all: the Four Tops, the Temptations, Smokey Robinson, Diana Ross. I still love seeing them. In fact, at my last two galas, the Temptations and the Four Tops were the post-game entertainment.

I also loved the Bee Gees. I will never forget the one time I was in my office at the Silverdome and they were out there performing—rehearsing for their show later that night. I was fortunate enough to meet them.

And you know who else rehearsed there? Michael Jackson. Now, when you talk about an entertainer, someone who can electrify a crowd, he was one of the very best ever.

Funny story about Tim McGraw and Faith Hill. My wife and I were in Beverly Hills, and I was celebrity-hunting, as usual, looking for stars. Well, we decided to go to the Beverly Hills Hotel to sit and relax in the lounge. They say that is "star heaven." In fact, the day we were there, Reggie Bush, Tim Tebow, Warren Beatty, and Annette Bening, plus a host of others were there, too.

Even though we didn't immediately recognize them, Lorraine and I were thrilled to meet Faith Hill and Tim McGraw.

Anyway, Lorraine went off to do a little walking tour of some of the shops. I was sitting in the lobby by myself, and who walks in the main door? Two people. I didn't know who they were, but they were holding hands and came right toward me. I say, "Hi, how are you doing?" and they asked what I was doing there.

I told them I was in town for a speaking engagement. I thought they were just fans. So, in the middle of the conversation, the woman says to me, "Well, if you're not doing anything, why don't you come see Tim this weekend. He's performing out here."

I said, "Tim? Wait a minute. You're not Tim McGraw and Faith Hill?"

I was shocked because early in the day my wife said two of her favorites were McGraw and Hill. I said, "Look, can you do me a favor. Just wait here five minutes. My wife will be back here. She would go wild to meet you guys."

They said, "Yeah, we're not going anywhere." Well, Lorraine came back, and I said to her, "Hon', I want you to meet Tim and Faith."

My wife had no clue who they were, so she just says, "Oh, hi, nice to meet you."

Then, it hit her. "Wait a minute. Tim McGraw and Faith Hill."

I can tell you, the photo of that situation is on my Wall of Fame.

Then there's Frankie Valli—I went to see him. In Sarasota, we have a beautiful concert venue, the Van Wezel Center, and I got a chance to go backstage and share a few words with him. He's amazing—he told me he does over 100 shows a year. He is quite an inspiration for all of us in the "seventies club."

I saw *Jersey Boys* on Broadway—five times. *Motown The Musical*—three times. It was off the charts.

I've also seen Donny and Marie Osmond. I hadn't realized it, but she's a big basketball fan. Gave me a big kiss on the cheek. Her husband, Steve Craig, played for BYU and was drafted by the Philadelphia 76ers. He played in the Danny Ainge era. She asked if she could take my picture to mail to her husband. To me, that's just unreal. She told me her husband would get a kick out of her meeting me. And I didn't even know she knew who I was.

Can't forget Lionel Richie. All night long, baby. All night long.

I love entertainers. I just love watching people perform, having an audience in the palm of their hand. I really like Chesney, the country-and-western singer. He's an entertainer deluxe. I bet I've seen him more than 10 times.

Recently, I went to see one of my idols—Tony Bennett. If you'd told me his age, I wouldn't have believed you. His voice sounded phenomenal, fantastic, just like it always has.

The one entertainer I didn't see was Elvis. However, I did get a tour of Graceland, his mansion in Memphis. I got a big hug and kiss from, yes, Priscilla. I never met the King. But I met the Queen.

Now, I'll tell you who I loved and whose passing made me so sad: Danny Gans. He was an impersonator out of Vegas—the best I've ever seen. He was so talented. He could impersonate everyone to perfection. We went to the Danny Gans Theater at The Mirage to see him many times. I never got tired of him, and we became friends.

I saved the best for last.

Over the years, my favorite entertainer has always been the Chairman of the Board, Francis Albert Sinatra. I mean, he had that special way about him. When he walked into the room, the room was his. When he walked onto the stage, the stage was his. He had a presence that no one else could match. He was as good as it gets. Movies, music. I saw him in concert five times. I even met him once in suburban Detroit when I presented him with a basketball. I got my picture taken with him, too, even though I'm sure he had no idea who I was.

I saw one show in Tampa that just blew me away. It was Frank Sinatra, Liza Minnelli, and Sammy Davis, Jr. It was one of the last times I saw him perform. They did a routine at the end I will never forget: Can You Top This? Liza came out, did her thing, and said to Sammy, "Can you top this?" He did his "Mr. Bojangles" routine, then said to Frank Sinatra, "Top this."

Then, Frank came out and did all his signature songs—"Chicago," "New York, New York," "My Way."

Top that.

My favorite song of all time? "My Way." I love the words. I listen to them over and over again. I feel that song sums up my life. I've tried to do the right things in my life. I know I'm not going to make everybody happy, but I've always done it my way.

Right now, if you're in my car and you hit my disc player, there's always a disc of Frank Sinatra with all his top hits, and, of course, I have Ol' Blue Eyes singing, "My Way."

The Chairman of the Board. Do I need to say anything else? Frank Sinatra was the man. Period. Here I am with the Chairman and former Pistons owner, Oscar Feldman. Meeting Sinatra was a real thrill for me.

CHAPTER 29
AT THE STARTING GATE

What little boy didn't want a horse, growing up? I was no different. For me, it was a golden Palomino.

When I was 10-11 years old, I worked at a pony track near our house, taking people for rides. So, for the longest while, that was the closest I came to my dream of owning a horse.

I was interested in horse racing, too, and in 1996, Lorraine and I went to the Kentucky Derby for the first time. That was the year the trainer D. Wayne Lukas won his sixth consecutive Triple Crown race. Lukas was a former teacher and basketball coach, a friend of Robert Knight's. He'd started training horses back in the late '60s during summer vacations. Known as "The Coach," he was elected to the National Museum of Racing's Hall of Fame in 1999.

The Kentucky Derby. The Run for the Roses. Mint Juleps. Women in hats. We went for two days. I was there with ESPN, but Rick Pitino (he's not only a Hall of Fame basketball coach; he also knows a little bit about horses) saw to it that we met the right people, got into the right places. We went to a party the night before the race. George Steinbrenner was there. He had a horse in the race. George Strait stood up and started singing. There were movie stars walking around.

I felt like a rock star.

The race was on Saturday. It was run in front of more than 140,000 people. Lorraine and I were with Lukas in the paddock area before the race. Standing five feet away was Muhammad Ali, the Grand Marshal of the Derby. Of course, I went over and got a picture with The Greatest. What a thrill.

We were talking to Lukas, and he said, "Wait a minute. I have to talk to my jockey." I felt bad we were keeping him from his work, so I said maybe we'd better leave.

"No, no. Stand here."

So we did. And we listened while he gave the jockey final instructions. I don't know all the terminology, but it was a typical coaching pep talk.

And guess what? His horse, Grindstone, won the Derby.

I remember going out to the area where they put a garland of roses around the horse's neck. Everybody was taking pictures with the horse, so we got our picture taken with Grindstone, too.

I had a blast.

Who would have thought I'd get to meet The Greatest, Muhammad Ali, at the Kentucky Derby?

So, about Rick Pitino. His horse, AP Valentine, ran in the 2001 Kentucky Derby. He knew I'd always been intrigued by horses. He also knew I was a regular visitor to the horse farms when I was in Kentucky to do a game.

He called me up one day in 2002—not to talk about basketball but to talk about me going in with him on owning a horse. He and his buddies had one share left. And, if I was in, I could name the horse.

He told me, "If you're interested in buying a quarter interest, then come in and have a little fun. But if you think you're going to make a lot of cash, don't come in. Not every horse is a Secretariat."

It was my boyhood dream come true. Of course I was in!

I named him It's Awesome, Baby.

I've owned five horses over my life, but this one was special. He was my first. He had good bloodlines and a former Kentucky Derby-winning trainer.

I went to Ocala to watch him train. I took my grandkids with me; I loved seeing my grandkids faces as they pet him and watched him train.

His first race—for two year olds at Calder Racetrack in Miami—was on July 4, 2003. The whole family came.

I knew zilch about horses. I couldn't tell a trifecta from an exacta. But sitting there with the other owners, I had a lot of fun.

I was watching them saddle MY horse, getting him ready for the race. Our trainer, Cam Gambolati, reminded me of the many coaches I'd known in my career—he was nervous, edgy. We said a few soothing words to It's Awesome, Baby, and then it was race time.

The horse started in seventh-eighth place. Rick's son, Michael, was saying what great shape the horse was in—I wasn't so sure.

All of a sudden, around the turn, on the outside, the horse started to take over.

And, sure enough, he won. We went nuts. We went to the Winner's Circle. The grandkids fed him carrots. We took pictures with the horse. It was a party atmosphere at the barn.

I remember thinking at the time that if he didn't win another race, I'd be OK with that. It had been such a thrill already.

Unfortunately, It's Awesome, Baby developed a breathing problem. My other horses didn't do well either. And so my days as a racehorse owner came to an end.

But the whole experience was wonderful.

Who says dreams can't come true?

A man and his horse. What more can I say? I loved owning It's Awesome, Baby.

CHAPTER 30

CARS, RACING, AND RACERS

I received a call one day from the organizers of the 2009 Indianapolis 500, asking me if I'd like to be the grand marshal of their parade.

Are you kidding me?

I told the officials of the Indy Racing League that I was very honored by the invitation, but I felt they could get a bigger name. They insisted they wanted me. So, the next thing I knew, it was Saturday of Memorial Day weekend, and Lorraine and I found ourselves sitting in an antique car, leading the Indy 500 parade down the streets of Indianapolis. It was spectacular. Thousands of people lined the streets, waving and cheering. Also making appearances were *EXTRA* Host Mario Lopez; *Dancing with the Stars* finalist Gilles Marini; Miss America Katie Stam, who was from Indiana; and Josh Duhamel, the star of the TV show *Vegas*.

Not to mention the drivers—Helio Castroneves, Danica Patrick.

It was unbelievable. I was in celebrity heaven. Of course, I got tons of pictures with everybody at the breakfast they held before the parade.

Later on Saturday, we toured the Speedway 500 Museum where famous race cars from the past were on display. Then, as a special treat, we were taken downstairs to the car vault—where the special, unique vehicles are held.

I was in awe. The cars ranged from a humble, do-it-yourself model you could have ordered from the Sears catalog to million-dollar luxury vehicles.

What a history the Indianapolis 500 has and how proud the officials are to show it off. It's easy to see why the Indy 500 is considered one of the most traditional and historic races out there.

And here's little Richie Vitale from New Jersey right at the heart of it.

It was just incredible.

Then came Sunday, Race Day. Over 250,000 people were gathered at the Indianapolis Motor Speedway. I got to walk along Pit Lane and in the garages, seeing all the drivers and their crews up-close. It was amazing to see the level of concentration shown by the mechanics. Everybody had a job to do, and they were all doing it—fine-tuning these amazingly complicated machines.

About five minutes before the start, I was with Ashley Judd—a big Kentucky basketball fan—and her then husband, Dario Franchitti, who'd won the Indy 500 three times. See, never underestimate the power of hoops, baby.

The Grand Marshal, baby! The organizers of the Indy 500 wanted me to be the grand marshal of their parade— what an honor. Here I am with Lorraine, leading the parade on the streets of Indianapolis.

Then came the time for me to participate.

As the grand marshal, I got to ride in the pace car to start the race.

That is something I will never forget. We were going really fast around the track with all the drivers following behind us, getting ready to begin the race. Once the announcer gave the world-famous direction, "Gentlemen, start your engines," they were off.

The noise of the cars and the speed at which they were going can only be appreciated when watching it in person.

Thank God for earplugs.

Castroneves was victorious at the end of 200 laps. He observed all the traditions of the Indy 500 winner. After he scaled the fence, he kissed the yard of brick (the start/finish line), and drank the traditional bottle of milk.

It was truly an unbelievable weekend—and an amazing sporting event, filled with excitement and tradition.

Maybe they picked me to be the grand marshal because they knew I'd always loved cars.

It must be a Vitale family trait, something in our gene pool. My dad liked cars. My brother loves cars. He owns a beautiful Corvette that he treasures. I've always loved convertibles. My wife, not so much. She thinks they mess up her hair. But I don't have that problem. I'm always tooling around town in a convertible.

I've always had new cars—or at least new to me. I get tired of a car after a year or two, so I turn them back in with maybe 8,000 miles on the odometer. I don't buy them; I lease them. I like to change colors and models. I just love getting a new car—the smell of it, the excitement of driving it.

I guess you could say I'm spoiled.

When I was a high school student, my father got me a used '55 red-and-white Ford convertible with a white Continental wheel on the back. I saw it in a used car lot and just fell in love with it. Putting the top down, driving around, listening to the Platters, Elvis Presley. Life didn't get any better than that.

When I started teaching, I bought a lime-green Pontiac. My students used to get a big kick out of watching their teacher pull up in the parking lot in his new convertible. I owe that car a huge debt: It gave me a chance to date Lorraine. She was intrigued by its beauty just like I was intrigued by hers. It was my favorite car of all time. But even that one—with all its sentimental value—I probably kept for just two years.

When I was coaching at the University of Detroit, in the Motor City where they make all the cars, the school gave me a new car every 6,000 miles. We had a deal with the Pontiac people.

My brother knows everything about cars. I don't know anything except to put the key in, step on the gas pedal, and fill the tank. I know nothing about what's under the hood. But that's really what I'm all about: enjoying the ride.

Well, I guess if the car fits, I drive it.

CHAPTER 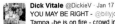 31

HERE A TWEET, THERE A TWEET

I'm old school.

I start my day off at either Another Broken Egg or the First Watch in Lakewood Ranch, Florida, where I live. I read five newspapers—the *New York Post*, *USA Today*, the *Lakewood Ranch Herald*, the *Sarasota Herald*, the *Tampa Times*—all over breakfast. I like having them in front of me. Then, I go to the internet and go through all the major papers through USsportspages.com—the *New York Daily News*, *The New York Times*, the *L.A. Times*, *The Detroit News* and *Detroit Free Press*, the Raleigh *News & Observer*, and the *Lexington Herald-Leader*—from the hot beds of college basketball.

Everything I read gives me lots of information and ammunition to fire off tweets.

Initially, my daughters had to convince me to get into social media to reach more people. They came in one day and said, "Dad, think of all the people you can have contact with in terms of raising dollars for your gala to help the V Foundation."

And they were right.

Since then, I've learned how to use Facebook, Instagram, texting, and Twitter. You could fill a massive photo album with all the pictures I've taken and posted. And I love meeting fans and posting their pictures on Twitter and Instagram. I have a blast. Where can you find me? I'm at dickiev_espn on instagram, twitter.com/dickiev, and my Facebook page is therealdickvitale.

More than anything else in the social media world, I'm a Twitter fanatic. I start tweeting from the time I get up—I tweet on all kinds of sports—tennis, baseball, basketball, even hockey. I just have fun with it. I've got to keep my nearly 700,000 followers informed. I'll be doing a game on ESPN and tweeting about the action during timeouts, tweeting during halftime.

I even tweet about Hollywood and the world of entertainment.

Sometimes, I can get a little carried away with it, like when Lorraine and I went to see Billy Joel in concert at the Tampa Times Forum. That's right, the piano man. I got so excited when he hit the stage— Here Comes Billy Joel—Sold Out, Baby—over 20 thou—that I started live tweeting his entire play list with commentary and the songs in caps.

Here's a taste:

Dick Vitale @DickieV · Jan 17
ONLY THE GOOD DIE YOUNG - @billyjoel is @MagicJohnson Larry Bird & MJ rolled in one Super sensational tonight @JL23TV #PIANOMAN @jksports
Expand

Dick Vitale @DickieV · Jan 17
YOU MAY BE RIGHT - @billyjoel having a @KingJames & @KDTrey5 night in Tampa -he is on fire - crowd in Palm of his hands Sing it #PIANOMAN
Expand

Dick Vitale @DickieV · Jan 17
IT IS STILL ROCK & ROLL TO ME - Keep rocking this house #PIANOMAN
Expand

Dick Vitale @DickieV · Jan 17
Time 4 A BIG SHOT #PIANOMAN
Expand

Dick Vitale @DickieV · Jan 17
Here it is Baby PIANO MAN - Billy Joel at his best #PIANOMAN
Expand

Dick Vitale @DickieV · Jan 17
SCENES FROM AN ITALIAN RESTAURANT #PIANOMAN
Expand

Hey, it must be the music. I found myself doing the same thing when we went to see Barry Manilow.

••

There are a lot of pros and cons about Twitter. It allows a lot of people to make off-the-wall comments. But it also helps me raise money for the Jimmy V Foundation.

After Lacey Holsworth—an adorable little eight-year-old girl who became an inspiration to so many—passed last spring from pediatric cancer, I called her father and told him we were going to raise a quarter of a million dollars for kids battling cancer. I sent that out to my Twitter followers, asking for donations to start a research grant in Lacey's name. Within three weeks, we had raised over $100,000. And, by the time of my gala in May, we raised the quarter of a million dollars.

The information gets out there so quickly. People break more news on social media than anywhere else.

And you'd be surprised how many comments you get if you post anything considered to be a little controversial. Reputations can be made and broken with the tap of a finger because there's no accountability on the part of most people who are posting.

Plus, there are no secrets anymore.

In 2013, I sent best wishes to Kanye West on his birthday to my followers. I couldn't believe all the hype about his wedding to reality star Kim Kardashian. So, I innocently tweeted, "I'm a dummy. I can't figure it out. Will somebody please explain to me why Kim Kardashian is such a celeb? What are her talents?"

My Twitter account just blew up. My ESPN PR guru, Josh Krulewitz, said they had over 4,000 retweets and 3,000 favorites to that tweet. But Kim got the last laugh because all this attention gave her more publicity and the cash register went ding a ling, ding.

Social media is here to stay, baby!

THE MOST INTRIGUING PERSONALITIES

I've met and enjoyed the company of a lot of famous people over the years. Just as many of them have been outside of sports as in it, and I've got a Wall of Fame in my house to prove it! But since I run mostly in the world of basketball, I'll stick to that. Baby, the people who I've had the privilege to rub elbows with are everything you'd think they'd be and more.

Hey, I'm letting some other people talk. On the set with Bob Ley, Coach K, and Jimmy V.

CHAPTER 32

COULD THIS BE MAGIC?

Some players are such mega stars that everybody recognizes them by their first name.

Think of the 1992 Olympic Dream team—Michael, Larry, Patrick, Sir Charles, and, of course, Magic.

I'm not saying he's the best of all-time, but I am saying if you ask me who I would have wanted to coach, have as a leader and play for me, it would have been Magic Johnson. Man, he had that superstar charisma. He was an extension of a coach on the court.

And he was all about winning.

Earvin Johnson got his nickname back when he was at Everett High in Lansing. In the seventh game of his sophomore season, Magic turned into a prodigy when he scored 36 points, grabbed 18 rebounds, and had 16 assists against Jackson Parkside, the preseason conference favorite. Fred Stabley, a local sports writer, figured he needed a nickname, and since "Dr. J," Julius Erving, and "Big E," Elvin Hayes, were taken, he decided to call him "Magic."

Stabley had no idea the name would stick—Magic was no illusion.

I got to know him when he was the star of stars in the state of Michigan when I was coaching at the University of Detroit. He was a 6-foot-8 franchise who ripped up the St. Cecilia's summer league in Detroit and led Everett High School to the state championship in 1977. Michigan had just been to the Promised Land, making the national championship game the year before and Magic grew up in the shadow of Michigan State, so I knew recruiting him was a long shot. But I wanted the winner's edge, so I grabbed my buddies Gaines and Brunker, and I said, "We're going up there at 7 o'clock to talk to Magic."

We had to leave early to make the two-hour journey from the Motor City, and we were battling snow and ice. I wanted to tell him just one more time how he would own the city of Detroit and be the man in the Motor City.

We knocked on the door of his house, and Mrs. Johnson answered. I said, "We just happened to be in Lansing. I'd like to have some words with Earvin."

She said, "I'm sorry, Coach, but Magic's not here."

"Magic's not here?" we said.

"He's at the playground," she told me.

It was snowing. There was ice on the court. And I walked out and looked at this kid working out in the freezing weather. Around the back. Between his legs. He didn't know we were watching him. I got down on my knees and called on St. Jude, the miracle worker. I said, "St. Jude, I've been a good guy this year. PLEASE let me have Magic."

But Magic let me down. He went to Michigan State to play with his buddies Jay Vincent and Greg Kelser after Jud Heathcote convinced him he could handle the Rock and orchestrate the break. I told him, "I would have given anything in the world to coach you because, as good as you were, I couldn't screw you up."

As I said earlier in the book, I told that story when I made my acceptance speech at the Naismith Hall of Fame. Magic was in the front row. He still had that infectious "Magic" smile on his face. After his Hall of Fame career, he should be all smiles.

On top of having that Michigan State championship ring, he won an NBA title and the Finals MVP award in his rookie season when the Lakers defeated the Philadelphia 76ers, four games to two. The Lakers had a 3-2 lead but their center, Kareem Abdul-Jabbar, who was averaging 33 points in the series, sprained his ankle in Game 5 and could not play in Game 6. Lakers coach Paul Westhead decided to start Johnson at center in Game 6. Magic went wild, going for 42 points, 15 rebounds, seven assists, and three steals in a 123-107 win while playing guard, forward, and center at different times—I love multi-position players.

Magic won four more championships with the Lakers during the 1980s. He won three MVP awards and made nine finals appearances. He led the league in regular-season assists four times and is the NBA's all-time leader in average assists per game, at 11.2.

And, here's one thing I didn't know: Reading Jack Ebling's book, *Heart of A Spartan,* I learned that Magic initially did not want to play professional basketball. He wanted to focus on getting into communications. He wanted to become a television commentator. Good thing he changed his mind. I don't need any more competition.

After he retired, he made the successful transition from the uniform to the business suit. He started a record label called Magic Johnson Music and co-promoted Janet Jackson's Velvet Rope tour in 2002. He was an NBA commentator for TNT and worked for ESPN. He runs Magic Johnson Enterprises, a company that has a net worth in excess of $1 billion and includes Magic Johnson Theatres, and Magic Johnson Entertainment, a movie studio. Johnson is also a minority owner of the Los Angeles Dodgers. He told me that whenever he signs a deal for a corporate sponsorship, he makes sure he has the right to sit on board meetings so he can learn how it works.

In 1995, Sonny Vaccaro asked me to introduce him as a speaker at a banquet honoring all the great high school players like Kevin Garnett and Kobe Bryant at his annual Roundball Classic. Magic got up, turned to them, and said, "I will never forget the time I was asked to play in the McDonald's All-American game. When I was in high school, two other players—Gene Banks and Albert King—got most of the ink. They were on the cover of *Sports Illustrated* in tuxedos. I was in awe. Now, I'm in warm-ups before the game and Gene throws down a reverse dunk and Albert is slamming home dunks, one hand, two-handed. And here I am shooting layups, left hand, right hand.

"Now the spotlight comes on and I'm saying to myself, 'Earvin, you don't play the game above the rim. You play it cerebrally. You play it in an intelligent way and just be who you are.' "

I am a big Magic Johnson fan.

Magic with the Lakers. Man, do I wish I could have coached him.

He paused. Then, he turned to the players.

"When it all ended, how many MVPs do they have and how many NBA championships do they have?" he said with a smile on his face, not trying to embarrass Banks or King. "I know how many I have, one for each finger. It's not how high you jump, how fast you run. All you guys here can run faster, jump higher. But I'll tell you, I can get my friend Larry Bird and the two of us will play any two of you and when it's all said and done, we will get the last laugh."

CHAPTER 33
THE GENERAL

I couldn't get through this book without singing the praises of The General, Robert Montgomery Knight.

Knight was so far ahead of his time. I first spotted him when I was coaching high school and he was at Army in the '60s. I could see he was a rising star after he had been named head coach at West Point when he was only 25 years old. The first time I heard him speak at a clinic, I was blown away by his concepts. He turned Army into a basketball school, a place where the sport wasn't a big priority, taking three of his teams to the NIT in the Garden and constantly maxing out his people.

They were a regular attraction in the city around March and about 2,000 of the cadets used to bus in to Manhattan to watch them play tough, intelligent basketball. Army had some good players back then: Mike Silliman, Bill Schutsky—who played for Rollie Massimino at Hillside, New Jersey—Jim Oxley, Mike Gyovai, and Mike Krzyzewski. Twice they advanced to the semifinals. They almost won it all in 1970. They had St. John's beat in the semis, were up, 59-58, with four seconds left. But Richie Lyons put up a desperation shot that had no chance of going in, and the officials called a controversial foul on Oxley. The Redmen made two game-winning free throws.

Many of his players found success in the military. Krzyzewski, the captain of the 1969 team, went on to enjoy big-time success as the head basketball coach at Duke.

The late Dick Schaap once said Knight had a fanatical desire to win, a la Lombardi of the Green Bay Packers, who grew up in my neighborhood.

A side note on Lombardi: Whenever I saw Vince Lombardi, I was reminded that when I coached East Rutherford, we played St. Cecilia High in Englewood, where his fame started. He didn't get his first head-coaching job 'til he was 40, but as a young coach, I would occasionally walk those halls and say to myself, "Wow, this is where Lombardi once worked and taught." I tried to use that as inspiration.

Knight inspires me in a similar way. When he was coaching, Knight was a brilliant teacher, a stern disciplinarian, and a purist who thought the game should be played the right way. The practice floor was his classroom; his players were his students. And he wouldn't put up with any distractions.

Knight was always searching for perfection.

And he found it in 1976 when his Indiana team won the national championship; they remain the last team to go

Photo Courtesy of Malcolm Emmons/USA TODAY

Robert Montgomery Knight during the 1976 season. What a coach, what a team.

unbeaten, finishing 32-0. Knight created some Hoosier hysteria in Bloomington, Indiana, with a starting lineup that all went on to play in the NBA.

Boy, were they good. They felt they could have won it all the year before if Scott May hadn't broken his arm 26 games into the season. That team was unbeaten before they lost to Kentucky, 92-90, in the Mideast Regional finals.

Some people will still tell you that 1975 team was Bob's best ever.

But I just loved watching that 1976 team.

They were my favorite team of all-time to watch as far as incorporating all the things I believe in as a coach—play unselfishly, make the extra pass, rebound, defend as a unit. They were so tough-minded, so fundamentally sound, so filled with character. Would they have beaten the UCLA teams with Kareem Abdul-Jabbar and Bill Walton? Who knows? But they dominated the Big Ten back when it was the best conference in the country with Michigan and Purdue, winning 36 straight conference games in 1975 and 1976.

Going undefeated is tough. Before that team, it happened only eight times in modern college basketball history—once with San Francisco in 1956, once with North Carolina in 1957, four times with UCLA in 1964, 1967, 1972 and 1973, and once with North Carolina State in 1973 when they were ineligible to participate in the tournament.

Regardless of the hype, Knight never let his guys lose focus; they wound up beating UCLA and Michigan (their biggest conference rival) in the Final Four at the old Spectrum in Philly. Michigan had twice played Indiana tough during the regular season and led the Hoosiers, 35-29, at halftime in the championship game. But Indiana rallied to win, outscoring the Wolverines 35-17 in the last 10 minutes to pull away for an 86-68 victory.

Knight went on to win two more titles and an Olympic gold medal in 1984. He also won the admiration of coaching legends like Red Auerbach, Pete Newell, Henry Iba, and Clair Bee. He's always had a temper, but if you are his friend, he is incredibly loyal to you.

He did something for me I will never forget. When I was rejected for the third time seeking induction into the Naismith Hall of Fame, I discovered he had conducted a letter-writing campaign to all living coaches in the Hall, lobbying for me to get in. He said to me, "Dick, you may not be selected to the Hall of Fame, but I want you to know what these coaches think of you. I am going to send you all the letters so you can have them." One of the letters, hand-written from John Wooden, strongly recommended me for induction as a contributor. It blew me away.

Photo Courtesy of ESPN/John Atashian

I've never forgotten about Knight doing that for me.

And I will never forget that 1976 Indiana team. Ironically, I wasn't in Philly to watch them hoist the trophy in person. I was out recruiting for the University of Detroit. I wanted to get players. I wanted to get to a Final Four and duplicate what The General had done. He set the standard.

Will another team go unbeaten? I won't ever say never, but it's getting tougher. The style of play, the three-point shot, and the one-and-done make it difficult to develop that major, monster team. But, for now, The General lives on as the last coach to do it.

Me and The General.

CHAPTER 34

LEBRON, 12 YEARS LATER

LeBron James is the best player in the world right now. Absolutely. It's not even close. He is the King, baby, an elite combination of size and strength, a 6-foot-8, 240-pound forward. While playing for the Miami Heat, he's won two NBA championships. His overall resume also includes four NBA MVP awards, two NBA Finals Awards, two Olympic gold medals, an NBA scoring title, and the NBA Rookie of the Year. And he made big news with his return to the Cleveland Cavaliers for the 2014-15 season as a free agent—it was on every channel, every website.

James was a high school football star who could have easily been an NFL tight end. Someone once said he was like a 600-pound steamroller coming at you. No wonder no one gets in his way when he attacks the basket.

And I did his first televised game.

LeBron was a 17-year-old teenage phenomenon who captured the imagination of a young generation of basketball fans like no one I can ever remember when he played for St. Vincent-St. Mary's High in Akron, Ohio. They were already calling him "King James" back then. I admit, I was a skeptic. When ESPN's Dan Steir brought up the idea of my traveling up to Cleveland to do the first big game of his senior year, I really didn't want to do it. I said, "Dan, we're making this kid bigger than he should be. He's a high school kid."

But Steir insisted. "No, no, they said they want you to call his game. There is so much interest in this kid. We want you to do the game with Dan Shulman and Bill Walton."

"Bill Walton?" I said. "We don't even do the biggest college games with Bill Walton. We're making this game bigger than a major college game."

St. Vincent-St. Mary's was playing Oak Hill Academy that night at Cleveland State. I could immediately tell this wasn't a typical high school game. There were more than 11,000 fans in the arena. Bill and I were talking before the game, and I said, "Can this kid be as good as everybody says?" We would soon see.

Oak Hill, the No. 1 ranked team in the country, had five studs. They were all going Division I. And LeBron dominates from the tip-off. He's treating them all like some high school JV team. He was just so dominant. About five, six minutes into the game, I turned to Bill and said, "Hey, Redhead, he's better than advertised."

James rocked the home of rock 'n roll with no-look passes and monster dunks. He scored 31 points, grabbed 13 rebounds, and dished six assists as SVSM beat up on Oak Hill, one of the top prep school programs in the nation, 65-45. It was a total mismatch.

After the game, we're getting ready to leave and a manager comes up to me and says, "LeBron would like to see you."

So, I go over to him, and he gives me a big hug and says, "Dickie V, I was so excited to have you come and do my game. I hope I didn't disappoint you."

I told him, "My friend, you were better than advertised, and I didn't expect to see that.

You are so talented. It's unbelievable." But I did warn him. "LeBron, watch out for all the vultures out there. They are going to be on you like you can't believe."

The next day, I'm reading Rudy Martzke's column in *USA Today*; in it, he asked Billy Packer of CBS about the fact that I was getting too overly excited about a high school kid. Billy responded, "What has he ever achieved? What has he accomplished?" But let me tell you, I could see greatness immediately, and by televising that game, ESPN really looked like it knew what it was doing. And the game was well received; the network had its highest rating in almost two years.

We've all seen what happened next. LeBron got Tiger Woods money to sign with Nike. $90 million to sign an endorsement deal right out of high school.

....

You know what I like about LeBron? I saw him a couple of years ago when I was in Miami to do a Duke game. I got a big hug from both him and his buddy, Dwyane Wade, who was also there. He's never forgotten where he's come from and a lot of his old high school buddies are still his friends.

As far as I can see, he's only made one misstep in his career, and that was in the way he handled his announcement that he was leaving Cleveland. He'd be the first to tell you today he should have done it differently.

He's made up for that by going back to Cleveland.

James has his roots in Ohio and owes a lot of his fame to the loyalty of the fans in Akron and Cleveland. After winning two NBA MVPs and playing in six All-Star games with the Cavs, he became an unrestricted free agent in July of 2010.

Me and LeBron. The first time I saw him play, I knew he was going to be a very, very special player.

Freelance sportscaster Jim Gray pitched the idea to James' management and ESPN for an hour-long show in which James would announce his decision. ESPN gave away the airtime, allowing James' team to sell ads in exchange for the news story. On July 8, 2010, ESPN aired a live special named *The Decision* that ran 75 minutes. At 9:28 p.m., James announced that he would play with the Heat in the 2010-11 season. James would be teaming with Miami's other All-Stars—Chris Bosh and Wade. Heat coach Pat Riley sold James on the idea he could be the next Magic Johnson.

Even though most of the money for the TV special went to charity and the show was a ratings success, the show drew considerable criticism because James didn't make his announcement for almost 30 minutes to keep up the suspense; the show turned into a spectacle with LeBron saying he was "taking my talents to South Beach." Cleveland fans considered his exit a betrayal that ranked second only in local sports history to Art Modell's decision to move the NFL Browns to Baltimore. Cavs owner Dan Gilbert wrote an open letter to fans, calling James' decision, "selfish," and he guaranteed the Cavs would win an NBA title before the self-declared "King."

We all know that didn't happen.

Photo Courtesy of Ken Blaze/USA TODAY

Congratulations to the fans of Cleveland, baby! After four years in Miami, LeBron is home.

James is under so much scrutiny, but since then, he's been like Derek Jeter of the Yankees, who has been amazing in the way he's handled New York City and all the pressure.

LeBron turns 30 at the end of 2014, and I firmly believe his book is not closed yet. I've always felt no one would ever be talked about in terms of greatest even comparable to Michael Jordan. But I've now changed my mind. When LeBron writes his last chapter, there will be people who will sit and battle over who was the best—Michael or the King?

CHAPTER 35
COACH K

The college comparisons between Mike Krzyzewski and John Wooden were inevitable.

Around the world, Coach K, who has coached the U.S.A. to two Olympic gold medals, has replaced Red Auerbach of Celtics fame as the face of American basketball. He deserves credit for the way he revitalized this country after a bronze-medal debacle in the 2004 Athens games and the way he has handled NBA stars such as Lebron James, Carmelo Anthony, Kevin Durant, and Kobe Bryant.

I feel he should be considered among the best coaches in sports history. Think about it: Why shouldn't he be up there with names like Vince Lombardi, Auerbach, Paul "Bear" Bryant, and Wooden? His legacy is firmly in place. He has won more games than any Division I coach. As of this writing, Duke has won four national titles, gone to 11 Final Fours, won 11 ACC titles, and 13 ACC tournaments; plus, Coach K has led Team USA to gold medals in the 2008 and 2012 Olympics. His ability to lead, motivate, and teach puts him on a different level. He should be included in a greater class.

But what puts him over the top, in my estimation, is the job he has done putting America back on top in the global game. He's brought back the passion and sense of pride in playing for the red, white, and blue, by getting NBA All-Stars to understand they are playing for the name on the front of the jersey, U.S.A. Since he's become coach, Team USA has played with the utmost sense of urgency, bringing back the gold medal to where it belongs.

It took a lot of courage for Jerry Colangelo, the head of USA Basketball, to select a college coach to lead a group of NBA All-Stars back in 2005.

But he figured Mike was the best man for the job.

Ironically, there was a time shortly after Coach K first arrived at Duke in 1980 when he was on the hot seat. Duke had been to the Final Four just two years earlier when Bill Foster was coaching there and the Blue Devils had stars like Gene Banks, Jim Spanarkel, and Mike Gminski, who all went on to play in the NBA. The alums weren't ready for any kind of slippage, especially after their rival, North Carolina, raised a banner after Dean Smith won his first national title in 1982. Mike was feeling the heat after Duke got off to a slow start in 1983, his third year on the job. He was under .500. If he had been coaching today, I have to wonder if he would have survived, especially with all the people ranting and raving on social media.

In this day and age, when fans and administrators want instant gratification, many coaches would not have been retained at that point.

Me and Coach K playing around a little before a game in 2001. I think he likes my beautiful head!

Photo Courtesy of ESPN/Jeff Camarati

But Mike was lucky. He had an AD, Tom Butters, who hired him on the recommendation of Bob Knight despite his having a losing record at Army his last year. Butters believed in him even though he'd came up a little short in recruiting high school stars like Chris Mullin and Bill Wennington, who both signed with St. John's.

Then, Mike struck gold with a recruiting class of Johnny Dawkins, Jay Bilas (my colleague at ESPN), David Henderson, and Mark Alarie in 1982, and once they added a quality point guard like Tommy Amaker the next year, they were on their way, advancing to the national championship game in 1986. It's been an incredible run; the Blue Devils won national titles in 1991, 1992, 2001, and 2010. With Duke, it's not about getting to the NCAA tournament; it's about cutting down the nets in the championship game.

Every time they get beat, like they did against Mercer in the first game of the 2014 tournament, it's a major story. Some people have the same feelings about Duke that they have about the Yankees, the Dallas Cowboys, and Notre Dame football. They can't wait to see them fail.

I am going to make a statement that anti-Duke fans are going to go wild about. They will scream that I am biased, and chants of "Dukie V" will come out. No matter what Mike Krzyzewski is making at Duke, it is not enough. He's underpaid! He is absolutely worth every penny he is getting. He is like a CEO of a major corporation when you think about his value to Duke University.

I get totally amazed at those who jump on me for praising Duke. What am I going to rip them for? You've got to be kidding. I loved it when the *Wall Street Journal* did a study trying to determine if I was biased toward Duke when I did their games on ESPN. And the results of the report showed if you listened intently, that I was as fair as I could be about both teams playing, which I could have easily predicted. You don't survive 35 years by being biased toward one team.

I have no idea how much longer Mike will be on the sidelines at Cameron Indoor Stadium.

But he doesn't show any signs of slowing down. He should be in the hunt for the Final Four in 2014-15 with a special recruiting class that features center Jahlil Okafor, point guard Tyus Jones, and forward Justise Winslow, who were stars on USA Basketball's grass roots teams that struck gold in the U-18 and U-19 world championships. And he signed on to coach the U.S. team that won the World Championships in Spain and then coach the Olympic team for a third time in Rio in 2016. Winning the gold is no cupcake city even with Lebron James, Kevin Durant, and all those great players.

This isn't 1992 anymore. Mike was an assistant on the Dream Team that year. I was in Barcelona with my family, doing radio reports for ABC. They had so many mega-stars: Magic, Bird, Jordan, Barkley, Ewing, and Malone. It was like the Beatles were in town. I firmly believe the presence of NBA stars in the Olympics elevated the status of basketball internationally. They won big, by an average of 44 points.

But the rest of the world is catching up.

It's a lot of pressure. Anything less than a gold medal is considered a disappointment. If you don't stand on the podium and hear them play our national anthem, you're going to get ripped from top to bottom on the talk shows.

I thought Mike might step down after the U.S. won the 2012 Summer games in London. I thought he might just want to be a consultant. But Colangelo is one of the key reasons why Mike said "Yes" again. Mike has such respect for what Colangelo stands for, and they have a fabulous relationship. That's why he came back and is going for the trifecta.

CHAPTER 36
JOHN CALIPARI

Let me say this up front: John Calipari of Kentucky belongs in the Naismith Basketball Hall of Fame. His resume speaks for itself.

One of the all-time Frank Lloyd Wrights, Calipari has taken three different programs—UMass, Memphis, and Kentucky—to the Final Four. He brought home the ultimate W when he coached the Wildcats to the national championship at Kentucky in 2012. Still, he's not on everybody's Christmas card list.

Sports Illustrated recently came out with a list of sports personalities who are the most disliked people in sports. Clippers' owner Donald Sterling was at the top of the list, which also included Lance Armstrong, Alex Rodriguez, Richie Incognito, and John Calipari in its Hall of Shame.

The blurb explaining Calipari's inclusion stated: "Calipari wins and recruits wherever he goes. He's also left a trail of NCAA violations in his wake at UMass and Memphis. His position at the forefront of college basketball's 'One-and-Done' era of recruiting has made him reviled among hoops traditionalists."

Calipari is college basketball's lightning rod, and he knows it.

He tweeted out this response: "Heard I made the SI Not So Liked List w/Saban, Belichick & one spot below Tiger. What's that tell me? I probably shouldn't run for office."

It's doubtful Calipari would ever give up this coaching gig to run for political office, but he would win in a landslide if he ran in the Bluegrass state as long as he continues to succeed. He could win four or five titles before he leaves the Commonwealth. He might have already won two more if his teams could shoot free throws better (a combined 13-of-37 during two losses to Connecticut, once in 2011 and again in 2014). His players need to watch me shoot them before games on ESPN. Nonetheless, he's better than most at what he does. Controversy or not, that should mean something.

Since coming to Lexington, he has coached the Cats to an Elite Eight, three Final Fours, and hoisted a gold trophy. He has coached three No. 1 overall selections—Derrick Rose, John Wall, and Anthony Davis. He's the only coach to have five first-round selections in the same draft (2010) and the only coach to send six players in the modern era (2012). When Davis and Michael Kidd-Gilchrist went 1-2 in the 2012 NBA Draft, Calipari became the first coach to have the top two players in the same draft.

He's turning out millionaires on a yearly basis. He gets them a better return on their investment than any brokerage firm on Wall Street.

Photo Courtesy of Robert Deutsch/USA TODAY

Sometime in the future when I'm doing a Kentucky game, I need to count how many times Calipari gestures. Baby, can he coach.

The coach received his own dividend, signing a long-term deal which would pay him $8 million in the final season of the contract. Calipari spurned overtures of a return to the NBA, passing on a lucrative offer by the Cavaliers worth a reported $60-80 million.

Remember, Calipari has to reload every year because he loses so many kids to the pros. It's amazing that he can take a new bunch of players who were all McDonald's All-Americans and No. 1 options on their high school programs and blend them into a cohesive team by March. The guy should teach psychology at Harvard because he has to keep all of his superstars happy and productive.

The one thing I find interesting about Calipari is, although he gets blamed for the one-and-done trend in college hoops, he's actually against it. He's just benefited from a rule that was put in place back in 2006.

Next, it's true that Memphis and UMass were slammed with recruiting violations for incidents that occurred while he was there, and both schools had to vacate their finishes. Calipari was vilified after UMass All-American center Marcus Camby took illegal inducements—an estimated $28,000 from a sports agent—but there was no proof Calipari knew about it. The NCAA also busted Derrick Rose for allegedly having somebody else take his SAT test for him, but Calipari was never linked to that either.

The NCAA came in and investigated Memphis three times, and the AD there said, "We want to make sure before we play him."

The NCAA told him, "Absolutely, we checked it out. He's fine. Play him." Then, in the post-season, they came back with what they said was new information. I have a deep problem with that.

To me, Calipari is going to win so big, the Hall of Fame committee is going to have to accept his career accomplishments, like they finally did for Jerry Tarkanian of UNLV, who won 80% of his games, went to four Final Fours, and won a national title in 1990 playing in a lower-tiered conference.

Calipari just better be careful and make sure he and everybody around him is dotting every "I" and crossing every "T" because the scrutiny he receives and the watchdogs on him are unbelievable.

He probably should cool it with the media, too.

When he went on ESPN recently to promote his book, *Players First: Coaching from the Inside Out*, he said he would like to ensure all college athletes' families can come to see them play in postseason games.

When he asked where the money should come from, he said, "The media...Make you people pay for your tickets. And you're eating popcorn and pretzels and drinking Cokes— buy your own meals."

The average ticket price at the Final Four was $279. So if the 2,000 or so media each paid, it would have raised just over a half million dollars, and somehow I can't see CBS or ESPN, who has broadcast rights, shelling out more dough for an event they already own.

I agree with Calipari from this standpoint: The players' families deserve travel expenses, hotel accommodations, and tickets to be part of the greatest moment in their youngster's careers—the Final Four. And I firmly believe the NCAA should pick up the tab.

Love him or hate him, you can't argue that he's left his mark on college hoops.

The late, great Jimmy V.

My sidekick. My colleague. My friend.

Jimmy was special.

I called him the Frank Sinatra of coaching. He was cool. He had that flair. The song "My Way" really epitomized his life. He truly was unique and different. He was more than just a guy who coached college basketball—x's and o's—though he was excellent at the basics. He loved being around a crowd, having an audience. Once he joined the Washington Speakers Bureau, he found an outlet for his talent. He traveled the country, giving speeches.

Jimmy was an entrepreneur of laughter. He had the gift. He could make people respond.

A caller on Jimmy's radio show asked him, "What should I do about a painful knee?"

Jimmy's response? "Limp."

When another caller asked, "Who's going to the Super Bowl?" Jimmy responded "My uncle Bruno. He's got tickets."

On State's chances against Houston for the national championship, he quipped, "Even my mother is taking Houston and laying points."

A lot of people think we were close from the beginning, but he and I didn't become friends until later in his life. I was aware of him though. He had played for Rutgers. He coached Iona, and we played them when I was at the University of Detroit. We didn't socialize back then, but when he came to ESPN, we bonded and became close friends.

In 1980, he became the coach of North Carolina State. And then came his remarkable win at the 1983 Final Four in Albuquerque, New Mexico.

His Wolfpack was playing the Cougars of Houston, coached by Guy V. Lewis. The Cougars were leading, 52-46, and appeared on the verge of breaking open the game. Jimmy's team committed several fouls; the Cougars were disastrous at the free throw line. NC State pulled ahead to win the game when Dereck Whittenburg—with just four seconds left—put up a 30-footer that was short and grabbed by Lorenzo Charles, who scored the game-winning dunk at the buzzer for the dramatic victory.

Basketball history was made.

Jimmy V spent the next minute running around the court, looking for someone to hug. Someone—ANYONE—to share that awesome, all-too-fleeting moment of victory.

That ultimate W was all the sweeter because no one

Photo Courtesy of MPS/USA TODAY

Jimmy V could really work over the refs when he was coaching.

expected it—except Jimmy. Who else would practice cutting the nets down before the tournament? Which Jimmy did, by the way.

And typical of Jimmy and his wonderful, wacky sense of humor, when the Wolfpack won, he had the perfect line ready.

"How do I like Albuquerque?" he was asked.

"Albuquerque is the greatest city the Lord ever made. My wife is pregnant and—she doesn't know this yet—I'm going to name the kid Al B. Querque."

Jimmy went on a winning streak after that, chalking up 20 or more wins in his first eight seasons at NC State.

But nothing lasts forever.

For Jimmy, who had then become AD, the hammer came down in 1990.

The book, *Personal Fouls* had come out the season before. It alleged that Jimmy and NC State officials had repeatedly covered up for failing students. It also alleged that the players had traded shoes for cash at a local store.

After "Shoegate" broke, the chancellor resigned. Jimmy resigned as AD but stayed on as coach for another year. When NC State played Duke, the Cameron Crazies threw sneakers all over the floor.

Movin' and shakin' on The Cosby Show. *Jimmy V and I made an appearance; we played the V and V Movers—ha!*

Jimmy received a letter from the NCAA enforcement office, saying he was not guilty of any involvement in recruiting violations. But the damage was done. Jimmy left NC State in 1989-90. His final record was 18-12. He was a heartbroken man, full of a lot of pain.

He kept his feelings hidden and joined ESPN for the 1990-91 season.

And then the fun started.

Like the time we were on *The Cosby Show*. Bill Cosby is a huge Temple fan and cheers for his alma mater. Jimmy had graduated from Rutgers and supported them big time. Cosby and Jimmy made a bet: If Rutgers made the tournament, he and I would be guests on the TV show. If Temple got in, Cosby would be on the "ESPN Tournament Selection Show."

Both teams were selected, and Jimmy and I did a segment of *The Cosby Show*; we played the V and V Movers. It was a blast. We were there to film from Monday through Thursday. I still get tweets from fans who just saw the reruns. And I still get residuals.

One night, we went to dinner with Bill Cosby, and it was eye-opening for us.

So many people came up to Cosby—wanting pictures, requesting autographs. He was extremely gracious, accommodating everyone.

People said to us, "Excuse me. Could you take a picture of us with Mr. Cosby?"

"What about us? We're on TV, too."

"We don't want your picture. We want Mr. Cosby."

It was an amazing night. I watched Jimmy V have the funniest man on television on the floor, laughing hysterically at his one-liners. I've said it so many times: Jimmy V could have been another Seinfeld on a sitcom.

••

People often ask why I am so dedicated to the V Foundation.

It was because of Jimmy and what he went through. I saw him suffer all that pain as he battled cancer. I remember him in his hotel room in Bristol, Connecticut, while he continued to try to work. Oh, my God, I don't want anyone to go through what he went through.

One minute he was listening to Sinatra as we'd be sitting in his hotel room, and the next moment, he'd be punching the wall, in agony.

I said, "Jimmy what is the matter?"

"Take your worst headache, toothache, and run it through your body. I feel that 24/7. I feel that every day."

When the doctor told him there was only a small percent of a chance that he could beat it, he said, "I'm going to be one of those guys."

He tried everything humanly possible—from exercise to prayer. But the bottom line was he wouldn't take morphine. He felt that was giving in. If he pumped that stuff into his body to kill the pain, he said it would be an admission that he was giving up.

The last game I did with Jimmy was Duke and UCLA at Cameron. It was Jimmy V, Brent Musburger, and me. What I remember most was that the Duke football team basically had to carry Jimmy to the broadcast booth, which was upstairs, overlooking the floor. He couldn't get up the stairs by himself.

He was in such distress during the broadcast, he had a friend behind him giving him Advil and painkillers to try to control the pain.

He said to me during the breaks, "Talk. Talk. I can't."

It was just unreal watching him go through that pain. But his strength inspired me.

The first time I found out Jimmy had cancer was when I got a phone call from the Washington Speakers Bureau, asking me to do some speeches in a hurry. I asked who I was filling in for.

They said, "We don't want to say anything, but it's Jimmy."

"Why would Jimmy be missing speeches?"

"We don't want to tell you. You've got to talk to Jimmy."

I called him up. He started to cry. I said, "What's going on?"

He said, "You're not going to believe this. I've got cancer, and it's bad."

We stayed on the phone for an hour—both of us crying.

Later, I got a handwritten note from him. "I appreciate your friendship," the letter read in part, "and, Dick, I'm going to give you a little bit of advice. Slow down, man: You go a 100 miles an hour with speaking, commercials, TV. Slow down. Enjoy your family. Life is so short."

On the set with Jimmy V—what a great friend, what an inspiration. I miss him.

Lorraine and I were so moved by this. Here's a guy with cancer, fighting for his life, who took the time to write me a letter.

He was a special guy. A very emotional guy—as he proved in his "Don't give up, don't ever give up" speech.

It's been over 20 years since Jimmy passed away, but he will always be a presence in my life. A reminder that we have only a limited amount of time on this earth and we should use our days doing the best we can for others.

All I can say is, I miss you, Jimmy V!

HISTORY LESSONS

One thing I've learned over the years is how much real sports fans love hearing about the history of sports. I'm no different. I love looking back and remembering magical seasons or heartbreaking moments. I've gotten to see a lot of history-making games, players, and coaches up close and personal, man, and while history does indeed repeat itself, especially in sports, it's those once-in-a-lifetime moments that are always the most memorable and most fun to share.

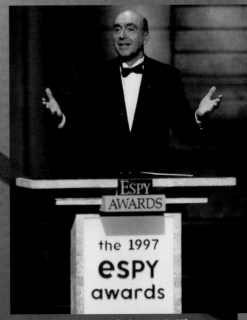

At the ESPY Awards in 1997. The awards have really evolved and grown through the years.

CHAPTER 38

DYNASTIES

When I was growing up in North Jersey, it was a foregone conclusion that the Yankees would win the World Series and the Boston Celtics would win the NBA playoffs. They had built up a tradition of invincibility over the years.

UCLA was like that in college basketball when John Wooden was coaching.

I got to see them play in person when Lew Alcindor was a senior in 1969 when I went to my first Final Four in Louisville. This was before he changed his name to Kareem Abdul-Jabbar. He was an All-American center who grew up in Manhattan and was the most publicized high school player ever from that city. Alcindor was the most dominant college player of his generation, and he needed to be towering in the national semi-finals that year when Drake, a smaller, huge underdog from the Missouri Valley Conference, gave the Bruins a rare scare.

But Alcindor never let UCLA lose in the post-season during his college career. Alcindor had 37 points, 20 rebounds, and was a human eraser defensively in his final college game as the Bruins breezed by Big Ten champion Purdue, 92-72, to win the championship. Purdue had All-American guard Rick Mount, but the Boilermakers never stood a chance.

Alcindor said later it was the biggest thrill of his life because no one had ever won three straight NCAA championships. Back then, freshmen weren't eligible to play varsity or UCLA might have won four in a row. The Bruins were 90-2 during the Alcindor era. He had a super supporting cast with Lucius Allen, Lynn Shackleford, Curtis Rowe, Mike Warren, and John Vallely, but he was at the heart of it all.

UCLA is the greatest dynasty in the history of college basketball, winning 10 championships in 12 years from 1964 through 1975. They won seven consecutive NCAA championships from 1967 until 1974. They also won 88 consecutive games at one point during the Bill Walton era (before losing to my former ESPN compatriot Digger Phelps).

Over the years, there have been dominant programs that have won

Photo courtesy Malcolm Emmons/USA TODAY

The greatest coach ever, John Wooden, poses with his first championship team, the 1964 UCLA Bruins, after winning the NCAA tourney in Kansas City.

When UCLA was king of the NCAA, Lew Alcindor (Kareem Abdul-Jabbar) won three titles with the Bruins. Here, he's celebrating after vanquishing Purdue in the 1969 championship game.

multiple titles—like Kentucky in the late '40s and again in the mid-'90s, San Francisco in the '50s, Cincinnati in the early '60s, Indiana in the '80s, Duke in the early '90s, Florida and North Carolina in the first decade of this century, and Connecticut, which has won four titles in the past 15 years. Duke has won four championships under Mike Krzyzewski and advanced to 11 Final Fours between 1986 and 2014, including two in a row in 1991 and 1992 when Christian Laettner and Bobby Hurley were in school.

But UCLA was on another planet. Rick Reilly of *Sports Illustrated* once wrote those UCLA teams with Walton and Abdul-Jabbar would beat any of the recent championship teams by 20, 30 points. And I agree with him.

It's hard to win a title these days ever since the field expanded to 68 teams. You must win six games to earn the crown. It's even tougher to win two straight titles. Billy Donovan's Florida Gators did it in 2006 and 2007 when all five starters, including three NBA first round picks—Joakim Noah, Corey Brewer, and Al Horford—decided to return for their junior year to make history. But they are the exception. These days, it's hard to pick a winner on Selection Sunday.

It comes back to the stability of the men's college game. There are so many incredible college players who leave early for the NBA, we've taken away any chance of having a great team again. The UCLA dynasty teams, the unbeaten Indiana team of 1976, or those Georgetown teams of the early '80's with Patrick Ewing are past history.

Today, it's a whole different ball game. It's even hard for the elite programs to develop any consistency when they are constantly reloading. The stars are gone before they become household names. It's a big thing when a player stays two years. The most intriguing names in the 2014 NBA draft were all freshmen—forward Jabari Parker of Duke, guard Andrew Wiggins of Kansas, and forward Julius Randle of Kentucky—all one-and-dones who stayed in college for one year and went in the Top 10. Can you imagine how much better they'd be in the NBA if they stayed through their senior year like Ewing?

As it stands, the only true college basketball dynasties since Wooden retired in 1976 occur in the

Pat Summitt put women's basketball on the map and, at the same time, made a place for herself in basketball's history books.

women's game, primarily because all the stars stay four years.

The Tennessee Lady Vols, coached by Pat Summitt, won four national titles in the '90s. The Connecticut Lady Huskies, who've helped Storrs, Connecticut, become the capitol of the college basketball world, allowed their school to complete a rare double the night after UConn defeated Kentucky to win the men's title by defeating previously unbeaten Notre Dame, 79-58, to finish off a perfect 40-0 season.

Geno Auriemma has become the women's version of John Wooden. His Huskies have won nine NCAA Division I national championships, advanced to 15 Final Fours, and won over 30 Big East

Photo Courtesy of Jim Brown/USA TODAY

Maybe he's better than Wooden? At the end of his career, UConn's Geno Auriemma will stand with the greatest coaches of all time.

regular season and tournament championships since he became coach in 1985. UConn has also been one of the leaders in women's basketball attendance and has produced numerous Olympians and WNBA All-Stars like Rebecca Lobo, Diana Taurasi, and Maya Moore.

There may be no end in sight to their domination.

CHAPTER 39

THE NCAA TOURNAMENT'S DEFINING MOMENT

The NCAA tournament was always considered a nice college-level event, a way to put a bow around the end of the season.

But the Michigan State-Indiana State championship game in 1979 changed everything. It helped the Final Four to grow up into the mega-event it is today with sold-out games played in football arenas, heavy corporate involvement, and TV rights fees worth billions.

The NCAA can't thank 6-foot-8 sophomore point guard Magic Johnson of the MSU Spartans and senior forward Larry Bird of the ISU Sycamores enough for that. They were the superstars of the two teams involved. Neither one of them had Jordan's athleticism, but they both knew how to play the game the right way and left an impact on the sport for the next decade with their involvement in the wild NBA rivalry between the Boston Celtics and the Los Angeles Lakers.

This game, played in Salt Lake City, had a perfect lead up.

Indiana State had only been playing Division I basketball for 10 years, but they were 33-0 and ranked No. 1 in the AP poll. They were a huge underdog to Michigan State, which was a traditional Big Ten power. America loves an underdog story, and fans wanted to see whether Bird, who grew up in Terre Haute, Indiana, and transferred to Indiana State from Indiana after his freshman year, could lift the little guy to a big W.

Bird was coming off a brilliant season—he finished second in the country in scoring with a 30-point average and was a consensus first team All-America. Not many people knew much about him, though, because he went out of his way to avoid the spotlight and didn't like talking to the media.

Magic was just the opposite. Just before the start of his sophomore year, *Sports Illustrated* flew a photographer into East Lansing to photograph him for the cover, wearing a tuxedo as he held a ball. Magic was only 19, but he already had a larger than life personality, which showed in the way he played.

The Magic Show was on TV all the time, but this game was the first glimpse America had of Bird, and they tuned into NBC in record numbers to watch the epic showdown

Photo Courtesy of Associated Press

Hey, we didn't know it at the time, but Magic Johnson and Larry Bird, shown here in the 1979 NCAA Championship game, would re-shape the landscape of basketball.

between a white superstar and a black superstar who both wore 33. The spotlight was on both of them.

Michigan State, coached by Jud Heathcote, won the game, 75-64. Magic Johnson was named the Most Outstanding Player after scoring 24 points. Bird did not have a typical "Larry Bird" performance as he scored 19 points but shot just 7-for-21.

The game took the tournament to another level. The Final Four became a national event that year. To this day, that contest remains the highest rated game in the history of college basketball. A quarter of all TV sets in America were turned in to watch Dick Enberg, Billy Packer, and Al McGuire do the game.

The 40-team NCAA tournament grossed $5.2 million in TV revenue. Two years later, the figure doubled when NBC renewed the contract. When CBS won the bidding in 1982, it paid $48 million for three years and the price just kept escalating. The tournament is now worth billions.

TV was the wave of the future, and I was glad to be part of it.

Seth Davis of *Sports Illustrated* wrote a book called *March to Madness* in which he noted how that game set off a six-year stretch that could be characterized as the golden era of the NCAA tournament. Between 1979 and 1986, he pointed out, the tournament introduced six players who would dominate the NBA for the next two decades—Johnson, Bird, Isiah Thomas, Michael Jordan, Patrick Ewing, and Hakeem Olajuwon.

Photo Courtesy of USA TODAY

America was watching. I was fortunate when the tournament became another Super Bowl; it helped my career at ESPN because of the increased interest in the sport and the fact we were taking it seriously.

I guess I owe Magic and Larry a personal thank you.

The Dream Teamers. Magic and Larry finally got to play together, and as members of the now-legendary USA Olympic "Dream Team," they helped dismantle the rest of the world's basketball teams.

CHAPTER 40

MY MOST MEMORABLE NCAA CHAMPIONSHIP GAME

The first 50 years of the NCAA tournament had its share of titanic upsets in the national championship game. Loyola beating Cincinnati in 1963, Texas Western beating Kentucky in 1966, and Villanova playing a near-perfect game to defeat Georgetown in 1985.

But the one that will always stick in my mind is the 1983 championship game at The Pit in Albuquerque, the night Jimmy Valvano and NC State crashed a fraternity party and pulled off the monumental upset of the University of Houston, or as they were called, "Phi Slama Jama."

Now, I'm a little biased here because Jimmy later became a friend, but this was a fantastic David vs. Goliath storyline. When you looked at Houston, it was easy to see why they were heavily favored. They were ranked No. 1 in the country by the AP, had won 26 straight games, and had just blown away Louisville, 94-81, in the semifinals.

NC State was flying under the radar, and no one gave them much of a chance.

The sports media was having a field day with them.

Dave Kindred of *The Washington Post* led his column this way: "Trees will tap dance; elephants will ride in the Indianapolis 500; and Orson Welles will skip breakfast, lunch, and dinner before State finds a way to beat Houston."

And Joe Henderson of *The Tampa Tribune* had this to say, "Rain would make it perfect. It always rains before an execution."

As I said in an earlier chapter, Jimmy loved playing the underdog. "Even my mother is taking Houston and laying seven points," he joked at the pre-game press conference.

In my own opinion, NC State was a lot better than most people thought. I had done their games in the ACC tournament for ESPN that year when they needed to win just to receive an invitation to the dance. In those days, kids weren't leaving early, and the league had the two best players in the country—7-foot-4 senior center Ralph Sampson of Virginia and Michael Jordan of North Carolina.

I watched a determined group of kids beat Wake Forest, North Carolina, and Virginia in three days, then beat Virginia again, 63-62, to win the NCAA Western Regionals. They had played nine teams that were ranked No. 1 at one time or another and weren't intimidated.

Jimmy V was able to unify his players—guards Sidney Lowe, Dereck Whittenburg, and Terry Gannon; forwards Thurl Bailey and Lorenzo Charles; and 6-foot-11 center Cozell McQueen—getting them to play together in a difficult season. They became the Cardiac Pack, emerging as America's unexpected darlings during March Madness.

Jimmy and Hall of Famer Al McGuire were similar in so many ways. They were fast-talking with funny one-liners who were both New Yorkers, baby. They had a fantastic feel for the game. They possessed such street smarts, and each had a great way of communicating in a positive way with their players. I was lucky enough to coach against both of them.

Jimmy V might not have had a player like Hakeem Olajuwon, the intimidating 7-foot junior from Lagos, Nigeria. But what he did have was Whittenburg and Lowe, a pair of cerebral guards who had played together at DeMatha Catholic under the legendary Hall of Famer Morgan Wooten. They formed one of the best backcourts in controlling the tempo of a game.

Valvano wanted to keep the score in the 50's, which he did. It helped that none of the three guards he started—Lowe, Whittenburg, and Gannon—committed a turnover. Houston went on to take a 42-35 lead with 10 minutes to play. But Houston played at such a frenzied pace that they looked exhausted. Houston coach Guy Lewis decided to give Olajuwon some rest and take some time off the clock by spreading the floor.

The Pack, as it had done earlier in the tournament, decided to make Houston earn the victory from the foul line. The Cougars couldn't do it. State tied the game at 52-52 with 1:05

Photo Courtesy of Associated Press

The slam that slammed the Slammers! Lorenzo Charles grabbed Derrick Whittenburg's 30-foot shot and slammed it home with one second remaining in the 1983 NCAA Championship game, giving NC State the title. A fantastic end to a gutsy win by the Wolfpack and their head coach, Jimmy V.

and pulled down the rebound after freshman point guard Alvin Franklin missed the front end of a one-and-one with 44 seconds left in regulation. It was Houston's ninth miss in 19 attempts.

Valvano immediately yelled, "One Shot." The crowd held its breath.

The last play of the game wasn't executed exactly the way he drew it up, and Whittenburg ended up launching a 30-footer with four seconds left that fell short of the basket. But Charles, who was standing under the basket, grabbed the ball and scored on a game-winning dunk.

When Jimmy V started running around looking for someone to hug in that crazy celebration, it reminded me of the time when I was coaching at the University of Detroit and we beat Marquette in 1977. He couldn't find a dance partner. I was a little more prepared; before the Marquette game, I was so confident that we were going to win that I told the team before the game that I would dance at center court with the cheerleaders after we won. And we won, our 21st game in a row, and baby, it became Disco Dick time.

They don't have coaches like Jimmy V anymore. No more Lou Carnesecca, John Chaney, Dale Brown, John Thompson, Rick Majerus, or Bobby Knight. I miss the originals. Now, every press conference is the same: "Yeah, we played with very little intensity"; "We didn't play with a lot of emotion"; "If we'd made our free throws..." There's none of that charisma, that pizzazz that Jimmy had when he was coaching.

Jimmy had a line for every occasion. When NC State visited the White House and met President Reagan, the President asked Jimmy, "Is it Val-van-no or Val-vane-o?" Jimmy replied, "I don't know, is it Ree-gan or Ray-gun?"

Maybe it's because they weren't expected to win and everyone said so. Maybe it's because Jimmy V and I became so close at ESPN. Whatever the reason, that 1983 championship will remain, in my mind, as the best upset the NCAA tournament has ever had.

Photo Courtesy of Malcolm Emmons/USA TODAY

The winners! The Wolfpack! Jimmy V! The coach celebrated with Derrick Whittenburg following NC State's great win over Houston in the 1983 championship game.

CHAPTER 41

THE GREATEST COLLEGE RIVALRY

I believe Duke-North Carolina is the best rivalry in all of college sports.

OK, I have to admit it: probably the best rivalry of all, if you include the pros, would be the Yankees-Red Sox. I know Buckeye fans and Wolverine fans will scream it's Ohio State-Michigan, and Alabama and Auburn fans will scream about the Iron Bowl. In the Bluegrass State, the fans would say it is Louisville against Kentucky.

But, to watch the Tar Heels and the Dukies battle it out at the Smith Center and Cameron Indoor Stadium is always special. It is filled with intensity because the two schools are located just eight miles apart in Tobacco Road country. They have a healthy dislike for each other, dating back to a brawl between Art Heyman of Duke and Larry Brown of Carolina in the

early '60s. On top of the setting and the history, you've got to factor in that North Carolina and Duke are usually among the elite teams nationally; there's always so much at stake in the ACC, it just raises the stakes of this storied rivalry.

As of 2014, the Tar Heels have won five national titles and been to a national record 18 Final Fours. The Blue Devils have won four national championships and advanced to 15 Final Fours.

Both teams have been ranked in the Top 10 in numerous meetings, and there is always excitement in the air any time Hall of Fame coaches Mike Krzyzewski of Duke and Roy Williams of North Carolina face each other. I give this rivalry a slight edge over Kentucky-Louisville because of conference implications.

There have been so many memorable moments. I can still remember the night in 1992 when North Carolina beat Duke, 75-73, at the Smith Center. That was the year the Blue Devils won their second national title. North Carolina's big center Eric Montross had blood streaming down his face as he was battling Christian Laettner and the undefeated, top-ranked Dukies. It was typical of the emotion and passion that is always on display when the two teams meet until the bitter end when Derrick Phelps hit several huge free throws.

I can also remember 1995; Duke got off to an uncharacteristic 0-7 start in the ACC and Coach K was out

Photo Courtesy of Bob Donnan/ USA TODAY

The 1992 game between the Tar Heels and Duke was one for the books, baby. Here, Carolina center Eric Montross (00) tries to pass as Duke's Christian Laettner (32) looks to stop him. The Tar Heels got the win, 75-73.

for the year with a back injury. But the Blue Devils gave the Cameron Crazies something to go wild about. They pushed second-ranked Carolina to the limit before losing 102-100 in double OT.

The Blue Devils were down eight with 17 seconds to play in the first overtime. But these games are never over until the final buzzer sounds. Suddenly, Duke comes back and it's 95-92 when North Carolina center Serge Zwikker misses two free throws. Jeff Capel rushes up the floor and launches a shot from just over half court that falls through the net at the buzzer, forcing five more minutes of play.

When Capel hit that shot, I jumped out of my seat with such excitement that I banged my head on a pipe up in the TV booth and blood started rolling down my face. Mike Patrick looked at me; he saw the blood. I told Mike, "Forget about it. Let the game go on." The intensity and play were special.

"I could stay here all night," I screamed into the mike.

North Carolina won, but not until Steve Wojciechowski's 10-footer bounced off the rim at the buzzer.

The rivalry has had a special, personal meaning in my life. The first game I did after coming back from surgery to remove the ulcerated lesions on my throat was Carolina and Duke in 2008.

It has been a privilege and an honor to watch the brilliance of coaches like Dean Smith, Roy Williams, and Coach K perform their magic. What a thrill it has been to see PTPers like Michael Jordan, Sam Perkins, Brad Daugherty, Kenny Smith, Tyler Hansbrough, Sean May, and Ty Lawson of the Tar Heels; and Laettner, Bobby Hurley Jr., Shane Battier, Jason Williams, and Grant Hill of Duke perform at such a high level.

I love big rivalries. I think they spice up the college season with their big-time emotion and adrenaline rushes. That's why I'm pushing for a renewal of the Indiana-Kentucky rivalry, which was canceled after an ugly court-storming incident in Bloomington back in 2011. The Cats and IU played every year from 1970 to 2012, but Kentucky coach John Calipari does not want to go back to Assembly Hall under any circumstances.

I have an idea to help motivate them: make part of the proceeds go to the V Foundation for Cancer Research. Here's another suggestion, based on what the VBDI (Vitale Bald Dome Index) spit out: set up a four-year series. Play one game at the campus in Bloomington, one game at Rupp Arena in Lexington on campus, one game at the Hoosier Dome, and one game at the KFC Yum! Center in Louisville. I know Calipari was upset when some fans acted poorly at the last game in Bloomington, but I don't think he should take it out on everyone. Get added security for the rivalry. I am talking about one trip to Bloomington in the four-year cycle.

The fans deserve it. The players deserve it. The media, alumni, and TV deserve it. All the people that love college basketball deserve it. THERE IS NO WAY THAT KENTUCKY AND INDIANA SHOULD NOT PLAY. Two people control that decision—Tom Crean and John Calipari. Hey, man, I respect them both, but please make this game happen.

The bottom line is that both Crean and Calipari have benefited in many ways from the great game of college basketball. It is time for them to set aside their egos and say this match-up is too good not to happen.

Rivalries excite everyone. They keep us interested, which is why I always love a good showdown.

CHAPTER 42
KEVIN OLLIE AND UCONN'S BIG SURPRISE

It's hard to believe Connecticut has won four national championships in the past 15 years. I remember doing their games when I first started working for ESPN back in 1979-80. They had just joined the Big East and had some good players like Corny Thompson, but I always thought of them as just another Yankee Conference team.

Now look at them.

The Huskies have joined teams like Duke, North Carolina, Kansas, Kentucky, and Louisville as one of the elite programs in the country. Look at their record in March—they've won it all in 1999, 2004, 2011, and 2014. Wow. Beyond being winners, in the American Athletic Conference, they lost twice to SMU and three times to Louisville, once by 33 points at the end of the regular season, but they rallied at tournament time.

Certain guys excel as tournament coaches. Jim Calhoun, a member of the Naismith Hall of Fame and one of my original Frank Lloyd Wrights, who built this program from scratch, is certainly one of them. Kevin Ollie is, too.

Ollie has to be one of the hottest coaches in the nation right now after coaching his seventh-seeded team to a 60-54 victory over Kentucky in the national title game. He was on everybody's radar after his team cut down the nets at "Jerry's House" in 2014. A lot of NBA teams, including the Los Angeles Lakers and the Cleveland Cavaliers, were salivating at the thought of him jumping to the NBA.

His is the classic survive-and-advance story. Why? Because for 13 years, he had to fight for survival to stick in the league, working on one-year deals year after year. So, nothing intimidates him. He built a reputation as a great practice player and teammate.

He built respect among UConn fans for the way he got his team to focus and win 20 games when the Huskies were banned from playing in post-season due to academic sanctions in 2013. Then, he restored the dignity of the program with UConn's latest run through March Madness where

Photo Courtesy of Robert Deutsch/ USA TODAY

Did he come out of nowhere to win the 2014 title? No, and more importantly, by winning the tournament, UConn's Kevin Ollie showed he's a phenomenal coach.

Photo Courtesy of Associated Press/Bill Shettle

Here, former UConn head coach Jim Calhoun hands over the reins to Kevin Ollie at his retirement announcement in 2012.

he maxed out the talents of players like guards Shabazz Napier and Ryan Boatright and forward DeAndre Daniels, who had a breakout March.

Napier did his best impression of Kemba Walker, who carried the Huskies from nowhere to the 2011 championship. He was fantastic in all six games and became the first senior in 12 years to win the Most Outstanding Player award in the Final Four.

Ollie, who played for Calhoun in the '90s and came back to campus to serve as one of his assistants for two years, made a huge impression on the UConn administration. They just bumped his annual salary to $3 million for multiple years. The new contract will almost triple Ollie's old salary and make him the highest paid coach in the American Athletic Conference. Ollie was originally given a seven-month deal when he replaced Calhoun, who retired in September 2012 and went on to join ESPN's college basketball coverage in 2014.

You know what really impressed me about Ollie? He never whined about the fact the Huskies couldn't play in the tournament during his first year. He just rolled up his sleeves and got to work. It couldn't have been easy following a guy like Calhoun, knowing you had nowhere to go that first year. But he got Connecticut to play hard every day and validated Calhoun's strong feelings about him. There was an element of the UConn fan base who wanted a bigger name and wasn't happy about Calhoun hand-picking his successor.

But they climbed aboard the express train, and now they're on cloud nine.

2014 was quite a post-season for the American as UConn won both the men's and women's title, Rutgers won the WNIT, and SMU finished second in the NIT.

While I was doing the NCAA championship game with Dan Shulman for ESPN International, I wondered what the Big Ten must have been thinking as the Huskies closed in on the title. The conference had a chance to grab Connecticut during that crazy realignment hysteria but said no.

Ollie remembers those days. And he'll always remember that special Monday night in Dallas. Winning a national title is a unique and special thing. A lot of quality coaches like John Chaney of Temple, Gene Keady of Purdue, and Bo Ryan of Wisconsin—who don't have to validate themselves—have never won one. Ollie has, which should be all the validation he needs.

In 2014-15, UConn should finish in the top three again in the American and should find their way into the Top 20 with the return of Boatright, the eligibility of transfer Rodney Purvis, a McDonald's All-American from NC State, and 6-foot-10 sophomore big man Amida Brimah, returning to form the nucleus of the team.

STATE OF THE GAME

When I started covering games for ESPN, there was no shot clock in college basketball, no three-point line, no NCAA tournament for women. There were NBA teams in Kansas City and San Diego, but no team in the state of Florida. Man, has the game changed over the past 35 years. What happened? Progress baby, progress. Basketball is as great as it ever was, but I'll admit that I still think it can be better.

I love the game more than ever, but I know it can still be better. Pass me the Rock!

CHAPTER 43
ONE AND DONE

It is time to end the one-and-done, baby!

For college basketball, it makes a fraud out of the term "student-athlete."

Come on, now… In the one-and-done scenario, it is basically "rent a player" for a year before he goes off to the NBA. Bye-bye. My friends, that is not what college basketball should be about. There are no positives in this situation.

College is supposed to be for those who want an education, for those who want to be there. It is unfair for an athlete who has no desire to be in the classroom to have to go to school for one year.

The current rules, put into place in 2006, make a mockery out of the term "student-athlete." If these kids are good enough and want to make themselves available for the NBA, then so be it. If the NBA sees fit to draft them, so be it. I would like a system in which the league determines which players in high school have a legitimate chance to be lottery picks and let them make the jump right from high school if they so desire. Look, we do an injustice to kids—no brainers like Lebron James, Kobe Bryant, and Kevin Garnett. Under today's rules, they would tease many by playing for one year.

But if a player signs a college scholarship and enrolls in school, he should have to stay in school for three years, a la college baseball. It would bring stability to a pro-game in which you have an increasing number of 22-year-old millionaires who are being drafted on potential after their freshman year only to find they aren't ready for the league and without getting that second contract. Too many guys wind up as basketball vagabonds looking for jobs in Europe or the minor leagues. But for things to change, everybody, specifically the NCAA and the Players Association, has to work together. If we had harmony in basketball like there is in baseball, where all entities unite—the NCAA, Major League Baseball, and the Players Union—it would work beautifully.

Being a Top 10 pick is no guarantee of success. Overall, the 2013-14 rookie class, for example, was billed as one of the worst in recent history. Guard Michael Carter-Williams of the Philadelphia 76ers, who was the 11th pick overall, was selected NBA Rookie of the Year. Guard Victor Oladipo, who was chosen by Orlando with the second pick overall, finished second.

Mark Cuban, the owner of the Dallas Mavericks, recently argued that the NBA Developmental League, not the NCAA, was the best path for an amateur athlete out of college. He called the NCAA hypocritical, noting most kids don't even want to go to class.

Mark made some good points—certainly, he's a very creative mind—and I like a lot of things about Mark, but I totally disagree with him. I believe in college and think the college situation is better for those who actually want to be there. College is also beneficial for players who need time to develop. College is not for kids who want to be rented out and move on after one year. If a young athlete feels basketball is a way to earn a living, why should we deny him if that is his goal or desire? If a kid is good enough, he should be allowed to play with the best. They do it in tennis, hockey, and baseball—the doors are wide open.

Adam Silver, the new NBA commissioner, is making a big push these days for a 20-and-under rule that would make players stay in school for two years before they can declare. Would it make a difference? Yes. It would give student-athletes more of a chance to develop. Certain kids, like Joel Embiid of Kansas who is from Africa and played only one year of high school basketball in the states, aren't ready after one year on the college court—Embiid still went third in the draft because scouts now select players on upside potential. He's a seven-footer who blocks shots, but he could still use more time.

I know everyone gets on John Calipari for recruiting so-called one-and-dones. I had one guy come up to me at the Final Four and say, "John Calipari ruined basketball." Ruined basketball? The only thing he's done is use the current rules to his advantage. Who in their right mind would turn down Derrick Rose of Memphis and John Wall, Anthony Davis, and Michael Kidd-Gilchrist of Kentucky? Nobody.

Calipari didn't make the rule. Plus, he has a great track record of preparing kids for the NBA. Rose, Wall, and Davis were all No. 1 picks overall. He walks into a house to talk to a kid and his parents, and his success with one-and-done players has become an incredible selling point. Turn on the NBA games; you see so many Kentucky kids involved.

Calipari has been trying to change the perception of the phrase "one and done" as a bad thing. So, the thing he's been talking about is "Succeed and Proceed." Calipari actually claims that if he had his way, he would coach players for four years because most of the young players aren't ready to make the transition to an 82-game NBA season.

That is so true, and let's not forget that by getting an education, they will be preparing for their biggest game, the game of life.

CHAPTER 44

SHABAZZ NAPIER MAKES A STATEMENT ON AND OFF THE COURT

Napier was the star of stars during the 2014 NCAA tournament, leading the Huskies to the NCAA tournament championship in an upset victory over Kentucky in the finals.

What a tournament he had. Napier won the Most Outstanding Player award and carried UConn the same way Kemba Walker carried the Huskies to the 2011 NCAA title. When the 6-foot-1 senior All-American point guard got up on stage, he started crying and gave his mother a huge hug. He had stayed in school because he promised her he would graduate.

Then, he gave an impassioned speech, the type usually reserved for the Oscars, talking about the plight of the student-athlete.

"Honestly," he told Jim Nantz of CBS, "I want to get everyone's attention. You're looking at the Hungry Huskies. This is what happens when you ban us."

Napier used national TV to point a finger at the NCAA for banning his program from post-season play the prior year, the result of poor academic graduation reports that they received during the tenure of the previous coach, Jim Calhoun. They dated back to 2008 and 2009, long before Napier and his teammates were part of the program.

"People know how I feel about the post-season ban," Napier said. "I really don't think that it was our fault. We had nothing to do with it. Everybody knows how I feel about it. And it created the Hungry Huskies."

I get what the NCAA is doing. It's a way to make sure coaches recruit kids who want to be in college and have a chance to make it. If kids don't want to be there, they're not going to work hard. You hear too many stories about kids who can't read or write.

But, in the case of Connecticut, I agree with Napier. The events leading up to the ban occurred before those kids were even enrolled. The kids who were being penalized had no part in what transpired. It's not fair

Photo Courtesy of Robert Deutsch/USA TODAY

Nobody on UConn's team deserved to hold the championship trophy more than Shabazz Napier. His play was stellar throughout the 2014 tourney, and he more than earned the Most Outstanding Player award.

to a current group or a current coach who steps in. You know, fine the school, take their cash, but don't penalize innocent people.

Napier also spoke about something else that really bothered me when he talked about stipends for student-athletes

"I don't feel student-athletes should get hundreds of thousands of dollars, but there are a lot of hungry nights when I go to bed and I'm starving," he said.

The NCAA Legislative Council has since approved a proposal that will allow Division I student-athletes to receive unlimited meals and snacks in conjunction with their athletic participation in an attempt to meet the nutritional needs of all student-athletes.

Previously, the NCAA had a bylaw allowing schools to offer bagels, fruits, and nuts to student-athletes. But, according to an interpretation, spreads like cream cheese were prohibited, according to a February report by the *Los Angeles Times*. The NCAA eliminated that interpretation last year.

I'll take it one step further. I would like to see the NCAA come up with a fund so student-athletes who have run out of eligibility and haven't graduated will have a shot to get their degree.

We have a pretty good system in college, except for this student-athlete issue. I have a problem with the fact that millions are being made at the Final Four and the athletes aren't sharing in any of it. When I go to the Final Four, I see a lot of executives from corporate giants in the stands. Yet, if a kid's parents want to go and can't afford to travel, can't afford a plane ticket or a hotel room, there's no money? It's time for the NCAA to lend a helping hand. Any player who has earned the right to play in the men's or women's Final Four should have the right to bring immediate family members to the games and have their flights and hotel rooms paid.

I firmly believe kids in the revenue-producing sports should get a stipend, not a salary, but cash in addition to their scholarship so they can live like normal college students. They're putting in a lot of hours a week for their sport over and above the hours they devote to class work. How many dollars? Some have thrown out the number $2,000, but I'm not a finance guy. Any stipend would have to be Title IX compliant, so all male and female athletes on full scholarship are eligible for the same benefits.

Bans and stipends have been an issue for some time; I'm glad Napier was able to bring them back into the spotlight.

CHAPTER 45

DOUG MCDERMOTT AND THE SENIORS WHO STAYED

Creighton's 6-foot-9 All-American forward Doug McDermott is definitive proof that seniors can still have a huge impact on college basketball.

He went wire-to-wire in the national Player-of-the-Year balloting. Creighton's all-time leading scorer and the eighth player in Division I history to score more than 3,000 points put on a huge show on Senior Night when he scored a career-high 45 points in a victory over Big East rival Providence.

McDermott was the first player since Patrick Ewing of Georgetown and Wayman Tisdale of Oklahoma to earn consensus first team All-American status three times. Now, he didn't come into college with the same ballyhoo as other guys. He was never as hyped like Kevin Durant, a Diaper Dandy from Texas who left after a year for the NBA.

He spent most of his career in the shadows at Ames High School in Ames, Iowa, spending his first two seasons on the JV and his junior year as a sixth man on the varsity. A lot of coaches visited the gym that year—Florida, Duke, North Carolina, Memphis, Kansas, and Iowa State—but they were all there to watch Harrison Barnes, a high school All-American who signed to play for the Tar Heels. McDermott was an unknown.

His father, Greg, didn't even recruit him when he was at Iowa State, partly because of the advice he received from other guys who had coached their sons. They told him if Doug wasn't one of the best players on the team or one of the worst, to take a pass. McDermott was all set to go to Northern Iowa. He had visited Creighton, but the previous staff wanted him to walk on as a freshman with a guarantee of a scholarship his sophomore year. All that changed when Greg decided to take the Creighton job after Dana Altman left for Oregon in the spring of 2010 and offered to take Doug along.

McDermott became a true coach's kid, a fundamentally sound gym rat who busted his gut, constantly working to improve his game and respond to every challenge. He was a lot like David Robinson of Navy and Tim Duncan of Wake Forest, who both came out of nowhere to become consensus All-Americans in college.

Photo Courtesy of Brad Penner/USA TODAY

Creighton's Doug McDermott was named the 2014 Player-of-the-Year, an honor the 3,000-point scorer completely deserved.

One game during the 2013-14 season, he went off for 39 points in a 101-80 win over Big East regular season champion Villanova. Wildcat coach Jay Wright was so impressed; he said McDermott was as complete a player with size he had ever seen because he could take players off the dribble, score inside, guard, rebound, and move without the ball.

Seniors are supposed to be dinosaurs in college basketball. But 2014 was a very unusual year. When the AP announced its first team All-Americans, there were four seniors—McDermott and guards Russ Smith of Louisville, Sean Kilpatrick of Cincinnati, and Shabazz Napier of Connecticut.

I'm rooting for all of them to make it, especially McDermott. I love everything about him. Great kid, great attitude, great family. And he should be a 10-year pro, landing with the Chicago Bulls.

CHAPTER 46
COACHING STRESS

Mike Krzyzewski of Duke and Jim Boeheim of Syracuse are Hall of Fame coaches who have both been at the same schools for over 30 years.

It may never happen again. Most coaches don't reach senior citizen status.

For as much success as they have had in their careers, coaches are constantly under the microscope these days because of social media. Twitter, Facebook, radio talk shows, TV. It's become a 24/7 cycle—everything you do on and off the court is scrutinized.

Boeheim coached Syracuse to 25 straight wins at the start of the 2013-14 season and when the Orange slowed down and lost to Dayton in the third round of the tournament in Buffalo, the heat started coming. The same with Coach K, the winningest coach in college basketball, heading for his 1000th win. The Blue Devils won 30 games but made the mistake of losing to Mercer in the second round of the tournament. Tobacco Road was up in arms because those two teams from the ACC failed to make it past the first weekend of the tournament, which meant no team from the ACC made it to the Final Four for a fourth consecutive season.

The best coaches are making big dough these days, sometimes over $7 million.

But when John Calipari, who won the national championship in 2012, failed to make the NCAA tournament and then lost to Robert Morris in the NIT in 2013, you would have thought the sky was falling in the Bluegrass state.

The pressure to win is enormous. Everybody wants instant gratification. And ADs have less patience. Between 30 and 50 Division I coaches get a pink slip every year.

Let me tell you a story about Tennessee last year. Cuonzo Martin coached the Vols to a Sweet 16. They won three games in the tournament and almost beat a really solid Michigan squad in the Midwest Regionals in Indianapolis. But it wasn't all roses. Midway through the season, his team went into a slump in the SEC and looked like they might not get an invite to the big dance. The fans turned on him big time. They wanted to bring back Bruce Pearl, who had been one of the most successful coaches in school history before he got the ziggy after it was proven he lied to NCAA investigators.

Martin had always been loyal when he was a player and an assistant to Gene Keady at Purdue. And he expected the same type of loyalty from the fans. When he felt he didn't get it, he began looking around. He talked with Marquette after Buzz Williams left for Virginia Tech, then eventually took the Cal job after Mike Montgomery retired.

Here's another one.

Rick Barnes won nearly 70% of his games at Texas, but after finishing 16-18 in 2013 and missing the NCAA tournament for the first time in 15 years, he received criticism for his lack of success in the recruiting front in talent-rich Texas. His future was uncertain. The Longhorns had a new AD in Steve Patterson and were predicted to finish eighth in the 10-team Big 12.

Patterson wound up forcing out popular football coach Mack Brown. But Barnes survived even though he lost two players to the NBA and had two others transfer. Barnes battled his way off the hot seat, turning himself into a national Coach of the Year candidate when he won 24 games and advanced to the NCAA round of 32 with a team that had big-time chemistry and work habits. At one point in 2014, his team beat four straight Top 25 teams.

• •

Everybody's blood pressure is up.

Mine certainly was when I coached East Rutherford and we had those outstanding state championship teams in Jersey with Cason. I could feel it all the time. I liked the winning, riding on the back of a fire truck, celebrating my head off at the crowd as we rode through the streets after our first state Group I championship. But the night before the regional finals, I was so nervous about the game that I found myself in the hospital with three bleeding ulcers.

It was like that my whole career. It happened to me again at the University of Detroit. I ended up leaving after our Sweet 16 season in 1977 because I had ulcers. I spent five days in the hospital with the same condition early in my short career with the Pistons.

I couldn't handle losing.

Every year, coaches are on the hot seat. Some survive and some don't. But coaches are always under stress—it's the nature of the job. These days, though, the 24-hour news-cycle seems to put more on their plates that is fair. I wonder if we'll ever have coaches last as long as Krzyzewski and Boeheim again.

CHAPTER 47
INFLUX OF FOREIGN PLAYERS

Bill Self of Kansas has always been one of the best salesmen in college basketball. But, in 2013, he took his recruiting to another level when he began going global, signing two players—versatile 6-foot-8 guard Andrew Wiggins of Canada and 7-foot, shot-blocking center Joel Embiid of Cameroon. The duo went in the top three of the 2014 draft.

Self is just trying to get the winner's edge and take advantage of the rapidly improving international market. In the spring of 2014, he added talented young 6-foot-8 wing Sviatoslav Mykhailiuk, a pure trifecta shooter, who was a big star in the European 18-and-under championships last summer. He averaged 25 points and opened a lot of eyes with his stroke at the Nike Hoop Summit in Portland, Oregon.

Mykhailuk, who will play for the Jayhawks in the 2014-15 season, just turned 17. He graduated from high school early but will have to wait two years before he can apply for the draft. That should give Self time to develop his game. If there's a criticism of Self's first decade in Lawrence, it's that he hasn't produced many NBA stars although Self has had plenty of kids drafted.

If Mykhailiuk becomes a star, that could be very powerful for Self overseas. This would indicate Self is not only one of the hottest recruiters in America, he's a star globally.

When I was coaching, most of us did our recruiting in this country. Aside from Tim Duncan and a few Canadian imports, international players were the exception, not the rule.

But, right now, it's turned into an avalanche. Players, especially from Canada and Africa, are coming over to this country to attend prep schools—where there are no transfer rules—to prepare themselves for college. And coaches are jumping on jets to go all over the world to find the next Dirk Nowitzki.

Wiggins was fairly well known from the AAU circuit when he crossed the border from Toronto to play his high school ball at Huntington St. Joseph Prep in Huntington, West Virginia. He was so good that he reclassified up a grade so he could graduate a year early. He wanted to get a head start on his collegiate career. He was voted National High School Player of the Year over Jabari Parker from Whitney Young High School.

Jayhawk fans were jumping for joy when he announced he wanted to play in Lawrence.

Embiid was a little more of a secret. When he arrived at Montverde Academy, he was a shot-blocker who had no idea how to play offense. During one early practice, he dribbled the ball off his foot, and his teammates started laughing at him.

Kevin Boyle, the coach at Montverde—who once coached Al Harrington, Michael Kidd-Gilchrist, and Kyrie Irving at St. Patrick High School in Elizabeth, New Jersey—immediately called time out and said to his players. "Laugh now. This kid is going to be worth $50 million

Photo Courtesy of Denny Medley/ USA TODAY

Despite his battle with injuries during his season with Bill Self at Kansas, Joel Embiid was still the third overall pick in the 2014 NBA draft. The 7-footer should do well in the NBA if he gets a handle on the injury bug.

someday," according to a *Bleacher Report* story written by Jason King.

Boyle's reputation for producing international impact players should continue this year with 6-foot-9 Ben Simmons of Australia, who committed to LSU as a high school junior. I personally saw Simmons play; they are going to flat-out love him in Bayou Country.

When Connecticut defeated Kentucky in the 2014 NCAA title game, I thought it was interesting that they had four international players on their roster, including two—forward Niels Giffey from Germany and 7-foot freshman Amida Brimah from Ghana—who both played roles in that 60-54 victory over the Cats in big D. The Cats, on the other hand, had no international players, not that John Calipari didn't try to recruit some. Back in 2011, when the Cats got to the Final Four in Houston, he brought a 6-foot-10 kid named Enes Kanter in from Turkey, who might have been the difference-maker if he had been eligible to play. The NCAA clearinghouse ruled he had signed a professional contract to play club ball in high school.

College basketball is truly becoming a global game.

We did an All-Canadian team for ESPN last year, which included Wiggins, Melvin Ejim of Iowa State, Nik Stauskas of Michigan, and point guard Tyler Ennis of Syracuse. Stauskas was the Big Ten Player of the Year. Ejim was the Big 12 Player of the Year. This brought a big smile to my Canadian buddies John Saunders and Dan Shulman.

And, this year, expect to see players like 6-foot-10 Domantas Sabonis from Lithuania, whose father, Arvydas, was a huge aircraft carrier for those last great Soviet Union Olympic teams. Sabonis' son will be a big name at Gonzaga.

The bottom line is this: basketball, unlike tennis and golf, for example, is not an expensive sport to play. All you need are your dreams, a ball, sneakers, and a hoop. Personally, I have no problem seeing international kids get a chance to play over here in college. We have Rhodes Scholars that go abroad to Oxford after all.

CHAPTER 48

MARCUS SMART AND THE LOSS OF CIVILITY

In February 2014, Oklahoma State's star sophomore guard Marcus Smart made big headlines. He got himself suspended for three games by the Big 12 office for violating its sportsmanship and ethical conduct policy. Smart shoved a Texas Tech fan in the final moments of the Cowboys' 65-61 loss to the Red Raiders at Lubbock, Texas.

The Cowboys were down two when Smart tried to block Jaye Crockett's dunk attempt from behind with 6.2 seconds to go, but he stumbled out of bounds behind the basket. As he was being helped up, he appeared to have a heated exchange of words with a fan who called him "a piece of crap." Smart shoved the fan with two hands. The fan, wearing a black Texas Tech shirt, stumbled backward but did not fall, though he did knock a woman off balance.

Smart then walked away, pointing back in the fan's direction. Officials assessed a technical foul but did not eject him, and he remained on the bench until the final buzzer.

The fan was later identified as Jeff Orr, an air traffic controller in Waco, who travels thousands of miles each year to attend Texas Tech basketball games.

Smart initially told Oklahoma State coaches Orr had called him a racial slur, but a videotape obtained by Texas Tech during an internal investigation proved that never happened.

This temporary loss of civility is just another sign we all need to calm down.

Most fans understand the logic of this—you have a ticket, you cheer and scream for your team, but you're always going to have a fan or two who gets carried away. Some of the things I hear coming out of the mouths of adults just blow my mind. When you start using profanity, referring to kids, families, making it personal, that's a no-no. Orr had that type of reputation of being a super fan who liked to tease the visiting teams and players. If you're a 19-year-old kid taking that kind of verbal beating, it can reach a boiling point.

Photo Courtesy of Tim Heitman/USA TODAY

Oklahoma State's Marcus Smart had a bumpy 2013-14 season, but the star guard was still the number six overall pick in the 2014 NBA draft.

185

But there is no situation where a kid can or should go into the crowd. It's indefensible. Once a player steps into the crowd like Smart did, you are asking for major trouble. You hope and pray it doesn't happen because it can get real ugly the way it did back in 2004 when the Pistons and Pacers got into that infamous brawl that is referred to as "Malice in the Palace." Nine players were suspended for a total of 146 games, and Ron Artest of the Pacers was eventually suspended for 86 games and fined $5 million after he went into the stands and started battling with a fan he thought threw a cup of beer on him.

Smart publicly apologized. Orr's statement, in part, read this way: "My actions last night were inappropriate and do not reflect on myself or Texas Tech—a university I love dearly. I regret calling Mr. Smart 'a piece of crap,' but I want to make it known that I did not use a racial slur of any kind."

I can't speak for Orr. From what I hear, Smart is a good kid. But he's emotional, and I think the pressure got the best of him in that moment. Smart could have been a Top 3 pick if he had declared for the NBA draft after his freshman year. Everybody was looking for him to be a Player of the Year candidate when he came back, and I think the frustration just built up inside him when he wasn't having the kind of year he'd anticipated. Hopefully, he will learn from it and grow. He was the number six overall pick in the 2014 draft, taken by the Boston Celtics.

The Oklahoma State-Texas Tech incident got most of the national attention, but there are increasing incidents of out-of-control fan behavior.

Just before the end of the regular season, an out-of-control fan at the UC Santa Barbara-Hawaii game ran onto the court during a stoppage in play and confronted the Rainbow Warriors coaching staff and players. The man, who wore a royal blue UCSB Class of 2014 t-shirt, was arrested after being quickly ushered off the court during the Gauchos' 86-77 Big West Conference win. Hawaii coach Gib Arnold said the incident was unlike anything he'd ever seen in his 22 years as a coach.

The incident came just a week after on-court violence involving fans and players at the end of Utah Valley's upset victory over New Mexico State when fans rushed the court and got involved in a brawl that broke out between the two teams. It led to the suspensions of two New Mexico State players.

It's time for universities to do a better job controlling outrageous fan behavior and provide a safe atmosphere for visiting teams and for visiting coaches. The schools need to make sure their players play within the lines, no matter what they hear during the heat of play.

CHAPTER 49
SECOND CHANCES

It's easy to say that 2014 was the year of forgiveness in college basketball.

Coaches like Bruce Pearl and Kelvin Sampson, who made mistakes in recruiting and were even given show-cause sanctions by the NCAA, are back on the sidelines. Their presence should make the game more interesting.

The biggest splash of the off-season occurred when Pearl was hired to re-energize Auburn after being fired by Tennessee in 2011 and receiving a three-year penalty once he admitted to lying to the NCAA about recruiting violations.

He owned up to his sins. And now he's back in the game. Pearl had pulled off miracles at Southern Indiana, Wisconsin-Milwaukee, and Tennessee, making 17 NCAA appearances in 19 years while taking the Vols to six straight trips to the big dance. The guy won 76.1% of his games. Plus, Auburn needed help and a burst of enthusiasm.

Pearl made a great move by bringing back former Auburn star Chuck Person, The Rifleman, to his coaching staff.

Since 2003, the Tigers have had eight losing seasons in the past 11 years, including five straight. I wonder what my guy Charles Barkley, who was the Round Mound of Rebound when he played there, thinks about that.

Barkley and Person were stars on the Plains when Sonny Smith was coaching them up, and the Tigers went to five straight NCAA tournaments. But that was 30 years ago.

When Auburn's AD Jay Jacobs met with Pearl, he saw a showman who could sell the product to recruits. Pearl could build a competitive team and start filling up the seats in the new arena. He hired him in the spring even though Pearl's show-cause, which prohibited him from recruiting, didn't expire until August.

Remember, Jacobs hired football coach Gus Malzahn, who led the Tigers to the national title game in the 2013 season, which was just his first year.

Pearl stayed in touch with the game in our studios. He paid his dues and he's ready to get back into the SEC wars, battling to make Auburn relevant again.

And he's ready to take on all comers by playing big name non-conference opponents. He's also added a number of transfers, including scoring whiz Antoine Mason from Niagara, who was second in the nation in scoring in 2013-14.

Sampson, who coached Oklahoma to the NCAA Final Four in 2002, falls into a similar category. He was given a five-year show-cause penalty and fired from Indiana in 2008 after the NCAA discovered major violations involving impermissible phone calls to recruits. Sampson escaped to the NBA, where he spent time as an assistant with the Milwaukee Bucks and Houston Rockets. Once his show-cause evaporated in 2013 and he was back in the NCAA's good graces, he started receiving feelers and eventually signed on to coach the University of Houston.

I will flat-out say no one has ever doubted the ability of Sampson to motivate, to inspire, and to teach the game of basketball. He just has to pay more attention to the rules

The rules make it harder to police our sport because many of them are open to interpretation. We waste time on the nickel-and-dime stuff.

Obviously, you need rules to run a legitimate organization. But the rule book is so big and so complicated even a lawyer couldn't figure it out. It used to drive me crazy just trying to keep up with the changes. I think it's wacky when a kid can't talk to an alum or a former great player about his experiences at a particular school so he can get a feel for what it's like.

Sometimes, coaches make mistakes that are not against NCAA rules but can potentially sidetrack their careers. Steve Masiello of Manhattan was one of the hot coaches in the country during the 2013-14 season when he won 25 games, captured the MAAC title, and played a tight game against his former boss Pitino. The Jaspers lost to Louisville in the second round of the tournament.

His reward? A million dollar offer from South Florida. But, before Masiello could sign on the dotted line, USF did a background check that showed he had not completed all of his coursework as an undergraduate at Kentucky. People at Louisville and Manhattan were totally unaware as there was no background check—even Pitino was shocked when he got the news Masiello had not graduated from Kentucky.

Manhattan could have thrown him under the bus, but the school showed compassion. President Brennan O'Donnell claimed Masiello executed poor judgment but did not intentionally misrepresent himself. Manhattan put him on unpaid leave in April and then agreed to rehire him once he competed the requirements for an undergraduate degree from Kentucky. Once that happened in May of 2014, Masiello was reinstated.

Hopefully, all three will benefit from their life experiences.

But I firmly believe—and I've said this for years—college basketball needs a commissioner who can deal with the NCAA over various issues and concerns that the coaches and the administrators have.

CHAPTER 50
TRANSFER MANIA

Florida coach Billy Donovan has changed his entire approach to recruiting in the past few years. He still gets most of the best players out of Florida, but he's now filling the gaps on his roster with blue-chip transfers so he can constantly remain competitive with Kentucky in the SEC.

Donovan took two more in the spring of 2014—adding former South Florida center John Egbunu and former Michigan forward Jon Horford.

The 6-foot-10 Egbunu will have to sit out the 2014-15 season, after which he will have three years of eligibility remaining. Horford is the younger brother of NBA forward Al Horford, who played for the Gators back-to-back national championship teams in 2006 and 2007. He is taking advantage of an NCAA rule that allows student-athletes who have graduated and have one year of eligibility remaining to transfer without penalty. He will be eligible to play for the Gators right away.

Florida has become the answer to lot of kids' prayers. Donovan has had at least one transfer on his roster in each of the last six years. He is not alone in embracing this new trend of taking transfers.

Top 25 coaches from all over are recruiting transfers the way they recruit prize high school stars, targeting once high-profile prospects who are unhappy with their minutes. *Sports Illustrated* calls it "up transferring" and backed it up with some research that shows 34.3% of the top 100 prospects in 2010 transferred from their original schools.

Transferring is becoming an epidemic. The number of transfers has tripled in the last 10 years. For the 2013-14 basketball season alone, more than 550 Division I players have opted to switch uniforms. That's the size of a small phone book. More and more, players are turning into Marco Polos, exploring for greener pastures.

What does this all mean?

Free agency is here to stay. Some are looking for instant gratification and leave for a bigger role. Some are junior college stars looking for that high-major scholarship. And some are recent graduates who have one year of eligibility left and are looking for one last shot at the glory with a higher-profile program.

In the 2014 season, a number of transfers played major roles on prime-time programs. Junior point guard T.J. McConnell, who started his career at Duquesne, helped Arizona spend most of the season ranked No. 1. Sophomore forward Rodney Hood, a Mississippi State transfer, averaged 16.1 points for Duke and was an NBA first-round pick. Iowa State's 6-foot-5 fifth-year senior point guard DeAndre Kane, who transferred from Marshall, helped lead the Cyclones to their first appearance in the Sweet 16 in 14 years.

Look, I get it. A coach leaves, he goes to a new school and gets a financial boost plus all the goodies—a beautiful new car, a country club membership. There's no sitting out for a coach. But a student-athlete doesn't have the same option. As it stands right now, if a kid wants out, he has to get a release or he has to sit out a year. If a school grants a kid a release because the coach emphatically feels, for example, Johnny Jones isn't going to play for him and it would be best for him to go elsewhere, I firmly believe that student-athlete should be able to play immediately. Now, if a coach feels a kid is vital to a team and he doesn't want to lose him, then I think the youngster should have to sit.

I have a real problem with schools that do not want to release athletes and want to hold them hostage. Why would you want to do that to a youngster? Shake his hand, suck it up, and let him leave.

When I was coaching at the University of Detroit, we had more time to evaluate players and there was no early signing period, so coaches knew more about the players they were signing. There was also less emphasis on immediate success because kids weren't leaving early. Back then, most players who left transferred to smaller programs closer to home to get more PT.

NCAA rule changes have helped increase the number of transfers. In 2006, the NCAA passed the graduate transfer rule, which allowed players who graduated to transfer and become eligible immediately as long as the school they were going to had a graduate program that their old school didn't offer. Well, you and I both know the rule is being abused. It's not so much about education. It's about playing basketball.

The other rule is the controversial transfer waiver rule for a sick relative, which allows a player to transfer closer to home and be eligible immediately if he can prove someone close to him is ill.

I got involved in a case a couple of years ago. Kerwin Okoro, a 6-foot-5 guard from the Bronx, transferred from Iowa State to Rutgers to be closer to his mother Eno and older brother Freddie. Okoro's 72-year-old father, Stanislaus, died last December of a stroke. Then, his 28-year-old brother Idiongo, died of colon cancer. Okoro applied for a hardship waiver so he could play immediately, but his application was initially denied.

When I heard about Okoro's story, I tweeted out support, calling on NCAA president Mark Emmert to change the ruling. The NCAA finally saw the light. It was only common sense. This ruling led to the NCAA making changes in its rulebook when there is a tragedy in the immediate family.

While some players, like Okoro, have legitimate reasons to transfer because of personal hardship, this rule has led to a flurry of sick relatives when a player didn't put up big numbers and eyeballs rolled around the sport. In men's basketball in the 2011-12 season, the NCAA granted 34 of 52 waivers, prompting many coaches to ask for clarity or a change.

The NCAA did just that in the spring of 2014. Instead of being able to potentially play right away, the NCAA now has proposed making everybody sit with an added year of eligibility. The NCAA says this is an academically oriented move, which allows students to take time to acclimate to their new team and academic surroundings before jumping into sports.

I understand the value of transfer players, but I also understand the importance of rules. I'm anxious to see how this issue develops in seasons to come.

CHAPTER 51
LETICIA ROMERO

The light bulb finally came on at Kansas State, which granted the transfer release of guard Leticia Romero. It came a week after the school had denied her appeal for a transfer. Under the terms of her release, Romero, a native of Las Palmas, Spain, could not transfer to another Big 12 school. *The Kansas City Star* and *The Manhattan Mercury* (Kansas) were on top of this story from the start.

It should have never taken this long.

Romero, an All-Big 12 freshman, sought a release from her scholarship after the school fired Deb Patterson, the coach who recruited her. She initially went to AD John Currie in March and presented him with a list of 94 schools she wanted to look at. He denied all 94 schools. However, Currie also said that he spoke with new Kansas State coach Jeff Mittie and that Mittie believed it would be in the best interests of the program if Romero was allowed to transfer.

"Although it is unprecedented," Currie wrote, "I believe that it is in this student-athlete's best interest for the committee to reconvene to consider this new information and potentially approve her request for a conditional transfer release."

But the Board still wouldn't budge. If Romero wasn't given a release, she would be barred from receiving a scholarship at another Division I university for a year. Kansas State's policy states that "except for the most compelling of circumstances, which place an undue burden on the student-athlete, it is the policy of the department of intercollegiate athletics not to grant a release for the purposes of a transfer or provide the one-time transfer exception."

K-State got a ton of well-deserved negative PR on this one.

Come on now. As I've said earlier, if a student-athlete doesn't want to be part of your program, why must you hold her hostage? Let her go. You do more damage to your school and program by fighting it. If you have kids who don't want to play for you, simply shake their hand and let them move on.

There is no rhyme or reason to transfer rules, which is why situations like this have led to student-athletes taking steps to unionize. If the NCAA won't step in and protect their rights, they may feel they have to do it themselves.

Photo Courtesy of Peter G. Aiken/USA TODAY

After refusing to allow Leticia Romero to transfer to another school, Kansas State finally relented; she'll be able to play in the 2015-16 season for Florida State, her new school.

Romero, an international student, didn't have the money to stay in this country without scholarship aid. Denying her the right to transfer by Kansas State's administration was wrong, shameful.

I am a big believer in defending the rights of student-athletes, so I had no problem jumping into the crusade. Neither did Jay Bilas. ESPN's *Outside the Lines* also did an investigative piece, calling out K-State, which seems to be unfair and subjective in the transfer process.

Romero eventually signed with Florida State and will be eligible to compete in the 2015-16 season.

CHAPTER 52
CHANGING THE RULES

I'm sure the NCAA rule book could use a few tweaks to make the college game better. But I can't believe the Pac-12 presidents and chancellors think they can slow down the tidal wave of freshmen declaring for the NBA draft by making all freshmen in the power conferences ineligible. At least, that's what they proposed in a letter to the other Big Five conferences.

What is this? The 1960s? I feel like I'm caught in a time warp. I thought we were way past turning back the clock like it's 1972 again.

The rule, if adopted, would affect hundreds of players when in fact it would only apply to a dozen or so blue-chip talents who would lose any incentive to attend a program in a power conference. Well, I guess that's one way to create parity. The one-and-done players would just sign with a school outside the power conferences or spend a year in Europe, making money until they became eligible for the draft. I will guarantee you the rule proposed by the Pac-12 will never become a reality.

College athletics has become a business, at least for the one-and-done players who want to put in their time so they can get started on their careers. And it is surprising some senior academic administrators with more brain power than me have such a Pollyanna view.

The college game is constantly evolving, and there are going to be a lot of wild ideas thrown around in the next few years.

And I have my own ideas to improve things.

First, cut down on the length of the season. It starts too early. I would love to see college basketball open right after Thanksgiving. Prior to that, all the talk is about college football—who's going to win the Heisman, who's going to be No. 1, who's going to play for the national championship. A lot of great early-season hoops games get lost in the shuffle and are not given the recognition they deserve. So why have them?

Does the length of the season create fatigue among the players? I don't buy that since kids are always finding a way to play hoops for hours. Every player is different, so I don't think you can generalize and say all players hit the wall due to a 28-game schedule plus conference tournament and post-season play. But adjusting the length of the season is still worth considering.

Remember, it is not just the physical problem. Mentally, the players are dealing with an adjustment period due to the academic pressures they face in transitioning from high school to college as well as the heightened level of play.

Also, players are being judged immediately. I'm as guilty as any other analyst of passing immediate judgment on many of these young talents arriving from high school. It made me smile whenever Andrew Wiggins or Jabari Parker had a bad game early in the year. Fans would say, "Gee whiz, they're overrated." Oh really? They are going to both be 10-year, solid gold pros. Players need time to adjust to a new environment, which means they will have bad games early on. Allowing players more time to adjust will elevate everyone's game and, maybe, cut down on early season screw-ups.

Second, I'd like to see the rules committee create more possessions in the college game by reducing the shot clock from 35 to 30 seconds. The 30 seconds works efficiently in the women's game. Why wouldn't it do the same for the men?

Third, the time has come to keep the star players on the floor. There should be a six foul limit at the college level, a la the NBA. However, in some cases, egos get involved and people don't want to follow the pattern despite it being the right thing to do.

How many times have we seen stars on the bench after picking up quick fouls? Fans come to see those stars play. A quick whistle can certainly alter the whole tone of the game, and that's not what basketball is supposed to be about. In no other sport are teams penalized by having players disqualified. It doesn't happen in baseball or football.

Ole Miss coach Andy Kennedy came with a variation of that rule during the SEC spring meetings. He wants to keep the Rolls Royce players in the game too for similar reasons. His plan is for unlimited fouls for players—with this catch: instead of fouling out with the fifth foul in a game, players could remain in the game, but each subsequent foul by that player would give the other team two free throws and the ball, much like a technical.

It could change the way guys coach because it would give them more options. It might also change how aggressive players are and the way officials call the game. Now it might also reduce the value of fouls and create a more physical game, as we saw when the Big East tried a one-year experiment with the six-foul rule and it turned into mortal combat. It could also increase the time of a game by creating more possessions with a parade to the free throw line, which no one wants.

Just giving you the pros and cons. My two cents.

CHAPTER 53

IS REALIGNMENT GOOD FOR THE GAME?

Once the dust settled in conference realignment, it didn't take long for Duke coach Mike Krzyzewski to re-invent the mythology of the the Atlantic Coast Conference while at the very same time piling dirt on the the legacy of the Big East.

With the addition of Syracuse, Pitt, and Notre Dame in 2014 and Louisville in 2015, Coach K is already envisioning mountains of success and predicting the ACC will be a 10-bid league in the future. "We're going to be the best conference in the history of the game," he said before last season.

It certainly looked like that on paper. The expanded 15-team ACC may have lost Maryland to the Big Ten, but with the Big East refugees and North Carolina, Duke, NC State, Wake Forest, Virginia, Clemson, Georgia Tech, Virginia Tech, Boston College, Florida State, and Miami—this should be a powerhouse for years to come.

Ironically, the ACC has been noticeably absent from the Final Four the last four years and only one ACC team—Virginia—made it out of the opening weekend of the 2014 NCAA tournament.

But it seems like just a matter of time before this league explodes like a giant volcano. ACC basketball was the big winner in realignment. Duke and Carolina, Virginia and Louisville could all be legitimate threats to make it to the Final Four in the 2014-15 season, and the ACC could challenge the record 11 bids the old Big East got a few years back.

I still have a hard time believing all the changing faces in the conferences. And not just the ACC. Both Maryland and Rutgers have left the ACC and the American Athletic Conference for the Big Ten. Missouri and Texas A & M left the Big 12 for the SEC. Connecticut is one of just three Eastern teams in the American Athletic. Utah and Colorado are now in the Pac-12. And West Virginia is in the Big 12.

The big losers in all this conference realignment are the fans because they lose so many of the regional rivalries they grew up watching.

No more Kansas-Missouri, Pittsburgh-West Virginia, or Maryland-Duke.

The landscape of college athletics is ludicrous and absurd. Geographically, it makes no sense.

A Rutgers in the Big Ten? Give me some logic. Penn State in the Big Ten? These Eastern schools are all over the place. BC and Syracuse are in the ACC, playing the likes of Clemson and Georgia Tech. I don't see it, but you just have to live with it and learn to adjust, I guess. It's all about football. It's all about the dollars, so tradition gets set aside.

Everything comes down to piles of George Washingtons. Piles and piles and piles. And then you get to the egos. Everybody wants to play in an elite power conference because they feel it will give them an advantage over the non-power conference schools.

Look at Connecticut. They could have been one of those schools to move on. The Huskies won both the men's and women's tournaments in basketball. You should have seen the support they got when they played in the NCAA regional at the Garden. I wonder if the Big Ten is having second thoughts about not inviting the Huskies into their conference. But, again, it's all about football. Connecticut football has been so-so lately, and they only play in a 42,000-seat stadium outside Hartford. And it's all about TV sets. The Big Ten figures to increase TV viewership in the Northeast corridor now that they have added Rutgers and Maryland and have a foothold in the New York City and Washington, D.C. markets.

Change can be good, but so much? I'm still not sure.

CHAPTER 54

REQUIEM FOR A HEAVYWEIGHT

When Dave Gavitt, one of the top minds in the history of college basketball, came up with the idea of creating the Big East back in 1979, he knew exactly what he was doing.

A Hall of Famer, Gavitt was truly a visionary.

He had been the coach at Providence College in 1973 when the Friars had flashy, exciting guard Ernie DiGregorio and perfect power forward Marvin Barnes. He led them to the NCAA Final Four that spring. They might have won it all, too, despite the presence of UCLA and Walton.

But the Friars never got a chance to meet UCLA on a neutral court in St. Louis. Midway through the first half of their semi-final game against Memphis, Barnes locked knees with Memphis forward Ronnie Robinson and had to be helped off the floor. Providence never recovered, and their dream of winning a national championship fell apart.

For the most part, back in those days, despite the fact that the East had some excellent coaches and teams, they were rarely a factor in the hunt for an NCAA tournament championship.

Eastern teams were either independents or they played in the Middle Atlantic Conference, the Ivy League of a loosely configured ECAC, which held a tournament at the end of the year to determine who could represent the league in the 32-team field. Prior to 1979, the last time an Eastern team won the NCAA tournament was La Salle with the late, great Tom Gola, in 1954, which probably happened because Kentucky chose not to play after two of its stars were ruled ineligible.

The Big East was smart. Gavitt, the league's first commissioner, got seven teams—Boston College, Providence, Connecticut, St. John's, Seton Hall, Georgetown, and Syracuse—in the first year and added Villanova in 1980. It had representation in every major city on the East Coast, and it didn't take long after the league formed a deal with ESPN to make every player and coach a household name across the country. Every game was a heavyweight battle and the Big East tournament, which was held in a sold-out Madison Square Garden, became the crown jewel of college basketball.

It was Broadway all the way. It had an impact.

Four of the original teams, Georgetown, Villanova, Syracuse, and Connecticut, went from regional powers to winning national championships. Connecticut won four. Three more—St. John's, Seton Hall, and Providence—advanced to the Final Four. In 1985, the Big East was so powerful with headliners like Patrick Ewing of Georgetown, Chris Mullin of St. John's, and Ed Pinckney of Villanova, that the league held its own block party at the Final Four with three teams—Georgetown, St. John's, and eventual champion Villanova—all making it to Lexington.

Gavitt and five of the larger-than-life Big East coaches—Lou Carnesecca of St. John's, John Thompson of Georgetown, Jim Boeheim of Syracuse, Jim Calhoun of Connecticut, and Rick Pitino of Providence—are in the Naismith Hall of Fame. They were giants, my friends. And Rollie Massimino of Villanova, who is in the College Hall of Fame, might have joined them if he had stayed at Villanova instead of leaving for UNLV in 1992. All-Americans like Ewing, Mullin, and Alonzo Mourning have found their way to Springfield, too. And there will be more to come like Ray Allen of UConn and Carmelo Anthony of Syracuse.

The Big East had a 35-year run where it was as good as any conference in the country. And, when the conference chose to expand to 16 teams for football reasons, it sent 10 teams to the 64-team field in 2010 and was still winning national titles as late as 2013 when Louisville cut down the nets in the conference's last year before the football and basketball schools got a divorce.

ESPN did an excellent 30/30 documentary called *Requiem for the Big East*. Every game was like rivalry week. And there were always fights. I can still remember an incensed Ewing throwing a punch at Syracuse's legendary guard Pearl Washington. And I'll never forget the prime-time Big East championship game I did in 1996 with Ray Allen of UConn and Allen Iverson of Georgetown.

The Huskies were 30-3 and ranked No. 3 in the country and the Hoyas were 26-7 and ranked No. 6. Allen and Iverson were both first team All-Americans. In the words of Thompson, this was a game for men. Allen wound up being the star, making a 13-foot jump shot with 13.6 seconds to play to give UConn a 76-75 victory.

It was the type of game you expected from that league when it was on top.

Eventually, the Big East collapsed because football controls the landscape. Maybe the Big East should have taken Penn State when it had a chance back in 2006. The ACC raided the Big East in 2003 and 2004, taking BC, Virginia Tech, and Miami, luring them with promises of big-time football. The Big East saved itself once under commissioner Mike Tranghese and had a chance to save itself again, but the presidents voted down a $13 million offer to stick with ESPN and decided to open the bidding for a new TV partner.

That fall, the ACC then came back again for Syracuse, Pitt, and Louisville, and took Notre Dame as a basketball member, offering them a new ESPN TV package for football and basketball, worth $24 million. West Virginia left for the Big 12, Rutgers bolted for the Big Ten, and the five remaining Catholic schools—Villanova, St. John's, Georgetown, Providence, Seton Hall—combined with DePaul, Marquette, Butler, Creighton and Xavier to form their own basketball league and brought the naming rights for the new Big East. Connecticut now plays in the American Athletic Conference.

The Big East doesn't even have a deal with ESPN any more. They signed on with Fox, which promised to do 150 of their games. But most of their prime time properties are gone.

The Big East was incredible while it lasted. But nothing, as we are discovering in college athletics, stays the same forever.

CHAPTER 55

THE BIG TEN DROUGHT

The Big Ten has arguably had the best conference—top to bottom—over the past two years.

In 2012, Indiana started the season ranked No. 1 with players like center Cody Zeller and guard Victor Oladipo. Both went among the Top 4 picks of the 2013 draft, and guard Trey Burke also went in the lottery. This past season, 2013-14, Michigan, Michigan State, Wisconsin, Ohio State, and Iowa all appeared in the weekly Top 25, and those five plus Nebraska made the tournament bracket.

But something crazy always seems to happen when these teams reach March Madness.

They start disappearing.

The Big Ten has not won a national championship since Michigan State, with the Flintstones (Mateen Cleaves, Morris Peterson, and Charlie Bell—all from Flint, Michigan), defeated Florida to win it all in 2000. Before that, you have to go back to 1989 when Michigan beat out my alma mater, Seton Hall, in the title game, and the flying Illini of Illinois also made the Final Four in Seattle.

It's hard to explain. The ACC will have four Hall of Fame coaches sitting on its benches this year, and the Big Ten might have the best group of teaching coaches in the meat grinder of conference play. Tom Izzo of Michigan State, John Beilein of Michigan, Thad Matta of Ohio State, and Bo Ryan of Wisconsin don't have to take a back seat to anyone, and there certainly was enough talent to merit six bids. Newer coaches like Chris Collins of Northwestern, Richard Pitino of Minnesota, Iowa's Fran McCaffery, and Tim Miles of Nebraska have all upgraded their programs to a point where there is so much parity that a team like Wisconsin could beat Northwestern in Evanston and turn around and lose to the Wildcats in the Kohl Center.

Maybe we should start measuring teams from the power conferences differently when we judge success or failure in a season. Perhaps how many teams from a league reach the second week or advance to the Final Four would be a fairer assessment.

Sometimes, Big Ten teams have just run into bad luck or better opponents.

Ohio State, with its dynamic freshmen duo of center Greg Oden and guard Mike Conley, who played together in high school, was good enough to make the title game in 2007. They ran into a defending national champion Florida team with every starter back and looking to make history. But it wasn't meant to be. The Gators became the first back-to-back champions since Duke, with an emphatic 84-75 victory.

Before the 2013-14 season, Izzo had sent every one of the players to the Final Four at least once during their career. His 2009 team, which saved the Final Four when it was held in the Motor City, might have been his best since 2000. The Spartans defeated Connecticut to ensure a crowd of 72,000 at Ford Field in the final. But they ran out of gas against a relentless North Carolina team with Hansbrough, Wayne Ellington, and Lawson.

In 2013, Michigan—the hottest team in the best league—dominated the first half of the title game against Louisville, thanks to Spike Albrecht. The freshman guard came off the bench to score 17 points and knock down four threes to give the Wolverines a 12-point lead. But the Cardinals pulled away in the second half for an 82-76 victory.

In 2014, I picked Michigan State to come out of the brackets and win it all. They certainly were impressive when they defeated Kentucky in the Legends Classic in Chicago. Even with several players hurt during long stretches of the season, they made it through. The Spartans battled a hot Connecticut team in the regional finals at the Garden. But the seventh-seeded Huskies looked like destiny's darlings, rallying from a nine-point deficit in the second half behind a 25-point performance by Napier to beat Michigan State, 60-54.

And the Big Ten drought continues.

CHAPTER 56
BREAKOUT OF THE MID-MAJORS

Gonzaga coach Mark Few hates the idea of having his program labeled as a mid-major.

TV might like Cinderella during the opening rounds of March Madness, but he would rather be the bully on the block.

The Bulldogs may be a small Catholic school from Spokane with an enrollment of less than 10,000 who plays in the West Coast Conference, but check this out:

Gonzaga, as of 2014, has been to the NCAA tournament 16 straight years. The Bulldogs were ranked No. 1 in the AP poll—an historic first for the school and the conference—and were the No. 1 seed overall in the tournament just two years ago during the 2012-13 season. Mark Few, who was elevated from an assistant to head coach in 1999, has a career record of 403-100 in just 15 years. That's a winning percentage of 80%, baby!

The only thing that's lacking from Few's resume is a Final Four appearance, and that could happen soon.

The Bulldogs have Top 10 talent and could be the next Wichita State, a team from a non-football playing, non-BCS conference with the potential to be a factor in the NCAA championship hunt. Few has taken a global approach to recruiting. Four of his key players have international roots. Przemek Karnowski, the Zags' center who averaged 10.4 points and 7.1 rebounds, is from Poland. Senior guard Kevin Pangos and forward Kyle Wiltjer, a transfer from Kentucky, are both Canadians. And incoming freshman center Domantas Sabonis, the son of Hall of Famer Arvydas Sabonis, is from Lithuania. Pangos, senior Gary Bell Jr., Byron Wesley, a graduate transfer from USC, and freshman Josh Perkins could give Gonzaga the best backcourt on the West Coast.

Photo Courtesy of Jeff Curry/USA TODAY

• •

The gap between the elite programs and good teams that don't grab the headlines or get mega air time until March Madness is not that big any more. Since 2006, George Mason, Butler, VCU, and Wichita State have all reached the Final Four.

Wichita State won 35 straight games in 2014 and was ranked No. 1 in the AP poll. The Shockers, who shocked Gonzaga in the third round of the 2013 NCAA tournament and advanced

Wichita State coach Gregg Marshall led his Shockers to a 35-0 regular season record before falling to Kentucky in the tournament. Just awesome!

Photo Courtesy of Christopher Hanewinckel/USA TODAY

Here's Mark Few talking with his players during the second half against the San Diego Toreros in 2014. Man, his program is going places!

to the Final Four, were no fluke. They could have been a national championship team, but Kentucky derailed those hopes in the third round of the 2014 tourney.

But I can see the day when a so-called mid-major wins it all because, in those programs, kids usually stay in school for four years and build chemistry. They aren't affected by the one-and-done. You get a couple of kids who can shoot the three, kids who get overlooked by the big schools who don't think they are quick enough, kids who can turn a game around, anything can happen.

In March 2014, six double-digit seeds won early round games. Mercer defeated Duke. Do you think any player from Mercer was recruited by Duke? How about Wichita State? How many of those kids were recruited by Kansas?

All these teams want is a chance to be more than an afterthought with the selection committee. In 2014, BYU from the WCC was the only team outside the RPI's top 10 leagues to make the field as an at-large team. Some schools like Creighton, Butler, VCU, and George Mason have tried to solve the problem by moving to higher-profile multiple-bid leagues.

Gonzaga is not going anywhere. Neither is Mark Few. He's happy where he's at. Just don't call his team a mid-major.

CHAPTER 57
IS UCLA STILL AN ELITE PROGRAM?

UCLA basketball has become a Hollywood script ever since John Wooden retired back in 1975. It has been filled with too much soap opera drama and unrealistic expectations.

Wooden won 10 national championships in his final 12 years as a coach, and the fans out there expect the Bruins to hang another banner every year.

Nine different coaches have tried to follow in his footsteps since with varying degrees of success. Guys like Gene Bartow, Jim Harrick, Steve Lavin, Gary Cunningham, Larry Brown, Larry Farmer, Walt Hazzard, and Ben Howland. Now, Steve Alford is the ninth. For all the talent that showed up on its doorstep, the program has only produced one more title, back in 1995, almost 20 years ago and 20 years since Wooden retired as head coach.

It's like Rick Pitino said when he was trying to rebuild the Celtics: "Larry Bird and Bill Russell aren't coming through the door." Neither are Kareem Abdul-Jabbar and Bill Walton.

But first-year coach Alford inherited enough future NBA players with versatile Kyle Anderson and Jordan Adams—then signed a third, Zach LaVine—to keep the ball rolling and brought excitement back to Pauley. The Bruins went 28-9 and reached the Sweet 16 in 2014 before losing to Florida in the South Region.

Can Alford be magical?

It is tough because there is so much to do in Tinseltown. You have so many teams to follow, like the Lakers, the Kings, the Dodgers, the Clippers, and the Angels. You are also dealing with the power of the movie industry. People in that area want only to deal with superstardom.

Howland took UCLA to the Final Four three consecutive years—from 2006 through 2008— and that wasn't good enough. He got the ziggy five years later after the program experienced some slippage. He missed out on the tournament twice (in 2010 and 2012) and made some miscalculations in recruiting. He looked like he had it turned around when the Bruins won the Pac-12 regular-season title in 2013, but he had lost the trust of the fans. They were ranting and raving about his style of play. Even though he was producing pros like Kevin Love and Russell Westbrook and had 14 guys playing in the NBA, they were getting on his back because they felt he was losing some of the best kids in Southern California.

The Bruins' loss to Minnesota by 20 in the first round of the NCAA tournament gave AD Dan Guerrero the opening to make a change. Alford wasn't their first choice. Guerrero made phone calls to Shaka Smart of VCU and Brad Stevens of Butler, hoping to lure them to the West Coast. But they weren't interested.

UCLA, like Kentucky, is tough in a different way. Once you set a standard, people want you to duplicate it all the time. I have people come up to me and say, "What happened to Duke?" all the time after that loss to Mercer in the big dance. The situation at Duke is that they have won so much people have become totally spoiled. UCLA has a similar problem.

I got into a Twitter war with some Bruins fans when I tweeted about all the empty seats in Pauley Pavilion. I wrote how embarrassing it is for a school of that status getting only seven thousand fans to their home games. I don't care to hear the argument that they didn't play tough competition in the pre-conference schedule. If you are an elite program like Kentucky, North Carolina, and Duke, the crowds come to see you.

I felt it was unfair to new coach Alford, so I tweeted what I thought, and a lot of fans got upset—"Look who they're playing"…"What is this?" Well, that type of attitude, to me, is not one fans of such a historically elite program should have. Anybody can come and support you when you are 30-0. That's easy.

Can they get it back to where they get to a Final Four? Absolutely. Alford has done a solid job. He learned his basketball under The General, Robert Montgomery Knight, at Indiana; he played for Knight in the 1984 Olympics as a sophomore and was a star when Indiana won a national title. He's grown into the job, too. He's a much better coach now than he was when he was at Iowa. He re-energized the program at New Mexico even though they lost to Harvard in the first round of the 2013 NCAA tournament.

Alford has been around long enough to know how to get things done. He's shown he can recruit top players. He's gone to a fast break style of play like the Showtime Lakers.

I don't know if it will happen overnight. But I think it will happen because UCLA still has those classical four letters on the front of the jersey: U–C–L–A. And that plays a big role in recruiting blue-chip superstars.

CHAPTER 58
RISING COACHING STARS

It is hard to believe what Shaka Smart has accomplished at Virginia Commonwealth in such a short period of time.

Smart coached the Rams to 137 wins in five years, four NCAA tournament bids, and one Final Four. That came back before VCU moved from the Colonial Athletic Association to a multi-bid Atlantic 10, which received six NCAA invites last season. The former Florida assistant also trademarked his suffocating "Havoc" defense the Rams use.

All of this by the age of 37.

Is it any wonder so many big timers have dialed his agent's number? He could write his own ticket, baby. Yet, he's comfortable where's he at. He's turned down every offer to stay put at a commuter school in Richmond. In fact, he just got another salary bump to $1.5 million through the 2023 season after turning down offers from UCLA and Minnesota. Smart also got raises for his staff and a commitment of $25 million for a new on-campus practice facility.

Smart was accepted by Yale, Harvard, and Brown after achieving a near perfect SAT score. He graduated magna cum laude with a degree in history from Kenyon College, a small liberal arts school in Ohio that is the alma mater of actor Paul Newman and former president Rutherford B. Hayes. He is smart enough to know where he is a good fit. He is the king of his campus and the biggest name among a new generation of young coaching stars who will inherit this sport after Hall of Fame legends like Mike Krzyzewski, Rick Pitino, Jim Boeheim, Tom Izzo, and Roy Williams walk off into the sunset.

He's a Michelangelo in training wheels and one of the five best young coaching minds in college basketball, along with Tony Bennett of Virginia, Sean Miller of Arizona, Pitino's son Richard of Minnesota, and Kevin Ollie of Connecticut. For those who are screaming, what about coaches like Gregg Marshall or Fred Hoiberg, let it be said that, to me, they have already reached stardom.

Bennett took the Virginia job in 2009 when he was just 39. He coached the Cavaliers to a 30-7 record and only their second outright ACC championship in 2014. Then, the Cavaliers beat Duke in the ACC tournament and were rewarded with a No. 1 seed in the NCAA East Regional. Virginia advanced to the Sweet 16. He is very cerebral, sharp, and the perfect fit for that school and the players who play there. Bennett recruits guys who fit seamlessly into his system. He's learned so much from his dad, Dick, who coached Wisconsin to a Final Four appearance in 2000 and was there in Greensboro to cheer his son on against the Dukies.

If you can win 69 games in three years — hear what I'm saying? — 69 games at Washington State in Pullman, Washington, you have accomplished something! They should put a statue up there for him.

Miller has put Arizona back in the national spotlight after taking over for Lute Olson back in 2009 at the age of 40. The Wildcats won the Pac-12, went 33-5, and were a top seed in the NCAA West Regional, marching all the way to the Elite Eight before they were beaten by Wisconsin. Miller has done an incredible job in recruiting, signing blue-chip players like versatile Aaron Gordon, who was a huge freshman star and an NBA lottery pick. He also picked up Stanley Johnson, one of the top prep players in America.

Miller was destined to be a success in this coaching business. He got the bug as a kid growing up in Beaver Falls, PA, where his father, John, was a successful high school coach who taught his son the discipline of coaching and the art of ball handling. Sean became so good, he appeared on *The Tonight Show Starring Johnny Carson* when he was fourteen years old and was featured in the 1979 movie *The Fish That Saved Pittsburgh* starring basketball star Julius Erving.

When I look at Richard Pitino, I see that he has a lot of the same mannerisms as his father, Rick, who has won two national championships (at Kentucky and Louisville). Richard was only 31 and had been a Division I head coach for just one year at Florida International when he was hired by Minnesota. He learned a lot by working as an assistant to both his father and Donovan at Florida before venturing out on his own. Pitino won a school-record 25 games in his first year in the Big Ten.

Finally, there's Ollie, the veteran NBA guard who succeeded Jim Calhoun at UConn when he was just 41. Ollie got to cut down the nets for his alma mater in 2014 at the NCAA tournament. He got them to play to their max this past season when the Huskies came out of the brackets as a seventh seed to beat Kentucky in the title game.

This guy is headed to big-time stardom. We've seen only the beginning of his success.

These are the rising stars, folks. I'm looking forward to seeing where they end up.

CHAPTER 59

GARY WILLIAMS AND NOLAN RICHARDSON: NAISMITH CLASS OF 2014

It's nice to see the doors of the Naismith Hall of Fame opening up for college basketball coaches.

In 2013, Rick Pitino of Louisville, former UNLV coach Jerry Tarkanian, and former Houston coach Guy Lewis were all inducted.

And, in the spring of 2014, former Maryland coach Gary Williams and former Arkansas coach Nolan Richardson were elected by the honors committee.

I'm always pushing for the college game to be honored in Springfield. There was a time, back in 2004, when no representatives from college were chosen; I was worried the Hall was becoming the sole property of the NBA.

But forward-thinking Jerry Colangelo, the chairman of the Hall, has done a great job correcting that.

Gary Williams was one of my best friends when I was doing his games in the ACC for ESPN. He was so feisty and was always ready to do battle with North Carolina and Duke, turning those games into huge rivalries. Williams loved the competition everywhere he coached, and he was successful at his first job at American U and then in the Big East, the Big Ten, and the ACC. How many people can say that? He was 653-258 in 31 years of coaching and was 447-240 in 22 years at Maryland from the 1989-1990 season through 2011. He passed Lefty Driesell as the winningest coach in school history. He coached the Terps to 14 NCAA consecutive appearances, their only two Final Fours, and won the school's lone NCAA tournament championship in 2002.

I can still remember the year they won it all with guys like guards Juan Dixon and Steve Blake, and forward Lonny Baxter. They beat Indiana, 64-52, in the finals at Atlanta, and finished 32-4. I remember watching him hug his daughter Kristin who was on the court for the playing of "One Shining Moment." Maryland won it all without a single McDonald's All-American.

Photo Courtesy of Matthew Emmons/USA TODAY

Gary Williams' coaching career was more than worthy of the Hall. Baby, this guy knew how to coach!

Juan Dixon, who scored 18 points and was selected the MOP of the Final Four, wouldn't let them lose. The kid was an inspirational story. He grew up in nearby Baltimore, and before he was 13, both of his parents died of AIDS. But Dixon stayed on track, becoming a skinny star at Calvert Hall. Maryland wasn't recruiting him, but Williams loved him when he saw him play in the Nike Peach Jam in Georgia.

Williams had taken his alma mater from the depths to the top of the mountain. When he left Ohio State to take the Maryland job, it was only a few years after Len Bias' tragic passing and Maryland was in the midst of a major NCAA investigation dating back to the Bob Wade era. Williams coached Maryland to an NIT appearance his first year, but then the school was hit with harsh sanctions, banned from post-season play in 1991 and 1992, and kicked off live TV in 1991. The school also docked itself several scholarships over two years.

It was hard to rebuild, but Maryland stayed competitive with Walt Williams and after making a surprise visit to the Sweet 16 in 1994, they were on their way.

The Terrapins became a fixture in the national rankings and featured future NBA players like Joe Smith, Steve Francis, Dixon, Steve Blake, Lonny Baxter, Terence Morris, and Chris Wilcox.

••

Nolan Richardson coached West Texas College to a 37-0 record and the Junior College National Championship in 1980. He took Tulsa to the NIT title in 1981 before leading Arkansas—President Clinton's favorite team—to the Division I NCAA tournament title in 1994. He also coached the Hogs to the national title game in 1995 and took his teams to 20 post-season tournaments in 22 years as a Division I coach.

He is known for wearing an assortment of polka dot ties, but he did something far more important for the growth of the sport in Texas.

Richardson was the first African-American coach at a major university in the South and the first African-American coach in the Southwest Conference. He was a pioneer in civil rights down there, always speaking up about the negative stereotypes he and other black coaches like Hall of Famers John Thompson and John Chaney encountered.

Richardson wasn't born with a silver spoon in his mouth. He coached high school and junior college for 13 years before he got a shot at his first Division I job. And he still likes to talk about his Bowie High School team in his hometown of El Paso, Texas, where he was the first black coach. Back then, he had a team of Mexican-Americans who were all shorter than six feet, so he installed a frenzied style of play that incorporated Henry Iba's defense with three-quarter court pressure.

As coach of the 1994 NCAA Champion Razorbacks, Nolan Richardson's "40 minutes of hell" defense landed him in the Hall of Fame. A great coach!

Photo Courtesy of David Butler II/USA TODAY

His Arkansas teams were like that, too. They played so hard.

Richardson got the Arkansas job after popular Eddie Sutton left for Kentucky. Arkansas got to the 1978 Final Four using Sutton's highly successful walk-it-up, half court style. Richardson replaced it with a wild, up-tempo system with full court pressure that became known as "Forty Minutes of Hell." It took forever for Richardson to be fully accepted by the Hogs. And some fans never did. Richardson constantly got racist hate mail. And, all the while, he had to deal with the fact his daughter Yvonne, who has since passed away, was diagnosed with leukemia at age 13.

Richardson finally won the fans over with his success, taking Arkansas to three Final Fours. He took them in 1990 when he was still in the SWC and in 1994 and 1995 when his teams overshadowed Kentucky in the SEC. His legendary Arkansas teams averaged 27 wins a season during the 90's and had four 30-win seasons in 17 years, making 15 NCAA appearances.

He solidified his legacy by beating Duke and Grant Hill, 76-72, in the 1994 finals on a big shot by Scotty Thurman in the final minute. After the game, Richardson and Clinton embraced in a hug.

I'm happy for both Williams and Richardson. I think it's fantastic when people get into the Hall while they can enjoy it.

There is one more thing I'd like to see the Naismith Hall of Fame do to celebrate our game: They should make a special category—the way they do for international players, women, and African-American pioneers—for players like Christian Laettner and Danny Manning, who had outstanding college careers but never had the same impact in the NBA.

CHAPTER 60

FUTURE HALL OF FAMERS

The Naismith Hall of Fame is a very exclusive club, but there is always room for deserving candidates from the world of college basketball.

In a perfect world, I think there are four coaches who should definitely be aboard an express train for Springfield. I've already shared my feelings on John Calipari. Now, I'd also like to mention Billy Donovan of Florida, Tom Izzo of Michigan State, and Bill Self of Kansas. They're all solid gold.

Like Calipari, they each have the greatest gift you can have as a coach. It's the ability to communicate with your staff, your players, your alums, the fans, and the media. If I'm an AD looking for a coach at the collegiate level today, communication is one of the biggest attributes, along with the ability to recruit and sell your program. It also takes a tremendous knowledge of the game and the ability to organize and handle practice situations as well as the talent to manage the game on the bench.

All of those guys are A-plus in those areas.

And, like Calipari, they've all won national championships. Sure, there are a lot of top-notch coaches out there who have never held the gold trophy, but in this day and age, it seems greatness is determined by winning the big prize.

Donovan has already won two, and he's only 48 years old. He won back-to-back in 2006 and 2007 when he was just 41 years old. Donovan is a Rick Pitino disciple who played for him at Providence where he developed from a chubby point guard into one of the Big East's most feared three-point shooters back in 1987. After a brief pit stop in the NBA and Wall Street, he got the coaching bug and joined Pitino's staff at Kentucky where they rebuilt the program from the ashes of NCAA probation into a perennial national contender.

Now, Donovan is creating his own legacy with the Florida Gators, down there in the O'Dome with the Rowdy Reptiles. He's been on a roll lately, taking the Gators to three straight Elite Eights from 2011 through 2013, and earning a spot in the Final Four in 2014. He has his program on track to make a deep run into March every season.

The Gators won 30 straight games in the 2013-14 season, won a sixth SEC regular-season title, and were ranked No. 1 in the country, beating Kentucky three times. We all know what Steve Spurrier and Urban Meyer did for Florida in football. Well, Donovan has embraced football, but he's also turned Florida into a basketball school.

I've been honored to have Billy Donovan in attendance at my Gala on numerous occasions.

Coach Tom Izzo brought his message to all those gathered at my annual Gala.

The fans are tough on their coaches in Gainesville. But the AD there, Jeremy Foley, pays well and expects success. I know he's happy Billy stayed on campus. A couple of years ago, he almost left for a job with the Orlando Magic. I won't say he'll be in Gainesville forever. I was just reading where he admitted speaking to a couple of NBA teams this spring, and he sounded intrigued by the possibilities. I'm sure the dollars are alluring, but Billy and the rest of these guys belong in college.

Izzo has been at Michigan State for what seems like forever. He started out as an assistant to Jud Heathcote, becoming the head coach in 1995, and then winning a national championship in 2000. He's part of the blue-collar culture that exists up there in East Lansing, and the kids he recruits reflect that toughness that always seems to show up in Big Ten games. In addition to his NCAA tournament championship, Izzo has led the Spartans to six Final Fours and seven Big Ten championships. As of 2014, he has 417 wins, the most in school history, and has been invited to 17 NCAA tournaments.

One of the best things about Izzo? He never forgot where he came from.

Izzo was born and raised in Iron Mountain, in the Upper Peninsula of Michigan where he met best friend and former NFL head coach Steve Mariucci. Both attended Iron Mountain High where they were teammates on the football, basketball, and track teams. At Northern Michigan University, where they were roommates, Izzo played guard for the men's basketball team from 1973 to 1977. In his senior season, he set a school record for minutes played and was named a Division II All-American. The two are lifelong friends.

Finally, there's Self, an Eddie Sutton disciple who's won big everywhere he's been. He won at Tulsa, at Illinois, and now at Kansas where he captured a national title in 2008 in that dramatic game against Memphis. Mario Chalmers hit that clutch three at the end of regulation to force OT in the championship game.

Bill Self has been Rockin' and Chalkin' since he took over the Kansas job, and—are you kidding me?—winning 82% of his games. Wow!

When he took over for Roy Williams in 2004, I really thought he might need mountain-climbing gear, that he might be in for an uphill battle because of what Williams had achieved. Williams was averaging 28 victories, winning 80% of his games and taking the Jayhawks to the Final Four.

I thought it was an impossible job, but Self came in there and proved me wrong. He continued what Roy had going, winning 325 games, an 82% winning percentage, in his first ten years as coach. During that time, he also won 10 straight Big 12 titles and made it to the Final Four twice. Kansas has always been considered one of the elite programs, and Self recognizes that. After he won the title, he received a lucrative offer from T. Boone Pickens to come back to his alma mater, Oklahoma State. But he couldn't pack his bags. Kansas continues to be one of the pillars of the college game, thanks to Bill Self.

I won't be surprised when these guys get their phone calls about the Hall of Fame.

CHAPTER 62
COURT STORMING

Court storming has become a new, disturbing trend in college basketball.

And I have mixed feelings about it.

On the one hand, you really want to enjoy the moment of having a special, special victory. But I see it getting totally out of control. Every night, there's another court storming. I was really taken aback, for example, when the Carolina students stormed the court after the Heels beat Duke at the Dean Dome. Given all the history and tradition of Carolina basketball, it surprised me. I know beating Duke is a major thing. It must be. Duke has lost 39 true road games since the 2003-2004 season. In 31 of those losses, the fans stormed the court. That's 79 percent.

I watched Miami do it two years ago. But this was North Carolina.

Mike Krzyzewski addressed the issue in 2013 when Duke lost up at Virginia and the Cavs' students went wild at the John Paul Jones Arena: "When we've lost in the last 20 years, everybody rushes the court," he began and went on to say much more…

> Whatever you're doing, you need to get the team off the court first. Celebrate, have fun. Just get our team and our staff off the floor before the students come down.

> Look, do you know how close you are to a problem—just put yourself in the position of our players or coaches. I'm not saying any fan did this, but the potential is there all the time for a fan to just go up to you and say, "Coach, you're a bleep" or push you or hit you. And what do you do? What if you did something? That would be a story. We deserve that type of protection.

> I'm always concerned with stuff like that. What if that happened and we get a kid suspended? That becomes a national story. It's not all fun and games when people are rushing the court, especially for the team that lost.

I personally feel court storming has become too abundant. This past season, after Utah Valley upset New Mexico State, 66-61, in OT at home, fans swarmed the court. A brawl erupted after a New Mexico State player hurled a ball at a Utah Valley player. Two New Mexico State players were suspended a total of three games by the Western Athletic Conference. Over in Tempe, Arizona State upset Arizona and fans rushed the court with time remaining on the clock. When the game resumed for seven-tenths of a second and ASU won, fans stormed the court…again.

A few players have been caught on video swinging at fans and vice versa. It's just a matter of time before we have "Malice at the Palace: College Edition."

After that famous brawl between the Indiana Pacers and the Detroit Pistons in an NBA game back in 2004, the SEC cracked down on court storming. When South Carolina fans rushed the court after their team upset Kentucky that year, the league fined the school $5,000. The scenario repeated itself in 2010, and the Gamecocks were fined $25,000. Students started going up to the athletic director and handing him $1 bills to help the cause.

Photo Courtesy of Brian Spurlock/ USA TODAY

And, like Coach K, I also worry about the danger.

The worst case on record occurred in 2004 when Joe Kay, a Stanford volleyball recruit, was buried under a pile of fans after he made a game-winning shot in a big high school basketball game in Tucson. Kay suffered a torn carotid artery and had a stroke. He survived, but his life as a Division I prospect was history.

Then, there was the scene in Bloomington on December 10, 2011, when

I thought I'd seen it all in college basketball, but the wild court storming by Indiana's fans after they upset Kentucky at Assembly Hall in 2001 was crazy... and scary.

Indiana upset top-ranked Kentucky at Assembly Hall on a last-second shot by Christian Watford. Dan Shulman and I did the game on ESPN, and the scene was crazy as IU fans poured onto the floor before officials could get to the review table.

Amidst all that joy and jubilation, I started to get worried. "Are we safe?" I said over the air. "I worry about the way they're coming out."

As it turned out, Megan Dills, a *Playboy* model and a life-long Kentucky fan who showed up wearing a Wildcats T-shirt and blue and white face paint, was injured.

She suffered a sprained ankle and some torn tendons after she was trampled in the mad rush and was knocked down five or six steps. The incident attracted major national attention and led John Calipari to go on his radio show the next week and set the wheels in motion to cancel one of the great rivalries in college basketball; he said the Cats no longer wished to play in Bloomington.

In January 2013, North Carolina State students, led by wheelchair-bound Will Privette, stormed the court after the Wolfpack knocked off No. 1-ranked Duke in Raleigh. The video went viral. Student body president Andy Walsh, who pushed Privette's wheelchair onto the court, told *USA Today* it was all one huge blur. "There were just so many people and it happened so quickly."

Privette, as it turned out, tumbled out of his wheelchair, and if it hadn't been for NC State player C.J. Leslie, who picked him up, there could have been a major, major problem.

These days, it seems like after any win, people storm the court. All I can say is act like you've been there, baby.

CHAPTER 63

IS RECRUITING BETTER OR WORSE?

I took a ride with my grandsons Connor and Jake to Ft. Myers, Florida, in December 2013 to watch the Culligan City of Palms Classic. I was amazed by the hoops hysteria that was taking place at this elite high school event. It was certainly fun meeting so many fans, signing autographs, and taking pictures with people who are so in love with high school basketball.

But I was hardly the biggest celebrity in the gym. That was Jahlil Okafor, the center from Whitney Young High School in Chicago, who had already signed with Duke. He is one of two kids from the Windy City, along with forward Cliff Alexander of Curie High who signed with Kansas, were on my pre-season All-Diaper Dandy team. I wanted my grandsons to see the stars of the future. They posed for a picture with Okafor and Ben Simmons, a highly-rated junior who has committed to LSU.

You can only imagine how good DePaul or Illinois would be if they sealed off the borders and kept the best kids in state. I think of the Illinois Final Four team in 1989—the Flying Illini with Nick Anderson, Marcus Liberty, all Chicago kids. I think of DePaul with Mark Aguirre and Terry Cummings in 1980 when they were ranked No. 1. I think kids sometimes don't realize the value of playing for a hometown team or a state school.

But it hasn't happened for a while. Derrick Rose went from winning back-to-back Illinois state titles at Simeon to being a first-team All-American point guard at Memphis as a freshman in 2008. Rose was the first pick in the draft and the youngest MVP in NBA history by his third season. Jabari Parker, who led Simeon to a record four straight state titles, signed with Duke and was a first-team All-American as a freshman before becoming the second overall pick in the NBA draft.

The assembly line just keeps going.

Okafor is the city's latest prodigy. DePaul actually offered him a scholarship in eighth grade, but the NCAA made them rescind it because it was a violation. Illinois offered Okafor in ninth grade, but he passed on both and signed with Duke to play with another Top 5 prospect, McDonald's All-American point guard Tyus Jones from Apple Valley, Minnesota.

It's like that in the NBA. The bluest of blue-chip players want to play with each other and play in the best programs. They want to play for a coach they feel can get them to the NBA as quickly as possible. Okafor is being projected as the first

Photo Courtesy of Brian Spurlock/USA TODAY

Duke landed Jahlil Okafor, who should be just outstanding. Coach K can still recruit.

Bill Self got a real gem in Cliff Alexander. Jayhawk fans will love him!

pick in the 2015 draft. It's one of the reasons John Calipari will have nine McDonald's All-Americans on his roster at Kentucky this year. And it's the reason Alexander chose Kansas over Illinois, Memphis, and DePaul.

Alexander was confused up to the night before his ESPN announcement when he decided on Kansas. He seemed undecided until the very second he told classmates at a packed high school gym he was going to be a Jayhawk. It was heartbreak city for Illinois fans, and they let him know how they felt with a negative outburst on Twitter.

Alexander said the deciding factor in choosing KU over runner-up choice Illinois was coach Bill Self's "developing his players, getting his players to the league" mentality. He's a kid in a hurry to move forward.

"One-and-done, then come back and get my degree," Alexander said of his future plans.

More and more high school superstars are looking for schools that can put them in the NBA as quickly as possible. They look at Kentucky, North Carolina, Florida, Kansas. Now, Duke is in it the last few years. Those kids come with the mindset of I'm a one-and-done player. They want to play in programs that are on TV all the time, where they can get some exposure. And, unfortunately, they don't stick around long enough so that their names develop. Can you imagine if kids like Andrew Wiggins and Parker stayed around long enough to become household names?

I remember when kids used to get excited about going to a college. Now, it's the league, the league, the league. It's like renting a player for a season. It's getting harder to forge a bond with a kid. Here today, gone tomorrow. Back then, you could build a national power with local players who stayed four years.

I'm so happy I'm not a part of it anymore. What happened to the good old days when recruiting was done with high school coaches involved? It was really done the right way. Today, you're dealing with a lot of shady people.

Andrew Wiggins was the top pick of the 2014 NBA draft. Cleveland chose him first and dealt him to Minnesota in the Kevin Love deal.

I have talked to a number of coaches, and they have spoken off the record about the incidents transpiring in summer basketball and the world of AAU teams ruling the highly regarded players. Recruiting has always been tough, but now, with the runners for agents and third-party involvement, it's beyond difficult, especially for the mid-majors, who are trying to compete on a playing field which is not level. Think about what is going on. You have donors, alumni from big universities, laying down big bucks to these AAU programs. It's legal, but not really ethical.

As a coach, you've got to play the game, kiss everybody's butt, and all that. It's sad in a way. You've got an 18-year-old super-talented player they are dangling in front of you, and he controls your life. If he says yes, you are on easy street. If he says no, you could end up looking for a job.

When I was at Rutgers, I always used to always think positively. I used to tell them if you think you're mediocre, you're going to be mediocre. If you think you're special, you're going to be special. You cannot convince me that I can't find two kids a year from New Jersey and New York City who want to play some games in the Garden, want to go to a first-class university. Come on. Give me a break.

When I went to Detroit, I sold the idea to recruits that many of them were going to make their living in the Motor City after college.

Today, kids live in their own little world and really do not evaluate the best place for them to go. Many times, they choose a place based on ego. They don't analyze the key factors in making a decision. For example, they don't spend time looking at academics, at the roster to see where they fit in, style of play, etc.

I think you get the picture about the wild world of recruiting.

The big programs will survive because of their reputations. The rules favor the elite schools. But, right now, recruiting has gotten out of control, and it's time to bring in a czar for college basketball to oversee the sport, someone who is strong enough to make certain that the rules are followed and work hand-in-hand with the NCAA in determining and enforcing policy.

CHAPTER 64
RAISING THE ACADEMIC BAR

Ever since the university presidents have gotten more involved in college sports, academics have become a more important part of the equation.

The presidents wanted more emphasis placed on achievement in high school classrooms so their universities won't be embarrassed by low graduation rates, which is why they began raising the bar for student-athletes who wanted to be eligible to play freshman year.

And they've kept raising the bar.

Starting in August 2016, prospective college athletes who do not come out of high school with a 2.3 grade point average, based on 16 core courses, will be forced by the NCAA to take a redshirt year. What this means is a college-bound student-athlete may receive an athletic scholarship in the first year of enrollment and may practice in the first regular academic term semester, but he or she cannot compete in the first year of enrollment.

Until then, students must still meet the NCAA's minimum 2.0 GPA, and the sliding scale with SAT and ACT scores is still currently in effect. Personally, I've always believed the university admissions department should have the final say on who gets accepted.

The NCAA wants coaches to recruit kids who want to be in college and have a chance to survive. A lot of kids just need a chance. We're supposed to be in the business of helping kids, not hurting them. Sometimes, when they are surrounded by motivated students, they fulfill their potential.

On the flip side, there have been a disturbing number of stories out there about athletes who can't read or write. Really.

The story that got the biggest headlines involved Kevin Ross, who played basketball for Creighton University over 20 years ago. I was really floored when I heard about this story, which appeared in the *Chicago Tribune*, and felt so bad for Kevin. He went on *60 Minutes* and told the world he had completed four years of college and was kept eligible even though he was illiterate.

Ross did an interview with ESPN's *Outside the Lines* a couple years ago and said when he opened up a book, he was scared to death because he didn't understand the words. Ross played on a state high school championship team in Kansas City and accepted a scholarship to Creighton, but the only thing he could read on his diploma was his name. He couldn't even read the name of the school he'd attended.

Ross played four years for Creighton, averaging just four points a game. When his eligibility was up, his passing grades stopped. His last semester in school, he got all F's. Ross wound up suing the university because Creighton did not live up to its obligations.

Six months later, Ross enrolled in Westside Prep Elementary School in Chicago, Illinois, founded by Marva Collins, and he asked for help. He had to start from scratch; he was learning in the same classroom with second and third graders and got special tutoring help from Collins. In nine months, Ross jumped 11 grades and eventually he graduated from high school. It was amazing how hard he worked to pursue his dream, learning how to read. But he never got his college degree and now works as a custodian.

There are a lot of sad stories like that.

ESPN did some research, and at one point, 10% of Division I programs had a zero graduation rate for their African-American athletes over a five-year period.

The NCAA has since taken steps to improve the situation, putting in an academic graduation rate requirement that would ban schools with poor academic performances from post-season play. The biggest name involved so far has been Connecticut, an NCAA tournament regular since 1990 and four-time national champion. The Huskies had to sit out the 2013 men's basketball tournament. Ironically, the kids on that team were punished for events that occurred back in 2008 and 2009. That was before they were even enrolled under a previous coaching regime, which bothers me. It's not really fair to the current group or current coach.

Fine the school. Take their cash. But don't penalize innocent people.

UConn officials knew they wouldn't make the cut in 2012 and sought a waiver when it asked the NCAA to use the two most recent years of data. But their argument was rejected.

In 2012-13, each of the record 10 schools that fell below the mandated four-year cut line of 900 or the two-year cut line of 930 faced additional sanctions. UConn had to replace four hours of practice time with academic activities each week

I thought it was interesting that Connecticut not only won the national title, but it also had a perfect score on the APR in 2014.

The NCAA came out with another banned list in the spring of 2014. Thirty-six teams in Division I are listed as ineligible for 2014-15 post-season competition. Nine football teams are among the 36, most notably UNLV and Idaho. Eight men's basketball teams are banned from competing in the NCAA tournament: Alabama State, Appalachian State, Florida A&M, Houston Baptist, Lamar, San Jose State, Central Arkansas, and Wisconsin-Milwaukee.

Historically, low-resource colleges and universities have produced lower scores than schools that bring in the most money. The most recent numbers reflect a similar trend. Of the 17 football and men's basketball teams facing the harshest sanctions, eight are historically black colleges—including the only two schools to face postseason bans in both sports: Alabama State and Florida A&M.

There has to be something done to help low resource colleges, and the NCAA needs to follow through with its plan to donate money to those schools for additional tutoring and an academic support staff. It is vital that the NCAA do everything in its power to provide these schools the necessary resources for helping student-athletes academically, especially if they're going to keep raising the bar.

CHAPTER 65
DIVISION IV

The NCAA is moving closer to a split between the Power Five conferences—which include the SEC, the Big Ten, the Atlantic Coast Conference, the Big 12, and the Pac-12—and the rest of Division I. An August 2014 vote gave the Power Five more autonomy to change the rules.

SEC commissioner Mike Slive said it was not something his conference wanted to do, but they needed a new model to support their vision of where college athletics needs to go.

Moving to Division IV would keep the major conferences under the NCAA umbrella but would give college football's biggest money makers more power to take care of their players. The SEC would like to pay full cost of college, provide long-term medical coverage, and offer incentives to kids who return to school and complete degrees. Slive isn't the first commissioner of a major conference who has threatened to bring his schools to a new division. Jim Delany of the Big Ten did the same thing in 2013.

Smaller Division I schools likely can't afford the changes the major conferences want. Division II and Division III have their own rules, but forming Division IV would create a wider gap between the universities in the power conferences and the rest of the 350-member Division I.

The NCAA and its member schools place far too much importance on competitive equity even though it doesn't exist right now. The poorer schools in the power conferences that are currently not competitive will veto certain rules for the sake of competitive balance, but they will never catch up with the likes of Texas, Alabama, or Ohio State, who have $100 million athletic budgets.

Slive claimed the Power Five wouldn't disrupt championship formats, including the NCAA basketball tournament, which is the crown jewel of the organization in terms of interest and money. Right now, we have growing parity with all kinds of upsets in the first weekend, and mid-majors are making a serious run at the Final Four. But what happens if a doomsday scenario takes place and the Power Five actually leave the NCAA altogether and form their own college football playoff and their own post-season basketball tournament? Think of the dough they would be able to generate if they negotiated their own deal with the networks. It might not happen overnight, but it is something to think about down the road.

As of 2014, the NCAA Division I men's basketball tournament has a 14-year deal worth $10.8 billion, and the new four-team football playoff should take in close to $500 million a year.

This could be worth way more to the richer schools, who could form their own cartel, eliminating the competition and creating a huge recruiting advantage because their teams would be on TV all the time.

CHAPTER 66
POP AND THE SPURS

The San Antonio Spurs are the best run organization in professional sports. There, I said it.

Gregg Popovich's team proved it with a dominant win in the 2014 NBA finals, dispatching LeBron James and the Miami Heat in five games. San Antonio's four wins all came by 15 or more points.

They are the first NBA team to win 50 games in a season for 15 straight years. And, in that time, they have won five championships and played in seven NBA finals.

Talk about consistency, man.

The Spurs have had their share of mega-stars over the years, like Tim Duncan, forward David Robinson, and guards Manu Ginobili and Tony Parker. In the 2014 finals, it was the emergence of Kawhi Leonard from San Diego State who, in just his second season in the NBA, captured MVP honors. Duncan won his fifth championship ring, the same as their outstanding coach.

....

I know people will argue for Bill Belichick of the New England Patriots as the best professional coach out there. But Pop gets my vote. And I think Krzyzewski's total resume, approaching 1000 wins, is above everyone in terms of being the best coach on the college level.

When you look at Coach K and Pop, there is a common denominator. Both went to school at service academies—Mike at West Point and Popovich at the Air Force Academy. They were both point guards. I think the discipline, the training, the mental toughness they received at the military schools have become part of their personalities, and they both transfer that to their players.

Popovich was the leading scorer and team captain at Air Force. He graduated with a degree in Soviet Studies and underwent Air Force intelligence gathering. He served for five years as an Air Force officer and, at one point, considered a career in the CIA. But, he chose coaching, returning to Air Force and serving as an assistant to Hank Egan for six years.

He was a student of the game who became a volunteer assistant at Kansas, so he could study directly under Larry Brown. Then, in 1988, when Brown left Kansas to become the head coach of the Spurs, he convinced Popovich to become his top assistant.

Popovich became the GM and vice president of Basketball Operations with the Spurs in 1994 after Peter Holt bought the team. He did two things immediately to change the culture of the team; he signed Avery Johnson to become the team's point guard, and the two won their first NBA title in 1999. Then, he traded loose cannon Dennis Rodman to Chicago.

After the Spurs got off to a 3-15 start in 1997 and Robinson was sidelined with a pre-season back injury, Popovich fired coach Bob Hill and took over the team as coach and GM. The team struggled over the rest of the season, but then they got lucky, winning the NBA lottery with their selection of Duncan from Wake Forest. Duncan and The Admiral, Daniel Robinson, formed the

Who's the best coach in pro sports? A great case can be made for Gregg Popovich, who not only has the championship rings but also has a team that is consistently one of the best in the NBA.

Twin Towers, and the Spurs began to blossom. They won 56 games in Popovich's first full season, then went on to win the title the next season.

They've been on a roll ever since. In all, five championships in 15 years.

In 2002, Popovich gave up the GM job, hiring R.C. Buford for the job. Popovich wanted to concentrate on coaching. Together, they have formed the best tandem in pro sports.

Buford's teams have a tradition of quality players and people who fit into his system. He's been able to keep the nucleus of his team—Duncan, Ginobili, and Parker—together. All three came from outside the borders. Duncan is from the Virgin Islands and was originally a swimmer. Ginobili is from Argentina and played on his country's 2004 Olympic gold medal team. Parker is from France. The Spurs have also managed to add players, like forward Leonard and guard Danny Green, who have been contributors. A lot of people didn't think Green could make it in the NBA when he graduated in 2009, the year North Carolina won the NCAA tournament. But he took advantage of his great shooting ability. You have to credit Buford for his evaluation skills; his roster has as much of an international flavor as any team in the NBA.

There is also such a sense of pride in that town. The fans in San Antonio love their Spurs. They love Popovich, who's become an institution there.

When it is all said and done, the Hall of Fame will call his name.

CHAPTER 67
KEVIN DURANT'S TRIBUTE TO HIS MOTHER

It seems the older I get, the more sentimental I get.

I was in tears when I heard Kevin Durant of the Oklahoma City Thunder give his acceptance speech after he was awarded the NBA's 2014 MVP award at a ceremony in Edmond, Oklahoma. I wanted to reach for the Kleenex, baby, when he started to talk about his mother, Wanda Pratt, and the sacrifices she made when he and his brother were growing up in the suburbs of Washington, D. C. With tears streaming down his and his mother's face, he went on to pay her an amazing tribute:

> And last, my mom. I don't think you know what you did. You had my brother when you were 19 years old. Three years later, I came out. The odds were stacked against us. Single parent with two boys by the time you were 21 years old.
>
> Everybody told us we weren't supposed to be here. We moved from apartment to apartment by ourselves. One of the best memories I had is when we moved into our first apartment. No bed, no furniture, and we all just sat in the living room and hugged each other, 'cause that's when we all thought we made it.
>
> When something good happens to you, I tend to look back to what brought me here. You woke me up in the middle of the night in the summer times. Making me run up a hill. Making me do push-ups. Screaming at me from the sidelines at my games at 8 or 9 years old.
>
> You made us believe. You kept us off the street, put clothes on our backs, food on the table. When you didn't eat, you made sure we ate. You went to sleep hungry. You sacrificed for us. You're the real MVP.

The words were so touching. The crowd gave his mother a standing ovation after Durant's heart-tugging speech was over. There wasn't a dry eye in the place.

Durant made his speech just before Mother's Day. The NBA was so moved, it created a new "Mother's Day" commercial. Because, while we

Photo Courtesy of Alonzo Adams/USA TODAY

Using the announcement that he'd won the 2014 NBA MVP award to acknowledge how important his mother was to him was special—it also showed that he truly deserved the award. A lot of us were crying with Kevin.

each can't thank our own mom with a touching speech after winning the NBA MVP award, we can certainly remind her that she's the MVP in our lives.

It's times like this we should appreciate our families. On my desk, I have a picture of my mother and father holding me as a youngster. It's the first thing I see when I go to work in the morning and the last thing I see before I leave at night.

Durant could have easily fallen through the cracks. He was always the tallest boy in his class—and very self-conscious about his height. His mother asked his teachers to put him at the end of the lines, so he wouldn't stand out as much. His grandmother Barbara told him his height was a blessing and to just wait and see.

Then, he discovered basketball and quickly became a star on the AAU circuit, playing with future NBA players like Michael Beasley and Ty Lawson. When he was 11, he told his mother he wanted to play in the NBA. When he entered high school, Durant began wearing 35 as his jersey number in honor of his AAU coach Charles Craig, who was murdered at the age of 35. Just before he entered his senior year at Montrose Christian Academy, Durant sprouted up five inches to 6-foot-8, and he also benefited from working out with his AAU coach at the time.

When Durant wasn't playing in organized games, he was given a set of drills to perform. He was a practice junkie, working out eight hours a day in the summer. And it paid off. Durant was the MVP of the McDonald's All-American game and Jordan Classic and got to meet his idol, Michael Jordan, before signing to play with Texas for a year before going into the draft.

Durant averaged 32 points per game during the 2013-14 season for a 59-win team that played most of the season without a healthy Russell Westbrook. Durant had one stretch of 41 straight games in which he scored at least 25 points. He scored 40 points 14 times in the regular season. He dominated the MVP balloting, picking up 119 first place votes. Lebron James, who won the award in 2012 and 2013, finished second with six first place votes.

"Everything in my life, I had to take it," he said. "They're not going to give it to you out of sympathy. I wouldn't want it any other way. This was another case, if I wanted to win the MVP, I had to go take it. I felt that this was the year I did that."

His mother was sitting in the front row for what Durant called a "surreal moment." At one point, as he thanked his teammates, he paused and said, "I don't know why I'm crying so much."

Photo Courtesy of Richard Rowe/ USA TODAY

There's nothing like acknowledging your mom. Kevin Durant and his mother, Wanda Pratt, celebrate after Oklahoma City won a game in overtime.

CHAPTER 68
THE INSTABILITY OF NBA COACHING JOBS

When you compare the college basketball scene to the NBA, there is a big difference in coaching security and stability. There is absolutely no stability in the NBA while there is some at the college level. Since the spring of the 2012-13 season, 21 NBA head coaching vacancies have been created.

Two franchises, the Cavs and Pistons, have made the list twice. The only teams not on the list are the Bulls, Mavericks, Rockets, Pacers, Heat, Pelicans, Thunder, Magic, Trail Blazers, Raptors, and Wizards. Rick Adelman retired from Minnesota, and Doc Rivers was traded from the Boston Celtics to the L.A. Clippers. But, other than that, all the openings were created by coaches whose contracts expired, were fired, or, like Mike D'Antoni of the Los Angeles Lakers, resigned before they were pushed out the door.

Even though they get the ziggy, one consolation is that coaches often have financial bonanzas in many cases. But, regardless of the cash, getting fired is a severe blow to your professional pride—believe me, I was there.

You can have a lot of success, even be NBA Coach of the Year, and be gone the next week. Ask George Karl. He won a franchise-record 57 games with the Denver Nuggets in 2013 despite its being the third-youngest team in the league. He was a brilliant leader and led the Nuggets to nine straight playoff appearances. But, instead of an extension, he got the ziggy because his team advanced out of the first round only once since 2005 when they lost in the conference finals. Karl wound up in broadcasting on ESPN instead of sitting on the bench.

In the 2013-14 season, Mark Jackson of the Golden State Warriors won 51 games and took his team to the playoffs for a second straight year, but he was out of a job after the Warriors lost to the Clippers in the first round. The Clippers prevailed despite the distraction of the Donald Sterling mess.

The list goes on, my friends. Guys like Vinny Del Negro and Lionel Hollins, who both won 50 games in 2013, got the pink slip. Hollins went on to coach in Brooklyn.

Ownership and front office personnel couldn't care less about awards like Coach of the Year. The regular season resume doesn't matter. It's all about the post-season. It is that simple.

Owners are constantly looking for coaches who can create magic, and teams are starting to move toward hiring coaches with no previous experience. The Warriors handed TNT analyst Steve Kerr $25 million for five years. He's never coached before. He still had his pick between two NBA jobs when the Knicks and the Warriors came calling. The Knicks hired Derek Fisher. The Brooklyn Nets gave Jason Kidd their job immediately after he retired from playing. Kidd went on to coach in Milwaukee. Jackson moved right from the TV booth to the sidelines. Brad Stevens of Butler was selected to coach the fabled Boston Celtics. Teams elevated assistant coaches like Steve Clifford, Mike Budenholzer, Brian Shaw, Brett Brown, and Mike Malone.

The ex-players like Kerr and Fisher, I understand why teams hire cerebral point guards. They have an innate feel for and understanding of the NBA game. Most former college coaches, like yours truly, have a different mindset of a practice session.

I remember vividly when Bob Lanier came in and told me, "Dick, we cannot practice with this intensity because this is the NBA and we play multiple times each week."

He was absolutely right. I had no clue about the lifestyle of the NBA player. It is also mandatory that inexperienced coaches hire experienced assistants. It is pertinent that Kerr and Fisher have experienced staffs.

The NBA coaching carousel has gone crazy. Owners are willing to pay big dough. But you can be yesterday's news quickly if you're not playing in late May.

On the collegiate level, do you think a coach is out on the street if he has one bad year? Guys like Mike Krzyzewski, Roy Williams, Jim Boeheim, Tom Izzo, Rick Pitino, John Calipari—do you think they will get the ziggy? Look at Kentucky in 2013, falling to Robert Morris in the first round of the NIT after winning the NCAA championship the year before. If that had happened in the NBA, he'd been fired. But Kentucky stayed the course, and Calipari bounced back and got his team into the championship game in 2014.

These guys have much more stability running their programs on the college level. They are truly in charge. Of course, they have to answer to the president and the AD, but their resumes and past successes mean something. Why would a guy want to jeopardize that by running to the pros? There is a long list of guys who did not enjoy success at the next level. Jerry Tarkanian, Leonard Hamilton, and Lon Kruger didn't when they made the jump. Calipari and Pitino proved better off on the college sideline, too.

There is the ego factor, the glamour of the NBA, and the bucks are a little bit bigger. But the top college coaches are making a nice living, too.

I think about the world of college basketball vs. the NBA, and it's pretty simple. The pros are all about the players. For example, look at the transition the Knicks are going through as Phil Jackson, who has all those championship rings, tries to instill a new mindset in New York.

I had a taste of the NBA, barely a cup of coffee with the Detroit Pistons, hardly enough time to put the milk in. Trust me, the NBA, with its 82-game regular season and all that travel, is very difficult.

Give me the college sideline anytime.

CHAPTER 69
THE NBA DRAFT GAMBLE

I might not be the best person to speak about the NBA draft.

When I was with the Pistons, our owner wanted Bob McAdoo badly. He then negotiated a trade with Auerbach of the Celtics where they ended up with two first-round draft picks in 1980. That led to their getting center Robert Parish from Golden State and forward Kevin McHale. They combined with Larry Bird to become one of the best frontlines in the history of the NBA and the catalysts for several championships. This was all part of compensation as M.L. Carr signed as a free agent with the Celtics.

Back then, before the birth of the lottery in 1985, at least half of the 22 teams in the league were pretty much assured of getting an impact player through the draft.

In 1984, the draft produced four Hall of Famers—center Hakeem Olajuwon of Houston, forward Michael Jordan of North Carolina, Charles Barkley of Auburn, and guard John Stockton of Gonzaga. Houston and Portland were involved in a coin flip, and the Rockets selected Olajuwon with the first pick. Portland, in need of a center, took 7-footer Sam Bowie of Kentucky, opening the door for the Chicago Bulls to take Jordan with the third pick.

Bleacher Report did an interesting story on free agency vs. building through the draft. Over the last 10 years, six different teams have won the NBA championship—the San Antonio Spurs, Detroit Pistons, Miami Heat, Boston Celtics, Los Angeles Lakers, and Dallas Mavericks. With the exception of two of them—the 2004 Pistons and the 2012 Heat—each of the winning teams either drafted or traded for the player who would win the NBA Finals MVP. The idea of building through the draft assumes that losing games and collecting lottery picks is a proven way to draft young players who will eventually blend together and become good enough to challenge for an NBA title.

The theory has worked in Oklahoma City, where forward Kevin Durant and guard Russell Westbrook have the Thunder in contention. The Thunder got help from the Portland Trail Blazers, who won the lottery in 2007 and chose Ohio State's 7-foot injury-prone Greg Oden over Durant, the league's MVP this year.

I look at the draft these days, and it's based strictly on one word—potential.

The last first overall pick who fell into a "can't miss" category was LeBron James, a high school prodigy from St. Vincent's-St. Mary's in Akron, Ohio, who was taken by Cleveland. James led the Cavs to the playoffs, but he didn't start winning titles until after he signed as a free agent with the Miami Heat. Interesting to note that LeBron recently returned to the Cavaliers via free agency.

Through 29 NBA lotteries dating back to 1985, only one team—San Antonio—won the NBA title with its own No. 1 overall pick. David Robinson won twice and Tim Duncan won five titles, two with the Admiral. That stat blows my mind.

Now, consider the Cavaliers.

They have defied logic by winning the lottery for three of the last four years with mixed results. They took freshman point guard Kyrie Irving from Duke in 2011, who is blossoming into a star. But, last year, 2013, they selected 6-foot-8 freshman Anthony Bennett, a Canadian

I first met Andrew Wiggins when he was a true Diaper Dandy. After one season with Bill Self's Kansas Jayhawks, Wiggins was the first overall pick in the 2014 NBA draft. He's going to be a good one!

import who was constantly injured and spent most of his time in the NBDL. In 2014, it was Andrew Wiggins who the Cavs selected first—they later traded him and Anthony Bennett to the Minnesota Timberwolves in exchange for Kevin Love.

Maybe Bennett will blossom into a big-time player, but his window is limited. Teams are guaranteed control of their first-round picks for only five years, and GMs begin thinking about whether to offer a second contract early on.

The Spurs have done an amazing job of keeping the nucleus of their team together over the years and remaining a champion with five titles in 15 years. But, in many cases, even if stars like Kevin Love make an immediate impact as a rookie, the way he did in Minnesota, there is no guarantee he will stick around if his team is not winning. The lure of free agency, fueled by enormous financial gain, can be tempting. So, in my opinion, the better way to go about putting together a winning team is in free agency.

Under the new collective bargaining agreement, contracts will be shorter and players will become free agents more often, so teams can turn their fortunes around quickly.

CHAPTER 70

SAY GOODBYE TO DONALD STERLING

Donald Sterling is out.

His Clippers franchise was officially sold to former Microsoft executive Steve Ballmer for $2 billion in August 2014. That ended a tumultuous time for the team.

As far as I'm concerned, the 80-year-old Sterling shouldn't have remained in charge of an NBA franchise after *TMZ* obtained and aired a now infamous recorded conversation. It was April 25, 2014; a voice identified as Sterling's tells a female friend he is angry over a photo she had posted on Instagram where she is posed with Basketball Hall of Fame player Magic Johnson.

Sterling told V. Stiviano: "It bothers me a lot that you want to broadcast that you're associating with black people," and, "You can sleep with them. You can bring them in, you can do whatever you want," but "the little I ask you is…not to bring them to my games."

My reaction was immediate. His remarks were offensive and a disgrace to the NBA. It was insulting to everybody, both black and white. It was flat-out embarrassing to think of anybody making those remarks and owning a team in the NBA, a league dominated by black players.

How in the world do you justify that?

Adam Silver, the NBA's new commissioner, did the right thing. After a quick investigation, he dropped the hammer on Sterling, banning him for life and fining him $2.5 million. Sterling's offensive, racist comments created a major scandal. Sterling was banned from entering any Clippers facility and attending any NBA games. Silver came down hard and said what the players and fans were hoping to hear. Almost immediately, Silver's stock went way, way up.

What a mess. And it came at a time when the NBA should have been celebrating the season, not trying to clean up a black eye. Sterling embarrassed and humiliated everyone in the NBA with his actions.

On April 26, the day after the tape was released, the Clippers held a team meeting to discuss the incident. Both the coaches and players briefly raised the possibility of boycotting Game 4 of their first-round series against the Golden State

Photo Courtesy of Kirby Lee/USA TODAY

Waving good bye to Donald Sterling. The Clippers were sold to former Microsoft executive Steve Ballmer for $2 billion in August 2014.

Warriors the next day. Rather than boycott, they decided to protest Sterling's remarks by wearing their shirts inside out in order to hide the team's logo during pre-game warmups.

Corporate sponsors also began to flee the scene.

Doc Rivers deserves a salute for a job well done in handling this situation. The psychology of his coaching was brilliant, from the night he found out about the Sterling recording to getting his team to perform at a high level and beat Golden State in Game 5. He made a great move after Game 4, calling off practice to allow his players to clear their heads.

There were a lot of angry words out there.

Reaction throughout the league was swift, with LeBron James saying, "There is no room for Sterling in our league." Magic Johnson said he would never attend another Clippers game as long as Sterling was in charge.

Even President Obama weighed in on this one, characterizing the recording as "incredibly offensive racist statements." Obama added, "When ignorant folks want to advertise their ignorance, you don't really do anything, you just let them talk."

I don't care if he was set up. I realize it was said in a private conversation, but the recording revealed the true nature of his personality and his thought process.

Sterling agreed to let his wife sell the team before the owners could vote to kick him out. Then, he did an about-face and reinstated a lawsuit to try to save his ownership. Well, it didn't work. Sterling lost his ownership for good. The NBA and Ballmer made the deal, and Sterling's appeal that closed the sale of the Clippers was denied.

And this was not the first time Sterling has been in the middle of controversy. He faced extensive federal charges of civil rights violations and racial discrimination in his business dealings. In 2006, the U.S. Department of Justice sued Sterling for using race as a factor in filling some of the apartment buildings he owned in Los Angeles County. The suit charged Sterling systematically drove Hispanics, African-Americans, and families with children out of those apartments. Three years later, in 2009, Sterling paid $2.73 million to settle the suit plus court costs.

That same year, Sterling was sued unsuccessfully by former longtime Clippers executive Elgin Baylor for employment discrimination on the basis of age and race. The original lawsuit, reported in the *Los Angeles Times*, alleged Sterling told Baylor that he wanted to fill his team with "poor black boys from the South and a white head coach."

And how about this? The Los Angeles chapter of the NAACP was supposed to present Sterling with a Lifetime Achievement Award May 15, 2014. Thankfully, they came to their senses and canceled that event.

I get sick talking about it. My hope was that Magic Johnson would have found a way to buy the Clippers. His group offered $1.6 billion but finished second to Ballmer. Everything Magic touches turns to gold. Magic would be able to step in right away. His smile alone would be so positive for the league as would as his experience as a player and a businessman.

But, as it stands now, I wish Ballmer the best as he takes over the Clippers.

GIVING BACK

At some point, I realized that I will never be able to fully give back to society all of the wonderful things it's given to me, but that doesn't mean I can't try. Whether it's my family giving back to our community, carrying on Jimmy V's "Don't give up, don't ever give up" legacy, or raising money for pediatric cancer research so that one day no child has to suffer, I'm always trying to do something, anything. All I can simply say is that I CAN make a difference, so I should be trying to make a difference.

I am so proud of the Dick Vitale Gala. Through the first nine events, we've raised in excess of $12 million for pediatric cancer research.

CHAPTER 71
BIRTH OF A GALA

When my broadcast buddy, Jimmy Valvano, first started complaining about a pain in his back at the 1992 Final Four, our group wasn't very sympathetic. We gave the usual rhetoric: "Take an aspirin," "You'll be fine," "Suck it up."

Little did we know that the pain would ultimately lead to bone cancer.

I cried like a baby when he called me and told me. We talked a lot back then—about our lives, our families, what we hoped for in the future. Jimmy cried, too. He couldn't believe this was happening. He was too young.

Jimmy kept fighting, and I watched him struggle with the pain, which was unbelievable. But the disease kept getting worse.

Jimmy was set to be in New York on March 4, 1993, for the first ESPY Awards, broadcast live from Radio City Music Hall—the ESPYS are ESPN's equivalent of the Oscars. Valvano was due to receive the first Arthur Ashe Award for Courage. The V Foundation was also going to be announced that night.

The night before the event, I came back from rehearsal and was in awe with the planning involved. I called to let him know how special everything would be. But Jimmy was in really bad shape. He told me he was miserable and did not think he could make it.

Valvano ended up flying up with his wife, Pam, and Mike and Mickie Krzyzewski. He'd been sick on the flight up to the city. In addition, he had just received the worst news imaginable: Instead of being one of the very few people in the world who could beat the disease, he learned that day that the cancer had spread throughout his body.

The ESPYS were the last thing on his mind. He was thinking about saying farewell to his wife and his family.

"Dick, you think I'm thinking about awards, man?" Jimmy said to me. "I'm thinking about my wife. I'm thinking about my kids—Nicole, LeAnne, and Jamie. I love them. I'm going to miss them so much."

"Please make sure you come to the event," I begged him.

He made it. And I'll always be grateful to Mike Krzyzewski for his help in getting Jimmy there. Before the telecast, I talked to some production personnel about making arrangements for a boom mic to be brought to Jimmy's seat so he could say a quick thank you and not have to struggle to the stage.

But he would have none of that.

"I didn't come here for a simple thank you," he told me. "I've got something to say. You get me to the podium."

Actor Dustin Hoffman introduced the award, describing what it meant. Then, he introduced me to present the award to Jimmy V.

Krzyzewski, Joe Theismann, and I carried Jimmy to the stage and then returned him to his seat after he received a standing ovation from everyone there. Now, I thought Jimmy would just say a quick thank you and sit down again after receiving his award. I should have known my friend better.

His speech was one for the ages. He positively electrified the crowd. Everyone there, and the audience at home, were treated to a fantastic speech by someone who meant every word. He talked about his battle with cancer. He talked about life—how one day you have it all, only to have it snatched away the next, as you're battling for your life. And Jimmy was still battling—believe me.

Then, he said, "There are three things we should all do every day. We should laugh every day. We should spend time in thought. We should have our emotions moved to tears—it could be from happiness or joy. If we laugh, we think, and we cry, that's a full day. That's a heckuva day."

He told the audience always to dream big dreams. Then, with his voice breaking, he said, "Don't give up. Don't ever give up."

I still get chills when I remember what he said.

Jimmy died on April 28, 1993. He was 47.

Before his death, with the help of ESPN, Jimmy created the V Foundation to raise money for cancer research. He'd told some friends his goal: "I want to beat cancer. I might not be able to beat it by myself, but I'm going to beat it by you guys not forgetting about me and raising millions of dollars to help find a cure."

I made my friend a promise that I would not forget him—or his valiant fight—and that I would do everything in my power to honor his wishes.

I eventually became a member of the Board of the V Foundation. Our first fundraiser was in New York. During the infancy stage of the Jimmy V Classic, John Saunders and I were very proud to host the event in Cary, North Carolina. One of Jimmy V's closest friends, Frank McCann, served as chairman of the event.

I loved meeting the youngsters and performers at Dallas Children's Hospital during the Final Four. It's tough not to clown around occasionally.

Then, in 2005, I got an idea: Let's throw a party at our house in Florida. We thought it would be a very simple party. We'd charge $1,000 a person. Then, I thought I'd get some of my friends to come and see how much money we could raise. I wanted to give more exposure and visibility to the V Foundation in Southwest Florida. Some 250 to 300 people came to the house. I had local celebrities there, too—like Billy Donovan from Florida and Ronde Barber from the Buccaneers. Nick Valvano, Jimmy's brother, as well as Jimmy's wife, Pam, came and spoke about the V Foundation.

Then, cancer got a face: Payton Wright, a little girl in my neighborhood. And I went into overdrive.

Payton was five or six years old when, on a trip to Sea World with her family, she started crying about the pain in her knee. Her parents, Patrick and Holly, took her to an orthopedist, who told them Payton was fine—just growing pains. But she was still in horrible pain, still crying from it. She had an MRI done of her body. The doctor walked in and changed the Wright's lives forever. He told them, "We have some bad news. The reason for her pain has nothing to do with her knee. She has a tumor the size of a grapefruit on her spine. And the worst of it is it's probably going to spread."

Lorraine and I are amazed when we visit children undergoing treatment. Even under tough circumstances the smiles are wonderful.

My heart just broke because I watched this little girl go from running around, having a ball—just like any other kid—to a point where she was in a wheelchair, paralyzed.

I can still remember when I first heard about her. After we had our first event at our home, there was a knock on the door. It was a friend of the Wrights who came to tell me about Payton. I asked them to give me a year. I'd just had an event. I couldn't call on my people again.

"We've got to help this kid," I told Lorraine. "Maybe throw a small party at our place, so we can raise a little money for the family."

We threw another party. It was a great time. The amount of money we raised shocked me. My daughters had balloons all over the place. Payton had just finished her chemo, and she came to our house. My God, she wasn't there more than a half-hour when she started crying and screaming like you can't believe. I remembered that scream because it was the scream I'd heard coming from Jimmy V one night when we were on the road. We were lucky. Her oncologist was at the house. He ordered her back to the hospital. The cancer had spread all over her body.

I called Dr. Joseph Moore, a Board member of the V Foundation, who holds a high position at Duke Medical Center. He requested her records from her doctors. When he received them, Dr. Moore said she had to go to Duke immediately. They admitted her. One day, while my family and I were on vacation in the Bahamas at the Atlantis, her father called. I was sitting, watching my grandkids having a ball in the swimming pool. He said, "Dick, I am so excited. I was able to take Payton to breakfast today after they put her in her wheelchair."

I lost it after I got off the phone. I shared the story with my wife and we were like water faucets as we cried hysterically. Life is so unfair. There I was watching my grandchildren having fun, and Patrick Wright was there with his daughter in a wheelchair.

She eventually lost her eyesight, and then her life.

My family and I went to her funeral. There is nothing worse than watching a mom and dad put their child to rest.

This photo was taken at a recent visit to All Children's Hospital in St. Petersburg. These children are so special.

Immediately after the funeral, I told Patrick and Holly Wright that we will be raising a million dollars for a research grant in her name to help other kids. We would not let her die in vain; we would help other kids in the future.

We've honed in on a pediatric cancer grant because kids should be out playing, having fun, not sitting in hospitals waiting for their chemo rounds.

In my first year of the gala, we honored Krzyzewski at the Sarasota Ritz Carlton and raised $1.3 million. I told him I wanted to hold a big gala—not just a party at my house—and wanted to honor Jimmy V. We wanted to raise a lot of money for the V Foundation.

After Payton passed, I was determined to dedicate myself to pediatric cancer research.

We raised $1.6 million in the second year of the event, honoring Pat Summitt and Bob Knight. That was the year after Payton passed away.

In 2008, the gala really hit home. I suddenly knew what it was like to wait—in my case for two weeks—for my biopsy results to come back. In the meantime, your life is on hold. All you can do is pray.

I was lucky. I was cancer-free.

But others aren't. And that's why it means so much to me to see how the gala has grown over the years. It's the most satisfying event I've ever been involved with in my life. And I promise you that I will do everything I can to keep raising money to fight cancer until my dying breath.

In 2014, we had our ninth gala and have raised in excess of $12 million for pediatric cancer research since the event's inception.

I'd like to be remembered—not just as a basketball personality—but as someone who wanted to help kids battling cancer, so the memory of those who've been lost along the way is never forgotten.

BOYS & GIRLS CLUBS

Because my family has been so blessed since we moved to Sarasota, Florida, Lorraine and I wanted to find some way to give back to the community for being so good to us.

We found it in the Sarasota County Boys & Girls Clubs. The Clubs provide after-school and summer programs for more than 5,500 children and youth ages 6 to 18. They are a place where youngsters can work hard to overcome their challenges.

I just love what they stand for—their motto is "Great Futures Start Here."

The late Roy McBean, a retired New York City policeman, loved kids, too, and sought to help them once he came to the Sarasota area. He recently passed, and my wife and I were so touched listening to the testimonials shared about his love for the Boys & Girls Clubs.

My involvement with McBean started one day when he and Mack Reid, who was the executive director of the Sarasota branch, came over to the house to ask for my help. They wanted to know if I could help them raise $25,000 to buy some computers.

I told him I would do better than that. "I love what you do, giving kids a chance to chase their dreams." I said I would help him raise $1 million to put toward a new building by running some charity events.

Lee Wetherington, who is a building contractor and a big supporter of the local clubs, gave his commitment to have a prominent role in building a new facility. As part of the new building, they built a physical education center with a basketball court and named it after me—the Dick Vitale Health and Wellness Center. I was very touched. They hired a famous sculptor to make a statue of me, which stands outside. When my grandkids go there to play basketball, they call me and say, "Papa, Papa. We just took a picture with you."

Then, Lorraine and I decided to do more. Every year, we donate $5,000 worth of scholarships for the kids in our area. Recipients are selected by the Boys & Girls Club. In addition to scholarships, we give T-shirts, videos, books, and basketballs to hundreds of kids in attendance.

It's not just about giving a check because that's easy to do. It's about taking the time to try to motivate and inspire them. Many of these kids come from single-parent homes and tough financial situations.

I love working with the Boys & Girls Clubs, and look at this, there's a statue of me holding the Rock with one hand, my other arm around a boy's shoulder. The sculpture is at the Sarasota headquarters, and let me say, it was a very humbling honor.

I love helping young kids, and I've been blessed in my life to be able to share and give back. My wife says I get as big of a kick as possible when I see the smiles on the faces of the kids.

The best part happens every Christmas. We hold a party for 12 hand-selected, needy kids in the Club at my home. We bring in Santa Claus to hand out the presents—wrist watches, clothes, bicycles, American Girl dolls, Kindle Fires. My daughters play a big role and find out what the kids' wishes are. The directors help as we get all of the presents. It's always a fun and inspiring time.

We sing Christmas carols while the kids open their gifts in front of a giant Christmas tree filed with gold and silver ornaments. Then, my son-in-law Thomas, who is a judge in the United States Circuit Court, and I come in and talk to them about making good decisions in their lives. We also talk to them about the value of reading, referring to sports heroes, like Peyton Manning, Jackie Robinson, and the late Arthur Ashe, who used education to improve their chances of making it in life.

It's become an annual tradition and is a wonderful way to spend part of the holidays in order to show my grandchildren the true meaning of Christmas.

We learned a lot of those values growing up. I had a lot of love in our household though we did not have financial riches. The holidays were always special.

But we had all kinds of love from my parents. That's why I loved Kevin Durant's speech about his mother when he received the NBA's MVP award.

I tell my friends to smack me across the head if I ever forget where I came from.

PRINCESS LACEY

One of the most touching stories in college basketball in 2014 was the special friendship between Michigan State star Adreian Payne and an adorable eight-year-old little girl, Lacey Holsworth. Sadly, she died that spring of neuroblastoma—a pediatric cancer she had been battling for three years.

The two met in 2011 when Payne and his teammates visited her room at Sparrow Hospital in East Lansing, where she was getting treatment. As the Spartans were leaving, Lacey asked Adreian to stay. She said she liked his smile.

Adreian said he felt she could feel his spirit.

In a lot of ways, he could see a lot of himself in her. Watching her struggle reminded him of the sadness he'd felt after he lost his mother at age 13 to asthma and the learning disability that almost prevented him from attending college.

Adreian gave Lacey his phone number that day, and two lives were changed forever. They began texting and tweeting back and forth. When Lacey got out of the hospital, he started leaving her tickets to his games. He said having Lacey there, with her face painted green and white and shaking her pom poms, motivated him. There were times he would bring her onto the court during warmups and give her hugs after the games to help her feel like a princess.

Which is what she became known as: Princess Lacey.

She called Adreian, "Superman."

I remember meeting her for the first time at the Breslin Center when I was there for ESPN calling a Michigan State game with Magic Johnson and Mike Tirico. The Spartans lost the game. But then, Payne came over to her. He started to hug this little girl. As I was signing autographs and taking pictures with some of the Spartan fans, I asked "Who's that cute little girl?" The fans said she has cancer and Adreian had become her friend. So, I walked over. I started talking to Payne, to the girl, to the family. From that moment on, we started to stay in touch.

I wound up inviting Lacey, her parents Heather and Matt, as well as Adreian and coach Tom Izzo to my fundraising gala for the V Foundation in 2013.

We brought her up on stage, and Dan Shulman interviewed her and Adreian. We had a video of them that appeared on national TV talking about their special relationship. She really played to the crowd. Let me tell you, there wasn't a dry eye in

Photo Courtesy of Associated Press/Al Goldis

This guy might be Superman. Adreian Payne, who was a senior at Michigan State in 2014, became great friends with little princess, Lacey Holsworth. Before she lost her courageous fight with cancer in April 2014, Lacey became a central part of the Spartan team.

243

Me and Princess Lacey. It was a privilege to know this inspiring little girl. She will never be forgotten.

the room. It was unbelievable. She had gone through two years of chemotherapy and yet was smiling and captivating everybody.

In November 2013, it actually looked like her cancer might be in remission. Lacey and her family took a celebratory trip to Disneyland. Then, she felt a familiar pain in her jaw. The cancer had come back and spread. And the prognosis was not good. After surgery, she'd slipped into a coma for a few days. According to *Bleacher Report's* Jason King's story, Payne came to visit his friend, bearing a stuffed animal. She looked very tiny and frail in the bed. When her mother told Lacey, "Adreian is here," Lacey rolled over, opened her eyes for the first time in days.

"Superman," she said, "you're here."

She rallied and became the inspirational face of Michigan State's season. She was there when Payne was honored on Senior Night. I was there, too. It was so emotional. She was his escort; he was like her adopted brother. Then, he picked her up and carried her around the court. She was also there helping Payne cut down the nets when the Spartans won the Big Ten championship. Lacey was at the team banquet; Izzo put his arm around her as he addressed the players and fans.

She got to go to the Final Four in Dallas in 2014 where she cheered Payne on in the College Slam Dunk Championship. At the end of the tournament, she told her parents she wanted to go home.

She went home and died there on April 8, 2014, in her parents' arms.

Adreian showed me the humanity of sports with the way he handled a difficult situation. And Princess Lacey showed what Jimmy V used to preach: Don't ever give up.

Lorraine and I were in the car, driving back from a speaking engagement in Orlando when the phone rang. It was King from *Bleacher Report*, who had become very close with the Holsworth family. He gave me the bad news that Lacey had passed. We were devastated.

I debated for about five minutes and then said, "I've got to call the family."

I didn't think anyone would answer, so I was just going to leave a little message about how my heart was with them at a difficult time. But her father picked up, and I'm telling you it was as tough a conversation as I'd ever had. Both of us were crying and talking about what an impact she'd made on people. At age eight, she inspired more people than most do in a lifetime.

I got emotional and told Matt, "I promise you we are going to raise a quarter of a million dollars a piece for research grants in Lacey and Eddie Livingston's names." (Eddie was a Sarasota child who had passed away earlier in the year.)

I told him, "We can't save your girl with the angelic smile, but we can try to save others with a research grant in her name."

Immediately after my conversation with Matt, I called Izzo; we shared stories on the impact she made. We were crying like babies, two grown men brought to tears by her courageous fight—the special girl who stole our hearts.

Though it was only a few weeks after her passing, her parents, attended the 2014 Dick Vitale gala. We paid tribute to Lacey's honor with that $250,000 research grant in her name.

Michigan State held a memorial service for her at the Breslin Center nine days after she passed. More than 2,500 people attended. There was a sign outside the Harrison Roadhouse that said, "Love Like Lacey." A celebration of her life was held inside the arena, and it included videos of her dancing to various songs from Taylor Swift, Bruno Mars, and Carly Rae Jepsen.

MSU junior guard Travis Trice told the story of the Spartans' loss to North Carolina in December, after which he left a grim locker room to see a smiling Lacey — about a month after finding out her cancer had returned. His misery was gone instantly. "That was one of her blessings," said Trice.

The team gathered together under a basket next to the stage and Payne performed a "silent dunk" to honor her. A MSU-produced video included words from the team to Lacey and pictures of her with Magic Johnson, Mateen Cleaves, Steve Smith, and others, and the family also produced a video with her mother interviewing Lacey and asking her what she would tell other kids with cancer.

"Just keep believing in God and keep praying," Lacey said, "and just try to stay strong."

May this little angel RIP. Trust me, she will never, ever be forgotten.

Michigan State coach Tom Izzo watching a tribute video of Lacey Holsworth, a wonderful celebration of her life and legacy. Everyone was choked up.

CHAPTER 74
THE 2014 GALA

I was thrilled. Our ninth annual gala for the V Foundation raised a record $2.1 million for pediatric cancer research, beating the prior record of $1.7 million we raised in 2013.

More than 870 people and 80 sports celebrities came to the Ritz-Carlton on Friday, May 16, 2014. The event was sold out for months. That's why I always say that on one special night Sarasota is the sports capital of the world.

Everywhere you looked, there were celebrities—college basketball coaches like Jim Boeheim of Syracuse, Steve Alford of UCLA, and Tom Izzo of Michigan State. Florida State football coach Jimbo Fisher was there, too, along with the Tampa Bay Buccaneers coach Lovie Smith and defensive end Gerald McCoy. The Lightning was represented by coach Jon Cooper. Former NBA coaches—and my old Jersey buddies—Mike Fratello and Richie Adubato—showed up. MLB star Gary Sheffield was in attendance. Nik Wallenda of high-wire fame was there. Stage and screen stars Audrey and Judy Landers also attended. Pro sports owners Jeff Vinik and Bryan Glazer joined former Nets owner Joe Taub.

After a while, I just stopped counting. It was wall-to-wall people—just the way I like it. And all for a great cause.

That year's honorees were Alabama football coach Nick Saban, Notre Dame basketball coach Mike Brey, and Indiana basketball coach Tom Crean. As you would expect from such high-caliber guys, their speeches were beyond eloquent, and I can't thank them enough for

When I pull together a crowd of celebrities like this, I know my Gala is going to be a big success.

being there. Izzo introduced me, and Saunders was our emcee. Did I mention that the Four Tops—one of my favorite all-time groups, played for me at my surprise 75th birthday party at the gala?

But that's not why we were there.

Nebraska's head football coach, Bo Pelini, introduced a special young man, Jack Hoffman, an eight-year-old boy who is a lifelong Huskers fan. He has been battling brain cancer, but that didn't stop him from running for a 69-yard touchdown with the help of the players in the annual 2013 spring intrasquad game. The video of his run got more than 8.4 million hits on YouTube—it even won the "Best Moment" award at the 2013 ESPYS.

Jack's tumor, which is located near the brain stem, is inoperable. Although he experienced a brief remission, Jack's cancer returned in the summer of 2014.

2014's gala was especially bittersweet for me since we lost three of the kids who'd attended last year—Lacey Holsworth, Eddie Livingston, and Dillon Simmons.

Izzo, along with Lacey's parents, Matt and Heather Holsworth, were there. I was very pleased to announce that we made our goal and presented a $250,000 grant in honor of Lacey, who had meant so much to the Michigan State basketball team. The money raised will be distributed to different hospitals for pediatric cancer research. We also donated $250,000 in honor of Eddie, a young boy from our area. The dollars will be concentrated on neuroblastoma, which took the lives of both Eddie and Lacey.

Eddie was 2 1/2 when he was diagnosed with stage four cancer. It had started in the adrenal gland of his left kidney, then spread to his bones. I met him at the Broken Egg when he was five in 2013 and was blown away by his will to live. He wanted to do five-year-old things—run, wrestle, ride a bike, swim, and eat chicken wings—his favorite food. But that wasn't to be. His bones were too fragile and he had a plastic tube protruding from his chest.

He died November 23, 2013, quietly at home in his mother's arms.

Dillon was at our gala in 2013. He told me he was hoping to come back and play hockey. He was 14 years old. He was in remission. Then, his cancer came back, and he was in a wheelchair. His father told me how hard the last week of Dillon's life had been. Finally, the family told him that it was okay for him to go. They told him, "Just relax. You're going to a better place."

But Dillon replied, "I don't want to go."

Heartbreaking. Simply devastating.

I told Mr. Simmons that we would honor Dillon next year at the gala with a grant in his name.

The evening is always very emotional. The stories you hear about the grit and determination of these kids moves me to tears.

There are happy stories, too.

Over the years, we are very proud when youngsters, like Jake Taraska from New Jersey, Tatum Parker from Indiana, and Kyle Peters and Erin Kisielewski from Sarasota, and many others, come back to the gala sharing positive stories about their battles with cancer. Their journeys inspire many.

I know Jimmy V would have been happy his legacy is still going strong over 21 years later.

CHAPTER 75

MOVING FORWARD

The clock, baby. The clock.

Tick tock. Tick tock.

Everybody has one. We can't outrun it. And, when it stops, we're done. The clock ultimately gets us all, and when it's finished, then—BOOM. It's over.

Well, my friends, as of this writing, I am 75 years old. Who'd have ever thought I'd get this far? Not me. Yet, here I am, still going strong. As I've often said, if I'd stayed in coaching, I'd have been dead by 50. But I didn't, and I'm not.

I was fortunate that Scotty Connal hired me in 1979 to do the first major college basketball game ever on ESPN. He told me at the time to remember to "enlighten and entertain" on the TV, with the emphasis on the latter. That was way back in 1979. And that's how it still is heading into the 2014-15 basketball season.

There's something about being on TV that's addictive. The excitement of being at the big game. Meeting the players. Interviewing the coaches. Interacting with the fans. Just being in the mix. I admit I'm hooked on it.

I also know I've been very lucky. After all, you don't last 35 years on a major sports network with just, "It's Awesome, Baby!" It simply doesn't happen. And the public knows it. I've prided myself on my basketball knowledge and preparation for games. Sometimes, I am too prepared because I want to get all of the information out. I've been told by many people in TV that I connect. I've asked, "What do you mean by connect?" Whether the fans agree or disagree, they go to the water cooler and discuss the things I say. That's the beauty of television and the essence of sports.

Even after three decades, I still have anxiety before every telecast, but that helps me. I get asked all the time when I give speeches: "When do you think you're going to step down?" And that bothers me big time because nobody would ask you that if you were 45, 50—even 60. They ask that only because 75 is such a big number.

My answer is very simple: "My bosses will dictate that. I have no clue. It could be today, tomorrow, next week. All I know is that as long as I'm here, I'm going to make the most of every day and control everything in my power, which means taking care of my diet, exercising, and doing things I think are positive."

I will challenge any of those youngsters out there to match my enthusiasm and energy. I feel like I am 25. OK—Stop laughing.

And I'm not alone.

My take-away is that people are keeping themselves in better shape these days. They're able to go on and work for a longer time. You see it with corporate executives. My feeling is why can a guy run for president in his 70's and not be able to coach basketball? Makes no sense to me. Let's face reality. Age is just a number.

I'm a part of that exclusive 70's club now. You're proud to get there, but you also do everything in your power to take care of yourself. Rollie Massimino and Larry Brown would probably tell you the same thing: If you didn't tell me my age, I wouldn't know it.

The bottom line is I attack every day with the same enthusiasm I've always had. I work out. I play tennis. I eat right. I don't smoke or drink. I'm known as "Mr. Cranberry Juice" at social functions.

I remember that in coaching, you get an incredible high but also an incredible low. There's nothing in between.

In TV, I don't get that feeling I had when I walked home after we beat Michigan my first year at Detroit, or going to Milwaukee and beating Marquette the year they won the national championship. I don't get that knot in my stomach either when my teams lost.

In TV, I coach every night, but I haven't had an L in 35 years. I have a better record than Coach K (ha,ha).

For me, one of the greatest gifts I've gotten from TV is the reaction of the fans. It's just unbelievable. It keeps me young. It keeps me enthusiastic and energetic. It keeps me passionate. And I think that's what has kept me on the air for so long. The fans keep me going—game after game, tournament after tournament, year after year.

It is difficult to put into words the high I get when the fans chant "Dickie V, Dickie V," in arenas all across America. It gives me goose bumps, baby!

I will do everything in my power to enjoy every moment and every game that I can while I can.

It's been an awesome ride, baby, and it isn't over yet!

EPILOGUE

Every morning, when I'm home, I start my day sitting at my desk, which has a picture of my mother and father as well as a Bible.

My faith has always been a source of strength to me. The Bible has some of the best stories and lessons ever written. And, when I look at my mom and dad—Mae and John—all I can say is a heartfelt thank you.

I would like to dedicate this book to the memory of the many youngsters I have met over the last decade since the inception my Dick Vitale Gala. The young people featured here have inspired me so much as I observed their incredible courage in battling that dreaded disease, cancer. They will never, ever be forgotten, and I want their families to know that they have inspired so many with their bravery.

May they all RIP.

David Heard
May 5, 2000 -
February 10, 2011

Lacey Holsworth
November 30, 2005 -
April 8, 2014

Caleb Jacobbe
February 4, 1998 -
May 10, 2006

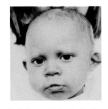

Adrian Littlejohn
February 4, 2010 -
May 1, 2011

Eddie Livingston
September 3, 2008 -
November 24, 2013

Justin Miller
April 21, 1992 -
April 3, 2013

Dillon Simmons
November 2, 1998 -
April 25, 2014

Johnny Teis
August 1, 2002 -
April 11, 2011

Lucy Weber
June 8, 2009 -
November 20, 2010

Payton Wright
May 7, 2002 -
May 29, 2007

– Dick Vitale

Photo Courtesy of ESPN/Joe Kapelewski

I've loved working games with the legendary Brent Musburger.

Photo Courtesy of ESPN/Jeff Camarati

John Saunders is a talented play-by-play announcer.

Photo Courtesy of ESPN/Bruce Schwartzman

Brad Nessler (right) and I called the NCAA championship game for ESPN International in 2013.

Photo Courtesy of ESPN/Rich Arden

Here I am with my go-to-guy Howie Schwab.

Photo Courtesy of ESPN/Rich Arden

I enjoyed doing College Gameday on the road with Jay Bilas (left) and Digger Phelps.

Photo Courtesy of ESPN/ Darren Abate

When you have three coaches together (Digger Phelps, me, and Bob Knight), there are always plenty of opinions. Rece Davis (far left) had the tough job of keeping us on task!

ACKNOWLEDGEMENTS

I want to sincerely thank the incredible efforts of Dick Weiss and his wife Joanie for their dedication to this project. My sincerest thank you goes to research guru Howie Schwab for the time and energy he devoted to the book. Also, thank you to ESPN's PR department for providing information and photos that have been utilized. To Bob Snodgrass, Publisher at Ascend Books, and Christine Drummond, Publication Coordinator at Ascend Books, thank you for being our Publisher of Choice and for keeping us on task to make sure this book became a reality. Finally, a sincere thank you to my wife of 43 years, Lorraine, and my entire family, for making these 75 years so special.

—Dick Vitale

I would like to thank the following people who have helped me while I reinvented myself: Joan, Dick and Lorraine Vitale and their daughters Sherri and Terri, Mike Flynn, George Raveling, Jeanine Reynolds and her children Tim, Andrew and Matt, Howie Schwab, Seth Davis of CBS and SI.com, Pat Plunkett, Bob and Elaine Ryan, the great John Feinstein, Steve Richardson of the FWAA, Mike Aresco and Chuck Sullivan of the American Athletic Conference, the incredible people at the Big Ten network, all the ADs and coaches—past and present—from the fabled Philadelphia Big Five, Larry Wahl of the Orange Bowl, Fairfield University, Sam Albano, Mike Sheridan and Jay Wright of Villanova, Tom Izzo of Michigan State, Ronnie Norpel, Lesley Visser, Robyn Norwood, John Akers of Basketball Times, Dick Jerardi, Mike Kern and Pat McLoone of the Philly Daily News, Dana O'Neal of ESPN, Mike Vaccaro, Steve Serby, and Fred Kerber from the Post, Lenn Robbins, Roger Rubin of the News, Lea Miller of the Battle for Atlantis, John Paquette of the Big East, Brian Morrison of the ACC, Steve Kirschner of North Carolina, Karl and Theresa Grentz, Mary and Patty Coyle, Tom Luicci, Mark Blaudschun, Dr. David Raezer, Chris Dufresne, Kenny Denlinger, Ray Didinger, Frank Bertucci, Dan Wetzel and Pat Forde of Yahoo Sports, Dennis Dodd of CBS Sportsline, my attorney Rick Tronciellitti, Melanie McCullough, Joe Cassidy of Rowan University, Craig Miller and Sean Ford from USA Basketball, Larry "the Scout" Pearlstein and Howard Garfinkel, Jerry McLaughlln, Allen Rubin, Adam Berkowitz and, of course, Charley and the guys.

—Dick Weiss

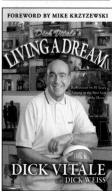

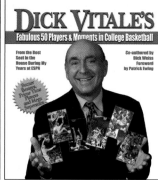

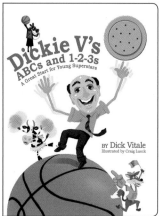

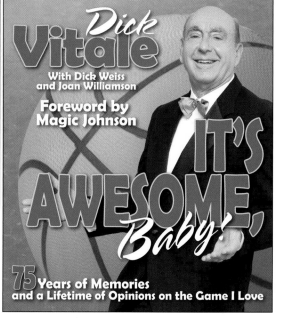